WHO?
WHAT?
WHEN?
WHERE?
WHY?

THE FIRST HALF

BY JOHN D.T. WHITE

PUBLISHED BY HERO BOOKS
DUBLIN
IRELAND
www.herobooks.digital
Hero Books is an imprint of Umbrella Publishing

First Published 2023
Copyright © John D.T. White

All rights reserved

Without limiting the rights under copyright reserved above, no
part of this publication may be reproduced, stored in or introduced
into a retrieval system, or transmitted in any form or by any means
(electronic, mechanical, photocopying, recording or otherwise)
without the prior written permission of the publisher of this book

A CIP record for this book is available from the British Library

ISBN 9781910827710

Cover design and formatting: jessica@viitaladesign.com
Photographs: Inpho

DEDICATION

I wish to dedicate this book to three very special people who are no longer with us.

Firstly, to Victor Coard, a fellow Red.
Miss your craic Big Lad!

Secondly, to Johnnie Beckett, a Big Linfield fan. I so miss our chats about football and the 'Good Old Days!'

Thirdly, to my father, John McDermott White, a Wolverhampton Wanderers fan, who had a soft spot for United just to make me feel happy. There isn't a single day that goes by that I don't miss you, Dad. Love You Always.

Victor, Johnnie and Dad –
Keep watching over your Loved Ones.

CONTENTS

ACKNOWLEDGEMENTS

FOREWORD
Alan Keegan

INTRODUCTION

PART 1	17
PART 2	55
PART 3	87
PART 4	123
PART 5	149
PART 6	169
PART 7	195
PART 8	217
PART 9	257
PART 10	281
PART 11	319

EPILOGUE

ACKNOWLEDGMENTS

I wish to say a huge *Thank You* to Gerry and Geraldine McCollum, my proof readers, who spent hours upon hours going over my entries to help me keep them as accurate as I possibly could.

And, not forgetting Jo, who had to put up with me when I was writing my book and who gave me the encouragement I needed to get the book finished.

Best Wishes
John

FOREWORD

ALAN KEEGAN
THE VOICE OF OLD TRAFFORD

They say that everyone has at least one book in them!

What does it say about a person that is about to publish his 21st book about Manchester United?

I first met John 'Chalkie' White many years ago at a Manchester United Supporters' Club event at Old Trafford which I was hosting on behalf of Manchester United. I was approached by what you might describe as a very confident United fan who wanted to tell me all about the Carryduff Manchester United Supporters' Club which was formed in 1991 and was based in Northern Ireland, and happened to be one of the biggest supporters' clubs not just in the UK but in the world.

I have a very strong Irish background and I had heard of Carryduff Branch and the great work that they were doing bringing together all sections of the community in Northern

Ireland and, more importantly, recognising that it didn't matter what religion you practiced, it was all about Manchester United… that was The Religion.

In 1998, I was asked by Manchester United to put together a football quiz for the matchday hospitality in the Manchester Suite and as part of my research (some people might call it plagiarism), I bought a book that was called, *The Official Manchester United Quiz Book* compiled by John White – the foreword of that book was written by a certain Alex Ferguson CBE, (the Boss hadn't been Knighted yet!) which makes it a special honour to be in such good company.

It was my go-to book for all things related to United; it was a brilliant book of facts, stats and questions and here we are 25 plus years on once again celebrating another Manchester United book by John White.

In May 2012, I had the honour of being invited to Belfast by John and the committee of Carryduff MUSC to attend and act as the stadium announcer at the Harry Gregg Testimonial game at Windsor Park, Belfast. The match was organised by Carryduff Manchester United Supporters' Club after John asked the Boss to bring the team over to honour Harry's 10 years at the club, which had previously gone unrecognised. It involved spending the day with Harry as he carried out a full schedule of media work prior to the game taking place in the evening – a memory that I will cherish forever.

I began these few words with a statement rather than a question about a person who is about to publish his 21st Manchester United book – John's book is a wonderful mixture of Manchester United facts, trivia and history. It is a book all

Manchester United fans will find very interesting with so many well researched entries.

And so, coming on for Manchester United is No.21, John 'Chalkie' White!

Alan Keegan
August 2023

INTRODUCTION

Sir Alex Ferguson, Boss – Thank You.

This book was made possible by Sir Alex Ferguson, who in 1998 agreed to pen the foreword to the first ever book about Manchester United that I wrote. That book is entitled The Official Manchester United Quiz Book. Many years later, and this is my 21st book about the club I have loved since I grew up and kicked a ball around on Harper Street, Short Strand in east Belfast, not too far from the home of my boyhood hero, George Best. What a footballer!

In 1991, I became the Founder Member of Carryduff Manchester United Supporters' Club in County Down, Northern Ireland. *The Troubles* were still ongoing at the time in Northern Ireland and not too many people ventured outside the safety of their own area. However, I wanted to create an environment where Manchester United fans could come together through their support for the club regardless of their religion.

So, I placed an advertisement in a local newspaper and stated my intention of forming a cross-community Manchester United Supporters' Club. I hired a room in Maysfield Leisure Centre, Belfast and invited like-minded Reds to come along and listen to my proposal. To my astonishment, around 50 people turned up and, within a week, Barry Moorhouse at the Old Trafford Membership Office granted official Branch status to the newly formed Carryduff Manchester United Supporters' Club. I was overjoyed. Eamonn Holmes was a Carryduff resident at the time and he agreed to become the Branch president. Eamonn always told our members that Ireland was neither Green (Roman Catholic) nor Orange (Protestant), but Red, Manchester United Red! How true this is still today.

Our first Branch trip was to see United play Norwich City at Old Trafford on Saturday 7 September 1991. We won the game 3-0 with goals from Denis Irwin, quite appropriate that an Irishman scored the opening goal of the game on our first visit to the Theatre of Dreams, Brian McClair and Ryan Giggs. A Branch trip back then involved us hiring a coach to take us from Belfast to Larne port, where we sailed from to Cairnryan, Scotland. Then a 225 miles coach journey to Sale, Manchester which took us around seven hours with a comfort break en-route. There was no such a thing as a smart phone then or the mobile game devices which are abundant today. So, to keep everyone on the coach occupied, my good mate John Dempsey, our Branch chairman at the time (now Branch president), would bring along VHS video tapes of *Only Fools and Horses* to play on the coach.

We were big fans of the show and still are today. Indeed, I recall one Trip when we practically played out our very own version of the episode entitled *The Jolly Boys Outing*. Del Boy was responsible for arranging an annual coach trip for all the patrons of the local pub, The Nag's Head in Peckham, and their destination was always an English seaside town. In this episode that seaside town was Margate. On their way to Margate, they stopped off for some light refreshments at a pub just off the motorway and when the lads were kicking a football about in the coach park their coach caught fire. Del Boy had sold the coach owner a Mustafa Radio/Cassette player which caught fire resulting in those on board watching their mates play football, quickly making their way off the coach.

I have a habit of sleeping on the floor of the coach, still do, and I will never forget our very own Jolly Boys Outing to Manchester! As we approached the Lake District, JD kicked me to waken me up. But, I couldn't see him as the coach was full of smoke. It had caught fire underneath and the smoke came up through the floor and into the main body of the coach. We all jumped off the coach and had to wait in a café for about five hours before a replacement coach arrived. Great memories.

Anyway, on those Branch trips which were not all as exciting as the one I just described, I used to compile a Manchester United quiz to entertain the Branch members during those long road journeys. I would make-up 20 questions and we would have a quiz on board. I did this for every trip and after about five seasons of travelling over to see Manchester United play, I had amassed a collection of around 500 questions about the club: its' history, managers, players and trophy successes. I wrote to a lot of publishers pitching my idea, but none of them were interested in a Manchester United Quiz Book. Enter Sir Alex, or Alex as he was at the time.

In the summer of 1997, JD and I attended the bi-annual Manchester United Official Supporters' Club Branch Conference at Old Trafford where two representatives from every official MUSC were invited by Manchester United to attend. A meal and complimentary drinks were provided and on this particular occasion, Alex Ferguson was the Guest of Honour. Not being shy, a bit like Del Boy himself, I printed all of my questions and answers and put them in an envelope along with a letter and marked the envelope:

FOR THE PERSONAL ATTENTION OF ALEX FERGUSON MANCHESTER UNITED MANAGER

My letter explained to the Boss – I still call him Boss to this day – that I was trying to get a publisher for my book but without any luck and I asked him if he would write the foreword to it. I shook his hand with my right hand and handed him the envelope at the same time with my left hand. Cheeky, I know, but sure, I am a Belfast Boy! Or as Del Boy always said, 'He Who Dares Wins'.

Can you imagine how surprised I was when, a week later, I receive a letter from the Boss in which he agreed to write the foreword to my book? As soon as the Boss was willing to support my idea, publishers became interested but naturally I opted for the Club's official publishers. And within a year my book was on sale in the Manchester United Megastore. I dared and I won!

This book is not a history book or a fact book or a trivia book. It is a combination of all of these things.

An entry in the book could be a player's debut for the club, a record score, a trophy winning match, a manager's first or last game, the club's first game in one of Europe's three main competitions, the first game at a new ground, a game remembered more for the incident than the football played such as Eric Cantona's kung-fu moment.

I also dip into what was happening in the UK Music singles charts at the time of the game, the No.1 movie of the year and I have used some famous quotes from history which suit the setting.

There are also a lot of interesting stories mixed-in in the book about managers, players and opponents.

At the end of each entry, I include a special *Did You Know That?* piece of trivia, which I hope you like.

As I said previously, this is my 21st book about Manchester United and I am very honoured to say that the Boss agreed to write the foreword to four of them. Very few people witnessed just how generous Sir Alex was and how much of his own personal time he gave up to spend with Manchester United fans. Indeed, JD and I organised several Sportsmans' Dinners in Belfast to raise monies for the charity which the Boss set up in memory of his late Mother and I am very proud to have spent time in his company, which included the Boss visiting my home on a few occasions.

I wish to thank Liam Hayes at Hero Books for his support in publishing my work, and a special word of thanks to Alan Keegan, The Voice of Old Trafford, for very kindly agreeing the foreword to this book.

To you my Fellow Reds, I hope you enjoy my book and it

brings back some truly wonderful memories for you of following our team, Manchester United.

And, Boss you made the *Impossible, Possible* for me.

Thank you once again Boss.

John D. T. White
August 2023

PART 1
YOU'LL NEVER WALK ALONE

UNITED NATIONS OF MANCHESTER

RED HERO TO RED VILLAIN

SEVEN REDS IN WHITE

SOLSKJAER'S YOUNG ONES

YOU'LL NEVER WALK ALONE

United fans everywhere boo every time they hear the song *You'll Never Walk Alone*. But that has not always been the case. The anthem of Liverpool Football Club was first sung at Old Trafford and not at Anfield.

MANCHESTER UNITED 1-1 NOTTINGHAM FOREST
ENGLISH FIRST DIVISION
OLD TRAFFORD
22 FEBRUARY 1958
ATTENDANCE – 66,124

In season 1957-58, Manchester United were the dominant force in English football, winners of the First Division title in seasons 1955-56 and 1956-57, FA Cup runners-up in 1957, and a side revered across Europe, having reached the semi-finals of the European Cup in 1956-57.

At the start of the 1957-58 season, Elvis Presley was No.1 in the UK singles charts with his first No.1 chart hit entitled *All Shook Up*. Matt Busby's young side, *The Busby Babes*, were all set to shake up not only English football, but European club football as well. United were the reigning First Division champions and had narrowly missed out on becoming the first team to win the Double in England in the 20th century after losing the 1957 FA Cup final to Aston Villa. Furthermore, in season 1956-57, United reached the semi-finals of the European Cup in their first season in competitive European club football. Although they were fondly dubbed *The Busby Babes* by the British press, their football abilities belied their youthful age.

> *Small boys become big men from the influence of big men who care about small boys.*

Eleven of the first team squad who missed out on completing the Double in season 1956-57, Bill Foulkes, Roger Byrne (capt), Jackie Blanchflower, Duncan Edwards, Mark Jones, Wilf McGuinness, Eddie Colman, Liam Whelan, David Pegg, Dennis Viollet and Bobby Charlton had all began their football careers as young boys playing for the Manchester United Junior Athletic Club which was run by Busby's right hand man, Jimmy Murphy. Busby was a manager who placed his faith and trust in the ability of his youth team players over and above buying players on a regular basis. In Murphy, United's teenagers had much more than a patriarchal figure to look up to, they had a second father looking after them and they would have done anything for their mentor. They may have been known as *The Busby Babes* but they were most definitely Murphy's Boys. Edwards, Whelan, Scanlon, Pegg, Charlton, McGuinness, Colman, Jones had all won FA Youth Cup winners' medals in teams assembled by Murphy. Murphy's young players were his vessel out on the pitch, finely tuned and sweeping all before them.

The Young Lions is a 1958 American World War II drama film directed by Edward Dmytryk. Murphy's Boys were only cubs but destined to be lions.

The Munich Air Disaster on 6 February 1958, claimed the lives of seven of Murphy's Boys – Byrne, Edwards, Colman, Whelan, Bent, Jones and Pegg – as well as the life of Tommy Taylor, who was signed from Barnsley. Just 13 days after the disaster, United had to resume their season with an FA Cup Fifth Round tie versus Sheffield Wednesday at Old Trafford. Matt Busby was lying in his hospital bed in the Rechts der Isar Hospital in Munich, West Germany recovering from the horrific injuries he sustained whilst Duncan Edwards was, like his manager, also lying in a hospital bed fighting for his life. Murphy was the manager of the Wales national football team and had not been on the flight as Wales had a 1958 FIFA World Cup qualifying game to play on the same night United drew 3-3 with Red Star Belgrade on 5 February 1958 in their quarter-finals, second leg tie. And so, back in Manchester he had the unenviable task of leading the club in Busby's absence and putting together a side to play Sheffield Wednesday on 19 February 1958.

Murphy looked to his youth players, who along with two survivors of the Munich Air Disaster, Harry Gregg and Bill Foulkes, beat Sheffield Wednesday 3-0 on a very emotional night at Old Trafford. Shay Brennan scored twice on his debut with Alex Dawson also scoring. The people of Manchester celebrated as one – red and blue sides of the football divide joined in the euphoria of watching a team rise from the ashes of a slush covered runway less than two weeks earlier. For the United and City fans, there was no 'Us' and 'Them', there was just 'Us' as many of the players who died were local lads and City also lost a former player in the disaster, goalkeeper Frank Swift who played for them from 1936-39 and was capped 19 times by England (plus 14 Wartime games), who was a reporter for *News of the World*, covering the game in Belgrade, Yugoslavia for his newspaper.

Two days later, 21 February 1958, Duncan Edwards died in hospital aged just 21 years and 144 days old. The following day a distraught Murphy, having lost yet another one of his Boys, had to field a team to play Nottingham Forest in the First Division on 22 February 1958.

> *Stab the body and it heals, but injure the heart and*
> *the wound lasts a lifetime.*
> (Mineko Iwasaki)

Jimmy Murphy was in a daze, a distraught man with a broken heart which had been stabbed eight times, a knife wound for each lost *Busby Babe*. But despite the club being in its darkest hour he had to carry on for his friend, Busby, his lost Boys, Tommy Taylor and the club officials who also perished in the disaster (Walter Crickmer, club Secretary, Tom Curry, Trainer and Bert Whalley, Chief Coach). Murphy was unquestionably the greatest ever signing Matt Busby made for Manchester United. In February 1945, after accepting an offer to become the next manager of United, Busby returned to the Army Physical Training Corps and in the spring of 1945, he took their football team to Bari, Italy. When he was in Bari, he took in a training session for a football team made up of non-commissioned officers which was led by Jimmy Murphy. Murphy was a former player, having played for West Bromwich Albion as a wing-half from 1928-39 and won 15 international caps for his native Wales (1933-38). Busby was hugely impressed by the Welshman's oratory skills and offered him the job of Chief Coach at Manchester United when the war ended. Murphy accepted Busby's offer verbally there and then, before joining the club officially in early 1946. Murphy led United's Youth team to success in the inaugural FA Youth Cup final in 1953 and in the following four finals.

The Manchester United side which played Nottingham Forest was: Harry Gregg, Bill Foulkes, Ian Greaves, Ronald Cope, Stan Crowther, Frederick Goodwin, Colin Webster, Ernie Taylor, Shay Brennan, Alex Dawson, Mark Pearson.

Foulkes, Goodwin, Cope, Dawson, Pearson and Brennan had all played in Murphy's youth teams. Forest were just establishing themselves in the top flight having won promotion to the First Division the previous season, after finishing runners-up to Leicester City in the Second Division. Murphy's selection was a very inexperienced side, a patchwork quilt of experience and youth, with Gregg playing in what was only his eighth league game following his transfer from Doncaster Rovers in December 1957, Webster was making his seventh league appearance of the season, Goodwin his fifth, Dawson his second, whilst Greaves, Cope, Crowther (made his debut in the Sheffield Wednesday game), Taylor, Pearson and Brennan were all playing their first league game of the season.

The loss of eight *Busby Babe*s traumatised the city of Manchester. What was the most appropriate way to celebrate the lives of eight young players who just wanted to play football for Manchester United? Many theatres up and down the country were staging their version of Richard Rodgers and Oscar Hammerstein II's 1945 musical *Carousel*. A popular song from *Carousel* was *You'll Never Walk Alone*, a song which is the anthem of Liverpool Football Club and is despised today by United fans across the globe. In February 1958, the New Mills Operatic Society in Derbyshire were rehearsing to perform *Carousel* in their local theatre. Jane Hardwick, a United fan and a teenage opera singer with the New Mills Operatic Society attended the Nottingham Forest game and when she began to sing *You'll Never Walk Alone* in tribute to the lost *Busby Babes*, her friends joined in and soon a large section of the crowd had also joined in the singing. For Jane and her fellow New Mills Operatic Society members they thought that the opening two verses of *You'll Never Walk Alone* was a fitting tribute to the lost lives of Geoff Bent, Roger Byrne, Eddie Colman, Duncan Edwards, Mark Jones, David Pegg, Tommy Taylor and Liam Whelan.

When you walk through a storm
Hold your head up high
And don't be afraid of the dark
At the end of the storm
There's a golden sky
And the sweet silver song of the lark
Walk on, through the wind
Walk on, through the rain
Though your dreams be tossed and blown
Walk on, walk on, with hope in your heart

*And you'll never walk alone
You'll never walk alone*

United were not facing a storm post the Munich Air Disaster, a tsunami had enveloped the club. Murphy, with his British Army background, set about steering United through a storm, ensuring his players held their heads up high, ignoring the darkness which clouded Old Trafford, to come out of the darkness and reach a golden sky. The game ended 1-1 with Dawson scoring for United. Murphy worked a miracle at Old Trafford as he began the process of building a new team for Busby and lift the club like a Phoenix rising out of the ashes of Munich. United ended the 1957-58 season in 9th place in the league, lost the 1958 FA Cup final 2-0 to Bolton Wanderers and lost 5-2 on aggregate over two legs to AC Milan (scorers: Ernie Taylor and Dennis Viollet) in the semi-finals of the European Cup. United's top goal scorer in season 1957-58 was Dennis Viollet, who found the back of the net 16 times in the league and 23 times in all competitions despite the fact that he was out of action for two months (missed 12 league games) as he recovered from injuries sustained in the Munich Air Disaster. On the international scene, Murphy's Wales team qualified for the FIFA 1958 World Cup finals where they reached the quarter-finals, losing 1-0 to Brazil whose goal was scored by a relatively unknown 17-year-old who would go on to become the best player in the world (well until George Best arrived on the football scene), Edson Arantes do Nascimento, otherwise known as Pele.

The United fans soon adopted *You'll Never Walk Alone* and would regularly sing it at Old Trafford, their way of remembering the eight players whose lives were so cruelly snatched away from them at such a young age. The Munich Air Disaster was the day a team died. However, when Gerry & The Pacemakers released the song as a single in November 1963 it gave the band from Liverpool their third consecutive No.1 hit in the UK Chart. *How Do You Do It?* and *I Like It* were their other top selling songs. When the Liverpool fans adopted the song as their anthem the United fans stopped singing it.

In 2007, Jane was interviewed by the *Manchester Evening News* about her and her friends singing *You'll Never Walk Alone* post the Munich Air Disaster. 'It has annoyed me so much that people think the song was first sung by the Liverpool fans. The Munich crash was so horrible and everyone was feeling down and despondent and it just seemed an appropriate song to sing. It was an emotional time and I managed to persuade my friends to join in with me. Soon the whole ground was singing it and many people, including me, were in tears. I never dreamed it would become the anthem of our old rivals but I wanted to put the record straight about where the song originated from on the terraces,' said Jane.

> *'The greatness of a man is not in how much wealth he acquires, but in his integrity and his ability to affect those around him positively.'*
> (Bob Marley)

Jimmy Murphy was not born into greatness, his was a journey to greatness and along that path he transformed many young boys from being promising players into great players. He helped Manchester United to five First Division Championships (1951-

52, 1955-56, 1956-57, 1964-65 and 1966-67), two FA Cup wins (1948 and 1963), five FA Charity Shields (1952, 1956, 1957, 1965 shared and 1967 shared), and the European Cup in 1968. As the manager of United's Youth team his Boys won six FA Youth Cups in 1953, 1954, 1955, 1956, 1957 and 1964, the last with two prodigious teenagers under his watchful eye, David Sadler (aged 18) and 17-year-old George Best. Murphy's Boys also won the Central League Championship three times in 1946-47, 1955-56 and 1959-60. Sadly, he passed away on 14 November 1989 aged 79. Quite fittingly in his honour the club commissioned the 'Jimmy Murphy Young Player of the Year Award' which is presented to the best player in the club's youth system in the previous season. It was first awarded in the summer after Murphy's death, with Lee Martin winning the inaugural award in season 1989-90. Manchester United's Carrington Training Centre has the Jimmy Murphy Centre and on 3 May 2023, a statue of Jimmy was unveiled outside Old Trafford.

Jimmy Murphy was a coach who was coveted around the world and despite being linked with taking charge of Arsenal, Juventus and Brazil (clearly they were impressed with his coaching skills of Wales at the 1958 FIFA World Cup finals) he never left his boys in Manchester and continued working in the background as the Assistant Manager at Old Trafford until his retirement in 1971.

Did You Know That?

GERRY & THE PACEMAKERS were managed by the same two men behind the success of The Beatles, manager Brian Epstein and record producer George Martin, and they almost never released *You'll Never Walk*

Alone as their third single. They were supposed to release The Beatles' *Hello Little Girl* but Gerry Marsden, who formed Gerry & the Pacemakers in 1959, along with his brother, Fred, Les Chadwick and Arthur McMahon was a big fan of *Carousel* and the songs from the musical ever since he first saw it as a young boy. The band were originally known as Gerry Marsden and the Mars Bars but after receiving a complaint from the Mars Company who made the chocolate Mars Bar, they were forced to change their name. In the second act of Carousel Nettie Fowler, the cousin of the protagonist Julie Jordan, sings *You'll Never Walk Alone* to comfort and encourage Julie when her husband, Billy Bigelow, the male lead in the show, falls on his knife and dies after a robbery attempt which went wrong. The song is then sung again in the final scene to encourage a graduation class of which Louise (Billy and Julie's daughter) is a member.

PISTACHIO OR TUTTI FRUTTI FLAVOUR?

Hugh 'Hughie' McLenahan was born in West Gorton, Manchester on 23 March 1909, one month before Manchester United won their first ever FA Cup. United defeated Bristol City 1-0 at Crystal Palace in the 1909 FA Cup final which was played on 24 April 1909. In February 1927, McLenahan joined Stockport County as an amateur but within three months of joining The Hatters, without making an appearance for the first team, he was on his way to Old Trafford. Prior to this his youth career had seen him play for several local clubs: Ambrose, Longsight A, Ashton Brothers and Stalybridge Celtic.

Manchester United, a First Division side in season 1926-27 – they eventually finished in 15th position in the final table at the end of the season – were struggling in the league and needed a decent half-back. Louis Rocca, was Manchester United's assistant manager at the time and he found out that Stockport County were in financial difficulties and had organised a bazaar in April 1927, to raise much needed funds to keep the club based in Greater Manchester afloat.

United weren't exactly cash rich themselves, but Rocca was also a very shrewd businessman. The Rocca family ran a very successful ice-cream business in Newton Heath and Louis offered a freezer of ice-cream to the cash strapped Lancashire club in return for their promising 18-year-old half-back. The Hatters needed all the help they could get and accepted the ice-cream in return for their player swap deal.

On 4 February 1928, Hughie made his debut for Manchester United, a 4-1 loss away to Tottenham Hotspur in the First Division (scorer: William Johnston). He went on to make a further 115 appearances, scoring 12 goals, including captaining the club several times. In December 1936, he moved to Notts County.

However, his playing career was interrupted by the outbreak of World War II when Great Britain declared war on Nazi Germany on 1 September 1939, and when the atrocities ended six years later, on 2 September 1945, McLenahan was 36 years old and was too old for a future in football as a career. He went on to work as a Machine Minder at the *News Chronicle* in Manchester and after his retirement he worked as a scout for Manchester United.

Sadly, Hugh McLenahan passed away in May 1988, aged 79.

Did You Know That?

NOTTS COUNTY WERE formed in 1862, 17 years before the formation of Newton Heath Lancashire and Yorkshire Railway Football Club (1878), and are the oldest professional football club in the world. They are nicknamed The Magpies due to the black and white colour of their home strip, which inspired the Italian club, Juventus, to adopt the colours for their kit in 1903.

UNITED NATIONS OF MANCHESTER

On 4 January 2011, Sir Alex Ferguson created Premier League history by selecting a team which took to the pitch comprising 11 players from 11 different countries. For the record the team that Tuesday evening at Old Trafford was: Tomáš Kuszczak (Poland), Rafael da Silva (Brazil), Patrice Evra (France), Chris Smalling (England), Nemanja Vidic, capt (Serbia), Luis Nani (Portugal), Darren Fletcher (Scotland), Darron Gibson (Republic of Ireland), Javier Hernandez (Mexico), Dimitar Berbatov (Bulgaria) and Ryan Giggs (Wales). Jonny Evans (Northern Ireland) was an unused substitute. Meanwhile, United's No.1 goalkeeper, Edwin van der Sar (Netherlands), Park Ji-Sung (South Korea), Antonio Valencia (Ecuador) and Federico Macheda (Italy) all missed the 2-1 victory which extended United's unbeaten run to 20 games and kept them top of the Premier League. Hernandez and Nani scored for United.

Did You Know That?

ONLY 22 NON-BRITISH players were registered to play in the inaugural season of the Premier League (1992-93) but in United's win over Stoke City in 2009-2010 there were 337 non-British registered players from 66 different countries. On 20 March 2021, Suriname became the 112th of the 207 foreign FIFA-affiliated countries to be represented in the Premier League by having a player capped for the country at full international level when Ryan Donk (West Bromwich Albion 2008-09, on loan), made his international debut for Suriname although he was born in Amsterdam, Holland.

PLAYER TO GAFFER

Four players who have played for Manchester United made their debut for the club against a club they later managed.

George Graham – Arsenal
Ian Greaves – Wolverhampton Wanderers
Joe Jordan – Bristol City
Lou Macari – West Ham United

Did You Know That?

ON 24 JANUARY 1973, Graham and Macari played in United's 0-0 draw versus Everton in the English First Division, with Brian Kidd coming on as a substitute for Ted MacDougall in the 56th minute of the game. When Sammy McIlroy made his Manchester United debut, in a 3-3 draw away with Manchester City in the English First Division on 6 November 1971, he played alongside Kidd and his idol, his fellow Irishman, George Best. Sammy scored the opening goal of the game in the 39th minute, Kidd made it 2-0 after 46 minutes and Alan Gowling put United 3-2 up in the 64th minute. It was the 85th league 'Manchester Derby' and a United win would have confirmed their position at the top of the First Division championship table, whilst a win for their neighbours would have seen them close the gap on United to just one point and confirm their challenge for the title. The legendary Manchester City player, Colin Bell, captained City for the first time in a derby game and City's Wyn Davies experienced his first Manchester derby. Davies went on to join United at the end of the 1971-72 season. Alex Stepney and Tommy O'Neill played in the game for United and, like McIlroy, they had also previously made their debuts versus City.

RED HERO TO RED VILLAIN

Only nine players have made the direct switch from Liverpool to Manchester United, or from United in the opposite direction, in the history of both of these famous clubs (up to the end of the 2022-23 season). Liverpool were formed in 1892, some 14 years after the formation of Newton Heath Lancashire and Yorkshire Railway Football Club.

August 1912: Tom Chorlton – Liverpool to Manchester United (no fee disclosed)

November 1913: Jackie Sheldon – Manchester United to Liverpool (no fee disclosed)

September 1920: Tom Miller – Liverpool to Manchester United (£2,000)

May 1921: Fred Hopkin – Manchester United to Liverpool (no fee disclosed)

February 1929: Tommy Reid – Liverpool to Manchester United (no fee disclosed)

January 1938: Ted Savage – Liverpool to Manchester United (no fee disclosed)

November 1938: Allenby Chilton – Liverpool to Manchester United (no fee disclosed)

February 1954: Thomas McNulty – Manchester United to Liverpool (£7,000)

April 1964: Phil Chisnall – Manchester United to Liverpool (£25,000)

Since Phil Chisnall made the reverse journey up the East Lancs Road (officially the Liverpool-East Lancashire Road, the A580), no player has been transferred directly between these two bitter rivals. Three other players have played for both of these English giants, Peter Beardsley (via Vancouver Whitecaps and Newcastle United), Paul Ince (via Inter Milan) and Michael Owen (via Real Madrid and Newcastle United). In 2007, Liverpool made an offer to buy Gabriel Heinze from United but the offer was rejected with United making it known that if their Argentinian star left Old Trafford, then they would only allow him to sign for a foreign club. Clearly the rivalry between the two Lancashire neighbours was bordering on a feud.

However, when Heinze decided to go public with his request to join Liverpool, quite understandably the United fans considered this nothing short of betrayal. Previously the United fans had proudly sang *Argentina* at home and away games in honour of Heinze despite the Falklands War (2 April 1982-14

June 1982) between Argentina and England, but when Heinze made it known he wanted to sign for Liverpool, then he was 'persona non grata' to United fans. It was seen as the ultimate betrayal, and Heinze moved to Real Madrid on 23 August 2007.

Did You Know That?

SIR MATT BUSBY, the manager of Manchester United from 1 October 1945 to 4 June 1969, and again for a second term from 29 December 1970 to 8 June 1971, was a Liverpool player from 1936-45 and declined an offer to join Liverpool's management team in February 1945, opting instead to become the new manager of United.

LOVING OUR CLUB CREST

On 14 August 1971, the Manchester United team took to the pitch at the Baseball Ground, Derby for their opening game of the 1971-72 First Division season. It would be the last season in which the players would wear a United shirt without a club crest on it. United drew 2-2 with goals from Denis Law and Alan Gowling. The game was also Frank O'Farrell's first game as the manager of Manchester United having succeeded Sir Matt Busby on 8 June 1971.

Alan Gowling won England caps at amateur, schoolboy and Under-23 level and also represented the British Olympic side in the qualifying tournament for the 1968 Summer Olympic Games hosted by Mexico. He was born in Stockport, Cheshire on 16 March 1949, and in August 1965, aged 16, he signed as a trainee for Manchester United. Whilst playing for the United junior side, he attended Manchester University where he studied and achieved a degree in Economics. His teammates nicknamed him 'Bamber' after Bamber Gascoigne, who was the host of the popular BBC TV show, *University Challenge*, at the time. He once scored seven goals in a 'B' game for United.

Gowling made his debut for Manchester United on 30 March 1968, aged 19, and scored in a 4-2 victory against Stoke City away in the First Division (George Best, John Aston Jnr and Jimmy Ryan also scored). Ironically, he made his last ever appearance for United against Stoke City on 29 April 1972, a 3-1 win in the First Division at Old Trafford when he came on as a substitute for Bobby Charlton (scorers: Charlton, Ian Storey-Moore and a penalty from George Best). Alan played 87 times for United and scored 21 goals. He played for Newcastle United in their loss to Manchester City in the 1976 League Cup final, being preferred by manager Gordon Lee to the legendary Magpies' striker, Malcolm MacDonald and scored 30 goals in 92 League appearances for the Geordies. During his time at St James' Park he was nicknamed 'The Galloping Chip' by the Newcastle fans.

Did You Know That?

THE BASEBALL GROUND was a stadium in Derby from its' opening in 1890 until it closed in 2003. As the name would suggest, the ground was first used for baseball games. It was originally called Ley's Baseball Ground and was part of a complex of sports grounds (Ley's Recreation Centre) built and owned by Sir Francis Ley, a local businessman, for use by the workers at his foundry, Ley's Malleable Castings Vulcan Ironworks.

Following a visit by Ley to the United States of America in 1889, he attended a baseball game and decided that his Vulcan Works foundry should have recreational facilities and so he paid for the construction of a ground where his workers could play baseball.

The Baseball Ground was the home of Derby Baseball Club from 1890 to 1898, but like most other imported sports during the Victorian era in England, it was never really accepted by the locals. Derby County Football Club was formed in 1884 by William Morley as an off-shoot of Derbyshire County Cricket Club. They shared the ground with their American neighbours from 1895 to 1898, with the groundskeeper busy changing the set-up of the grass from a baseball diamond to a football pitch every week. In 1997, after a 102-year tenancy, Derby County Football Club moved to their new home, Pride Park Stadium.

HIS FINAL WORDS – THANK YOU BOSS

On 12 May 2013, Sir Alex Ferguson addressed the Old Trafford crowed following a 2-1 win over Swansea City in the Premier League. It was his last ever home game in charge of Manchester United. Javier Hernandez and Rio Ferdinand scored for United.

'First of all, it's a thank you to Manchester United. Not just the directors, not just the medical staff, not just the coaching staff, the players or the supporters, it's all of you. You have been the most fantastic experience of my life. I have been very fortunate. I've been able to manage some of the greatest players in the country, let alone Manchester United. All these players here today have represented our

club the proper way – they've won the championship in a fantastic fashion. Well done to the players.

My retirement doesn't mean the end of my life with the club. I'll be able to now enjoy watching them rather than suffer with them. But, if you think about it, those last-minute goals, the comebacks, even the defeats, are all part of this great football club of ours. It's been an unbelievable experience for all of us, so thank you for that.

I'd also like to remind you that when we had bad times here, the club stood by me, all my staff stood by me, the players stood by me. Your job now is to stand by our new manager. That is important.

Before I start bubbling, I just want to pay tribute to Paul Scholes, who retires today. He's unbelievable, one of the greatest players this club has ever had and will ever have. Paul we wish you a good retirement and I know you'll be around annoying me! Also, I'd like to wish Darren Fletcher a speedy comeback to our club.

The players… I wish the players every success in the future. You know how good you are, you know the jersey you're wearing, you know what it means to everyone here and don't ever let yourself down. The expectation is always there. I'm going home, well, I'm going inside for a while, and I want to say thank you again from all the Ferguson family. They're all up there, 11 grandchildren. Thank you.

Did You Know That?

THE LEGENDARY SCOTTISh actor, Sir Sean Connery, who famously portrayed James Bond 007 in seven movies, paid his own tribute to Sir Alex, a fellow Scot, and chose the lyrics of the Beatles' song *In My Life*.

There are places I'll remember
All my life though some have changed

Some forever, not for better
Some have gone and some remain
All these places have their moments
With lovers and friends I still can recall
Some are dead and some are living
In my life I've loved them all
But of all these friends and lovers
There is no one compares with you
And these memories lose their meaning
When I think of love as something new
Though I know I'll never lose affection
For people and things that went before
I know I'll often stop and think about them
In my life I love you more
Though I know I'll never lose affection
For people and things that went before
I know I'll often stop and think about them
In my life I love you more

A SHIRT OF MANY COLOURS

Several Manchester United players have played international football for more than one country.

Johnny Carey: United 1936-53 (Republic of Ireland and Northern Ireland).

Tommy Breen: United 1937-39 (Republic of Ireland and Northern Ireland).

Andrei Kanchelskis: United 1991-95 (Soviet Union, Commonwealth of Independent States (CIS) & Russia)

Wilfried Zaha: United 2013-15 (England and Ivory Coast)

Did You Know That?

IN 1946, THE first post-war FIFA Congress saw the four UK associations welcomed back after an absence of almost 20 years. In honour of this return, a match between a Select XI from the UK and a team from the Rest of Europe was arranged for the following year. On 10 May 1947, a crowd of 137,000 fans packed into Hampden Park, Glasgow to see a friendly dubbed by the press as the '*Match of the Century*'. The Great Britain side was selected by the new England manager, Walter Winterbottom, who played for Manchester United from 1936-38, but no United players were selected by him. Great Britain won the game 6-1.

SEVEN REDS IN WHITE

On Sunday 28 August 2016, Sam Allardyce announced his first-ever England squad since he replaced Roy Hodgson as manager on 22 July 2016. Allardyce named three Manchester United players in his squad for the 2018 FIFA World Cup qualifier in Slovakia on 4 September 2016 – Luke Shaw, Chris Smalling and Wayne Rooney. A few days later, Allardyce confirmed that Wayne Rooney would retain the England captaincy; at the time, Rooney had captained England 19 times in his 115 appearances (up to and including their 1-0 defeat to Iceland at the 2016

European Championship Finals) but was a long way short of two other United England captains, Bryan Robson (65 caps as captain from 90 appearances) and David Beckham (59 caps as captain from 115 appearances). Robbo, Becks, Billy Wright and Bobby Moore remain the only players to have captained England more than 40 times. No doubt Robson would have challenged the Wright/Moore record of 90 captaincies had it not been for his aggressive style of play for club and country, resulting in several serious injuries, thereby reducing the number of caps he was awarded.

In February 2012, Fabio Capello resigned following the FA's decision to remove the captaincy of the national side from Chelsea's John Terry, and Stuart Pearce took temporary charge of the team in a caretaker role. Pearce selected four United players in his squad to face Holland at Wembley Stadium on 29 February 2012. England lost the friendly 3-2, with Chris Smalling, Danny Welbeck and Ashley Young starting (Young scored). Phil Jones came on as a substitute for Smalling.

Sir Alex Ferguson once sent eight United players to join-up with an England squad, a 2002 FIFA World Cup qualifier versus Albania on 28 March 2001 in Tiranë. Five Reds started in the 3-1 win (Gary Neville, Nicky Butt, David Beckham, Paul Scholes and Andy Cole), with two coming on as substitutes (Wes Brown for Sol Campbell and Teddy Sheringham for Michael Owen), meaning there were seven United players on the pitch at the same time. Phil Neville was an unused substitute. Two future United players also played in the game, Rio Ferdinand (Leeds United) and Michael Owen (Liverpool). The England scorers were Owen, Cole and Scholes.

Did You Know That?

ANDY COLE'S FIRST three full England caps were awarded by three different England managers: Terry Venables (England 0-0 Uruguay, 29 March 1995, 1 cap), Glenn Hoddle (England 2-0 Italy, 4 June 1997, 1 cap) and Howard Wilkinson (England 0-2 France, 10 February 1999, 2 caps). Cole was also capped six times by Kevin Keegan, again by Howard Wilkinson and five times by Sven-Goran Eriksson. His goal against Albania in a 3-1 away victory on 28 March 2001, ended his England goal drought at the 13th attempt, his only goal for his country in 15 international appearances.

THREE LIONS ON HIS SHIRT AND THE CAPTAIN'S ARMBAND

No Manchester United player had been given the captaincy of England prior to the Second World War. England played their first ever international game on 30 November 1872, a 0-0 draw with Scotland at Hamilton Crescent, the West of Scotland's Cricket Ground, Partick, Glasgow. However, since 1945, 12 Manchester United players have captained England.

Sir Bobby Charlton, Ray Wilkins, Bryan Robson, Peter Beardsley, Paul Ince, Michael Owen, David Beckham, Rio Ferdinand, Wayne Rooney, Chris Smalling, Harry Maguire and Marcus Rashford. On 6 June 2021, Rashford became the 125th England captain, and the youngest black and ethnic minority captain, when he led the team out against Romania in Middlesbrough. England won 1-0 thanks to a Rashford goal.

Did You Know That?

IN 1984, DAVID Platt signed as an apprentice for Manchester United after leaving school but was later released without having ever appeared for the first team who were managed by Ron Atkinson. On 23 February 1985, he joined Crewe Alexandra in the Fourth Division on a free transfer and spent over three seasons at Gresty Road under manager, Dario Gradi, before signing for Aston Villa for £200,000 in February 1988. Villa were promoted to the First Division at the end of the 1987-88 season and he stayed at Villa Park for a further two seasons, before becoming one of the rare players from England at that time to ply their trade abroad. On 21 July 1991, he moved to AS Bari in Italy's Serie A before moving on to Juventus and Sampdoria. During his time in Italy, he won the UEFA Cup (Juventus 1992-93) and the Coppa Italia (Sampdoria 1993-94). He then moved to Arsenal in 1995, and helped the London club to win their second 'Double' of League and FA Cup in season 1997-98 (also 'Double' winners in season 1970-71).

During his career, Platt scored 27 goals in 62 games for England, helping his country finish fourth in the 1990 World Cup finals and reach the semi-finals of the 1996 European Championships. He captained his country 19 times.

STAR SPANGLED UNITED

Up to the end of the 2022-23 season, four players who had a United States of America nationality, played for Manchester United.

James Brown (1932-34): 41 games, 17 goals (born in Kilmarnock, Scotland).

Edward McIlvenney (1950-51): 2 games, 0 goals (born in

Greenock, Scotland).

Tim Howard (2003-06): 71 games, 0 goals (born in North Brunswick, New Jersey, USA).

Jonathon Spector (2003-05): 8 games, 0 goals (born in Arlington Heights, Chicago, USA).

Did You Know That?

TIM HOWARD MADE his debut for Manchester United on 10 August 2003, versus Arsenal in the 2003 FA Community Shield at the Millennium Stadium, Cardiff. The game ended 1-1 after extra-time (Mikael Silvestre scored against his future club, 2008-10) and went to a penalty shootout which United won 4-3. Howard saved penalties from Giovanni van Bronckhorst and Robert Pires, to give United their eleventh FA Charity/Community Shield. Paul Scholes, Rio Ferdinand, Ole-Gunnar Solskjaer and Diego Forlan scored in the penalty shootout, but Ruud van Nistelrooy's spot kick was saved by Jens Lehman.

OLYMPIC GOLD MEDAL

Harold Hardman, Manchester United 1908-09, four appearances and no goals, won a gold medal with Great Britain at the 1908 Olympic Games which were hosted by London. He won four senior international caps with England between 1905-08, and scored one goal which came in a 1-0 win over Ireland at Goodison Park in the British Home International Championships. Ryan Giggs captained the Great Britain squad at the 2012 Olympic

Games in London where they lost out to South Korea in the quarter-finals, a 1-1 draw followed by a 5-4 penalty shootout loss at the Millennium Stadium, Cardiff. In 1906, Hardman won an FA Cup winners' medal when he played for Everton as an amateur.

Did You Know That?

 HAROLD HARDMAN WAS a solicitor by trade, and in November 1912 he was appointed as a Director of Manchester United Football Club until 1931, and again from 1934. He served as the Chairman of Manchester United from 1951 until his death on 9 June 1965, aged 83.

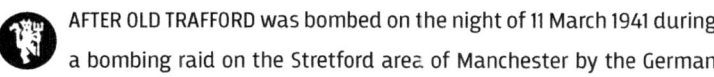

NO PLACE LIKE HOME

Since the club's formation as Newton Heath Lancashire and Yorkshire Railway Football Club in 1878, they have had three fixed home grounds.

1878-93 – North Road, Newton Heath, Manchester.
1893-1910 – Bank Street, Clayton, Manchester.
1910-Present – Old Trafford, Manchester.

Did You Know That?

AFTER OLD TRAFFORD was bombed on the night of 11 March 1941 during a bombing raid on the Stretford area of Manchester by the German

Luftwaffe, the pitch and stadium were so badly damaged that the club had to rent Maine Road, Manchester from their city rivals, Manchester City.

SHOW ME THE MONEY

The following lines are from the 1996 movie *Jerry Maguire* starring Tom Cruise as sports agent, Jerry Maguire, and Cuba Gooding Jr as Rod Tidwell, a wide receiver with the Arizona Cardinals and Jerry's client.

What can I do for you? You just tell me. – Jerry

It's personal and very important. Hell! It's a family motto. Are you ready, Jerry? – Rod

I'm ready. – Jerry

Here it is. Show me the money. – Rod

Show me the money was voted the 25th best quote in movie history by the American Film Institute.

Since sponsorship of football jerseys of English clubs began in the early 1980s, no fewer than six huge companies have been more than willing to show Manchester United the money.

It wasn't until the 1982-83 season that Manchester United wore the name of a sponsor on their shirts. In the summer of 1982, the club teamed-up with the Japanese electronics company, SHARP. Not only was the deal very lucrative commercially for the club, but SHARP also had a factory located in the heart of Newton Heath since the early 1970s, the spiritual home of Manchester United. The deal was actually worth £500,000 over five years.

Prior to the start of the 1982-83 season, the United manager,

Ron Atkinson and his squad took part in a photo-shoot on the Old Trafford pitch to promote 10 of the products manufactured by the Japanese electronics giant. These gadgets were considered to be 'must have' items for all homes at the time. They included a VC9300 VCR video recorder so as Reds fans could record United games shown on TV; a VZ3000 vertical record player, which could play vinyl LPs and singles, cassette tapes and picture discs (which were extremely popular at the time); a WFT audio radio/tape player with a double cassette deck which allowed you to record the UK Number 1 chart hits in the summer of 1982, which included *Come On Eileen* by Dexy's Midnight Runners, *Happy Talk* by Captain Sensible and *Eye of the Tiger,* the theme song to the *Rocky* movies starring Sylvester Stallone and performed by the American rock band, Survivor. Quite close to the feet of Big Ron was a cash register and less than a year earlier, 3 October 1981, United broke the British record transfer fee when they paid West Bromwich Albion £1.5 million for Bryan Robson

The deal with SHARP lasted for 18 years until season 2000-01 when Vodafone won the rights to place their company name on the most famous football shirt in the world, but not before the SHARP name was emblazoned on United shirts worn famously by Eric Cantona during United's two Double winning campaigns in seasons 1993-94 and 1995-96, and the club's historic 1999 Treble winning team. Vodafone paid United £30 million for the privilege, which ended before the 2006-07 season when AIG entered the arena, or rather, the Theatre of Dreams.

American Insurance Group agreed a four-year deal worth £80 million to become the latest club sponsor. It was the most lucrative club shirt sponsorship deal in the world at the time, but United decided not to extend it after the contract came to a close. It has been claimed that economic troubles at the time for the U.S. company resulted in Manchester United looking to find a more stable commercial partner.

Next up to the plate was another American company, AON, the world's leading risk advisors and human capital consultants. They are believed to have paid £80 million for a four-year sponsorship deal commencing in season 2010-11.

In the summer of 2014, a household name in the U.S., a beast of the motor industry, Chevrolet, who were already the club's official vehicle partner, agreed a deal to become the new shirt sponsor. In season 2014-15, the name of CHEVROLET adorned the famous red jersey of Manchester United. The deal was worth £47 million per year.

On 19 March 2021, Manchester United announced they had signed a new five-year deal with the German-based computer software company TeamViewer to become their principal shirt sponsor from the start of the 2021-22 season. The deal is believed to be worth an estimated £47 million each season to United, a total of £235 million over the 5-year term.

Did You Know That?

ON 28 AUGUST 1982, a Manchester United team took to the pitch for the first time with the name of a sponsor on their jerseys, SHARP, and they beat Birmingham City 3-0 in the English First Division. Kevin Moran enjoyed the honour of scoring the club's first ever 'sponsored goal, with Frank Stapleton and Steve Coppell also scoring.

TOP 10 GOAL SCORERS

1. Wayne Rooney – 253 (2004-17)
2. Sir Bobby Charlton – 249 (1956-73)
3. Denis Law – 237 (1962-73)
4. Jack Rowley – 211 (1937-55)
5. Dennis Viollet – 179 (1952-62)
6. George Best – 179 (1963-74)
7. Joe Spence – 168 (1919-33)
8. Ryan Giggs – 168 (1991-2014)
9. Mark Hughes – 163 (1983-86 & 1988-95)
10. Paul Scholes – 155 (1994-2011 & 2012-13)

Did You Know That?

BETWEEN THEM, BILL Foulkes, Alex Stepney and Joe Spence only won four senior international caps for England. Spence won two caps and scored one goal, in a 3-3 draw versus Ireland in the 1926-27 Home International Championship at Anfield.

SCORING AT THE WRONG END

Two former Reds jointly hold the unwanted record of scoring the most number of own goals as a Manchester United player. Bill Foulkes (1952-70) scored five own goals in 688 appearances for the club, the fourth highest number of games for United in the history of the club. Nobby Stiles (1960-71) also netted five times against his own goalkeeper during his Old Trafford career in 395 games.

John Clements was the first player to score an own goal for the club when Newton Heath drew 2-2 away to Accrington Stanley in the First Division at Thornleyhome Road, Accrington, Lancashire on 26 November 1892 (scorers: James Colville and Thomas Fitzsimmons). On 27 November 1902, Thomas Read scored United's first ever own goal, in the Second Division, a 1-1 draw at home (Bank Street, Clayton) with Glossop (scorer: Daniel Hirst). Thomas Jones (1924-37) became the first player to record an FA Cup own goal when United beat Brentford 7-1 at Old Trafford in Round Three on 14 January 1928. James Hanson scored four times, whilst William Johnston, Francis McPherson and Joe Spence also found the back of the Brentford net.

On 15 October 1963, Manchester United beat Willem II 6-1 in the First Round second leg of the European Cup Winners' Cup at Old Trafford. All seven goals were scored by Reds, with Noel Cantwell, United's 1963 FA Cup final winning captain, scoring for the Dutch visitors. Denis Law scored a hat-trick, with goals from Maurice Setters, Bobby Charlton and Phil Chisnall. It was the first own goal scored by a Manchester United player in European competition. Shay Brennan scored the club's first own goal in the European Cup when United beat SL Benfica at the Estadio da Luz, Lisbon, Portugal on 9 March 1966. United won 5-1 in the quarter-final second leg tie with George Best (two), John Connelly, Paddy Crerand and Bobby Charlton scoring.

Jimmy Nicholl was the first Red to score an own goal in the League Cup when they lost 4-1 to Norwich City at Carrow Road,

Norwich in a Third Round tie on 26 September 1979. Martin Buchan, the club captain, also scored at the wrong end in the game, with the United goal coming from Sammy McIlroy. Gary Pallister was the first player to score an own goal for the club in the Premier League, a 2-2 draw away to Arsenal on 22 March 1994. Lee Sharpe scored twice for United. In the Champions League era of the European Cup, Roy Keane was the first Red to score past his own goalkeeper when they lost 3-2 at Old Trafford to Real Madrid in a quarter-final second leg tie (scorers: David Beckham and Paul Scholes penalty) on 19 April 2000.

Mikael Silvestre became the first, and only player, to score an own goal in the FA Charity Shield for United when they lost 3-1 to Arsenal at the Millennium Stadium, Cardiff in the 2004 final played on 8 August 2004. Alan Smith scored for United in the game. On 28 November 2019, Bernard Di'Shon became the first player to score an own goal as a Manchester United player in the UEFA Cup/Europa League; United lost 2-1 away to FC Astana in a Group L game (scorer: Jesse Lingard).

Did You Know That?

'ACCRINGTON STANLEY... WHO are they?' spoken in a distinct scouse accent by a young boy is a famous slogan that was used in a TV advertisement for milk by the Milk Marketing Board in the 1980s. The commercial shows two young Liverpool fans adorned in the Liverpool home kit, in the kitchen of one of their homes, after they had just played a game of football. The visiting kid asks his mate if he has any lemonade to drink and he is handed a bottle. The other kid starts pouring milk from a glass pint bottle and his mate says, 'Milk? Uuuuhhh'.

His mate then says milk is what Ian Rush, a major star for Liverpool at the time, drinks and that Rush told him that if he didn't drink milk, when he grew up he would only be good enough to play for Accrington Stanley. The other kid then says, 'Accrington Stanley... who are they?' to which the first kid replies, 'Exactly'. The second kid then says, 'Give me some', but he is told... 'Get off!' According to one of the producers of the television advertisement, Tottenham Hotspur were going to be named but they objected, resulting in Accrington Stanley being chosen as they were a non-League side at the time.

It is believed that the commercial earned Accrington Stanley £10,000.

MANCHESTER UNITED'S WAR HERO

John Scott joined Manchester United in June 1921, a £750.00 transfer from Bradford Park Avenue. He only stayed one season at Old Trafford, playing 24 times without scoring. In June 1922, he moved north of the border to join St Mirren in his native Scotland. He was born in Motherwell. During World War I, Scott was awarded a Military Medal.

Did You Know That?

THE ORIGINAL BRADFORD Park Avenue was founded in 1863 as the Bradford Football Club, playing rugby football and won its first major trophy in 1884 when they lifted the Yorkshire Cup. Bradford Football Club began playing association football in season 1895-96 and shared the West Yorkshire League Championship with Hunslet in 1895–96, also winning the Leeds Workpeople's Hospital Cup in their inaugural season.

BROTHERS ON THE SCORESHEET

On 7 April 1890, Newton Heath Football Club beat Small Heath 9-1 at home in the Football Alliance. Thomas Craig, Jack Doughty (two), Roger Doughty, Alf Farman, Alf Stewart (three) and Edgar Wilson all scored for The Heathens. It was the first and only time two brothers scored for Newton Heath Football Club/Manchester United in the same game.

Did You Know That?

 SEVEN PAIRS OF brothers have played in a Premier League game in the same team: Shola and Sammy Ameobi (Newcastle United), Andre and Jordan Ayew (Swansea City), Christian and Jonathan Benteke (Crystal Palace), Shaun and Bradley-Wright Phillips (Manchester City), Gary and Phil Neville (Manchester United), Kolo and Yaya Toure (Manchester City) and Rafael and Fabio Da Silva (Manchester United).

UNDER THE LIGHTS

Newton Heath Football Club/Manchester United played their first ever floodlit game in season 1899-1900, at their Bank Street, Clayton home. Newton Heath Football Club were an English Second Division team at the time and the game under lights was a benefit match which was organised for two stalwarts of the club, captain Harry Stafford and Walter Cartwright, in recognition of their services to The Heathens. Stafford was the one who asked for the game to be played at night because he knew more fans would turn out after finishing work earlier that day. The club hired the Wells Lighting System and used a gilded football so as the fans could see all of the action.

A Wells light was a large paraffin-fuelled (kerosene) blow lamp used for engineering work, particularly for illumination during the Victorian era. In 1900, widespread electrical lighting had not yet become available in England, and so the Wells lighting system was the most common form of high-powered portable illumination used at the time. It was mainly applied for construction work, particularly railways, civil engineering, shipyards and ironworks.

On the evening of the benefit game a strong wind enveloped the ground which meant the match stewards found it extremely difficult to keep the numerous lamps lit. As they re-lit one lamp another one went out. When it got to the point that only one lamp stayed lit, the referee blew his whistle and brought the game to an end.

Harry Stafford played 200 times for Newton Heath/Manchester United from 1895-1903, and scored one goal in a 3-0 home win against Portsmouth on 5 January 1901 (when the club were still known as Newton Heath Football Club) in an FA Cup Supplementary Round match. Walter Cartwright made 257 appearances for Newton Heath/Manchester United from 1895-1904, and scored eight times.

Did You Know That?

WHEN THE MATCH officials returned to their changing room area, they discovered that 10 of the 22 players who started the game had already showered and were dressed for the post-match buffet and drinks reception. The lighting was so bad none of the match officials even noticed them walking off the pitch.

SOLSKJAER'S YOUNG ONES

On 28 November 2019, Manchester United fielded the club's youngest ever side in a competitive European game away to FC Astana. In season 1956-57, Matt Busby defied the orders of the Football League not to play any European games and entered United, the reigning English First Division Champions, in the European Cup. The competition was first played in season 1955-56, but Chelsea, English First Division Champions in season 1954-55, declined the invitation to participate in the inaugural European Cup because of the pressure applied on them by English football's hierarchy. Real Madrid won the first edition of the competition when they beat Stade de Reims 4-3 at Parc des Princes, Paris on 13 June 1956. Busby's side, famously dubbed 'The Busby Babes' pioneered European club football for English teams. However, Hibernian had already represented Scotland in the tournament in its first competition and lost 3-0 over two legs to Stade de Reims in the semi-finals.

Before him Busby, Dave Sexton, Ron Atkinson, Alex Ferguson,

David Moyes, Louis van Gaal and Jose Mourinho had all selected a Manchester United side to play in Europe.

Solskjaer's team to play FC Astana away in the Europa League mirrored Solskjær's nickname 'The Baby Faced Assassin' when he sent his own team of babes out on to the pitch. He handed debuts to six members of United's Youth team who were Di'Shon Bernard (19), Ethan Galbraith (18), Ethan Laird (18), Dylan Levitt (19), D'mani Bughail-Mellor (19) and Largie Ramazani (18). Bernard and Levitt started the game. Bughail-Mellor came on as a substitute for Tahith Chong (65 mins), Ramanzi came on as a substitute for James Garner (84 mins) and Galbraith came on as a substitute for Angel Gomes (89 mins). United lost the tie 2-1. Jesse Lingard scored United's goal.

Did You Know That?

WITH AN AVERAGE age of 22 years and 26 days, United's team was the youngest they have ever named for a match in major European competition, excluding qualifiers. The team was: Lee Grant, Ethan Laird, Luke Shaw, Axel Tuanzebe, Di'Shon Bernard, James Garner, Dylan Levitt, Tahith Chong, Jesse Lingard, Angel Gomes and Mason Greenwood.

PART 2

SIR BOBBY'S RECORD BEATEN

OUR TOP BOY

UNITED BANNED FROM OLD TRAFFORD

WITH BAT AND BALL

OUR DEADLIEST MARKSMEN

LIKE FATHER, LIKE SON

FOOTBALL MATCH
TURNED BOXING MATCH

On 20 October 1990, United, the reigning FA Cup holders faced Arsenal, English First Division Champions in season 1988-89, at Old Trafford in the league. The Gunners won 1-0 in what proved to be an ill-tempered affair and the beginning of a fierce rivalry between these two English giants of the game. Nigel Winterburn made a tackle on the United left-back Denis Irwin to which the Republic of Ireland international's Old Trafford teammate, Brian McClair, took great exception. McClair squared up to the Arsenal left-back and quite quickly a number of other players joined the fracas. In fact, 21 players got involved in the melee with only one, United's goalkeeper, Les Sealey, not becoming directly involved with the numerous confrontations on the pitch.

The United side was: Les Sealey, Clayton Blackmore, Denis Irwin, Steve Bruce (Captain), Gary Pallister, Mike Phelan, Neil Webb, Paul Ince, Lee Sharpe, Brian McClair and Mark Hughes. Substitutes: Mark Robins for Sharpe 66 minutes and Lee Martin for Irwin 79 minutes.

Sealey was actually acting as a peacemaker in the melee and

put his arms around the Arsenal midfielder, David Rocastle; sadly, both of these players have since passed away. Rocastle died on 31 March 2001, aged only 33, whilst Les died on 19 August 2001, aged 43. Ironically, if any of the 22 players on the pitch that day were destined to lose their temper with an opposing player, it would almost 100% definitely have been Sealey. He had already started writing, presumably an autobiography, entitled *DEFINITELY MENTAL*.

Arsenal fined Anders Limpar, the goalscorer, Paul Davis, Rocastle, Winterburn and manager George Graham two weeks wages. The Football Association acted swiftly and deducted United one point for misconduct by their players, whilst Arsenal were deducted two points. However, both clubs ended the season with silverware. The Gunners claimed their second league title in three seasons with 83 points, seven clear of runners-up Liverpool. United beat FC Barcelona 2-1 in Rotterdam, Holland in the 1991 European Cup Winners' Cup final.

Did You Know That?

ARSENAL MANAGER, GEORGE Graham and his assistant manager, Stewart Houston were both former Reds. Graham played 46 times for United from 1972-75 and scored two goals. His fellow Scot, Houston, made 250 appearances for United from 1973-80, scoring 16 times.

SIR BOBBY CHARLTON'S RECORD FINALLY BEATEN

When Bobby Charlton decided to retire at the end of the 1972-73 season, he had made a record 758 appearances for the club and scored a club record 249 goals (1956-73). When Ryan Giggs replaced Paul Scholes in the 87th minute of the 2008 Champions League final versus Chelsea in Moscow on 21 May 2008, it was his 759th game in a Manchester United shirt. United went on to beat their fellow Premier League side 6-5 in a penalty shootout after the game ended 1-1 after extra time. Cristiano Ronaldo had given United the lead in the 26th minute but was the only Red to miss from the spot kick. Ironically, it was Giggs who scored United's sixth penalty to give them their third European Cup/Champions League success, 50 years after the Munich Air Disaster which claimed the lives of eight young Busby Babes. After the trophy presentation, Sir Bobby Charlton was the first person to walk up to Giggs and congratulate him. It was Giggs' 18th winners' medal as a Manchester United player and he went on to make a staggering 963 appearances for the club, scoring 168 goals.

Did You Know That?

A YEAR AFTER he retired, Bobby Charlton was persuaded to return to the game and take-up the position as player/manager of Preston North End.

TOP BOY

The following British and Irish Reds are among their country's leading marksmen.

Wayne Rooney (Manchester United 2004-17): England top goal scorer with 52 goals. He scored three goals more than the legendary Sir Bobby Charlton, who notched up 49 goals to be No.2 in the list of England goalscorers, but unlike Rooney who scored eight goals for his country as an Everton player and 44 goals as a Red, Charlton scored all of his international goals when he was at Old Trafford.

David Healy (Manchester United 1999-2001) Northern Ireland: top goalscorer (36 goals).

Denis Law (Manchester United 1962-74) Scotland: joint-top goalscorer along with Kenny Dalglish (30 goals).

Mark Hughes (Manchester United 1980-86 and 1988-1995) Wales: joint-seventh top goalscorer along with Robert Earnshaw, Cliff Jones and Aaron Ramsey (16 goals).

Frank Stapleton (Manchester United 1981-87) Republic of Ireland: fourth top goalscorer (15 goals).

Did You Know That?

DWIGHT YORKE (Manchester United 1998-2002) is joint-seventh in the list of top goalscorers for Trinidad and Tobago with 16 goals, but Robin van Persie (Manchester United 2012-15) is top of the Dutch list with 50 goals.

UNITED BANNED FROM OLD TRAFFORD

On 24 April 1971, Manchester United played their last home game in the First Division Championship during the 1970-71 season. Ipswich Town were the visitors to Old Trafford and a crowd of 33,556 turned out to see the game. United won 3-2 with goals from George Best, Bobby Charlton and Brian Kidd. However, during the match some Reds threw knives into the away end. Football hooliganism was rife in English football in the early 1970s, with many clubs up and down the country having gangs, better known as Firms, associated with them. Not surprisingly United's firm was called 'Red Army' and they were among the most feared in the land, with thousands of Reds going to away games ready to rumble once they stepped off their coaches and from train carriages. Every time the Red Army visited a town or city, hundreds of uniformed police officers marched them to the ground with police dogs ready to attack any Red who stepped out of line.

As a result of the incident during the game versus Ipswich Town, the Football Association ordered Manchester United to play their opening two home games of the following season away from Old Trafford. On 22 August 1971, United walked out of the home dressing-room at Anfield to face Arsenal in their first home game of the 1971-72 First Division campaign. It was United's third league game of the season, having drawn 2-2 away to Derby County at The Baseball Ground, and winning 3-2 over Chelsea at Stamford Bridge. On 22 August 1971, Liverpool's world famous and iconic, Spion Kop, was a sea of red and white scarves as Reds crammed into it behind one of the goals. But on this occasion, for the first time in the history of Liverpool Football Club, founded in 1892, the Reds in attendance were Manchester United fans.

The Spion Kop was built in 1906 as a reward to the fans after Liverpool had clinched their second First Division Championship title in season 1905-06 (also champions in 1900-01). It had 100 steps and towered above the Walton Breck Road behind the ground. The name came from a small hill in South Africa known as Spion Kop where in January 1900, during the Boer war, a battle left hundreds dead. Many of the soldiers killed came from Lancashire regiments, with a strong contingent from Liverpool.

United beat Arsenal, the reigning First Division champions, and FA Cup holders, thanks to goals from Charlton, Alan Gowling and Kidd. The match programme still carried the title of 'The Anfield Review'. Speaking to the *Guardian* newspaper in 2010, Alex Stepney, who was in goal for United in the game when Frank McLintock opened the scoring for the other visiting team, said he could not really remember the game, saying, 'I vaguely remember that we had to play two games away from Old Trafford, but I can't recall that match. I thought I'd only ever won one match at Anfield, when we beat Liverpool 4-1, so I can add a second win now'.

United beat Liverpool 4-1 at Anfield in the First Division on 13 December 1969 with goals from Charlton, Willie Morgan, Ian Ure and an own goal. Liverpool Football Club received 15% of the gate from the United versus Arsenal game which was attended by 27,649 fans. On 23 August 1971, United played their second exiled league home game at The Victoria Ground,

Stoke and beat West Bromwich Albion 3-2, with Best (two) and Gowling on target.

Did You Know That?

IN 2005, THE movie *Green Street* was released. In the movie an American college student (played by Elijah Wood from the *Lord of the Rings Trilogy* of movies), falls in with West Ham United's GSE firm of fans (Green Street Elite), which is being run by his brother-in-law's younger brother. In the movie, West Ham United are drawn against arch rivals, Millwall in the FA Cup. The GSE and the NGO (the Millwall Firm) meet up before the game for a hand-to-hand battle.

IN THE DOCK

In June 1892, Newton Heath Lancashire and Yorkshire Railway Football Club signed James Brown from Dundee Our Boys. On 3 September 1892, Brown made his debut for The Heathens, a 4-3 loss away to Blackburn Rovers at Ewood Park in the First Division (scorers: James Coupar, Robert Donaldson and Alf Farman). It was the club's first ever match in League football. On 19 October 1892, Brown played for the club's reserve team versus Darwen Reserves, a local Lancashire rival. A. H. Albut, the secretary of The Heathens, wanted to see what his young Scottish full-back was made of and the reserve league was a brutal one, in which no prisoners were taken in games. It was a man's game, a working man's game, played by men who played for the love of the game and without any monetary award.

During the game, Brown accidentally collided with Joseph Apsden, the opposing centre-forward. Brown missed the ball and his knee struck Apsden in the stomach. It was an innocuous incident, no malice was intended by Brown, but Apsden was taken off the pitch to the medical tent. There was no such a thing as substitutes at the time. Apsden was too unwell to go back on the pitch, the game ended, and he went home. Within a few hours of returning home, he died. Brown was served with a summons to attend the Coroner's Court and give evidence. He was devastated when he learned of Apsden's death and attended the hearing which handed out a ruling of 'Accidental Death'. In season 1892-93, Brown won a Manchester Senior Cup winners' medal with the club, their fifth win in the competition's history which was first won by Ashton United in 1885.

Did You Know That?

IN 1893, DUNDEE Our Boys merged with Dundee East End and formed Dundee Football Club in order to participate in the Scottish First Division. The Scottish First Division was formed in season 1893-94, although the Scottish Football Association was established in 1890. In the inaugural Scottish First Division season (1893-94), Dundee Football Club alternated between the two kits of their merger clubs, the sky blue and white stripes of Dundee East End and the all navy blue of Dundee Our Boys. They ended the season in 8th place in the League (10 teams competed), which was won by Glasgow Celtic.

TOP 10 APPEARANCE MAKERS FOR UNITED

1.	Ryan Giggs	963
2.	Sir Bobby Charlton	758
3.	Paul Scholes	718
4.	Bill Foulkes	688
5.	Gary Neville	602
6.	Wayne Rooney	559
7.	Alex Stepney	539
8.	Tony Dunne	535
9.	Denis Irwin	529
10.	Joe Spence	510

Did You Know That?

GARY NEVILLE was awarded an Honorary Degree by Bolton University for services to football.

DUAL INTERNATIONALS WITH BAT AND BALL

Three Manchester United players represented their country at international level in a cricket Test Match. Noel Cantwell, Manchester United's 1963 FA Cup winning captain, played football at international level for the Republic of Ireland and also represented his country at international level in cricket in 1956. He was a left-handed batsman and a right-arm medium pace bowler. Cantwell played for his country 36 times in football internationals and scored 14 goals.

Arnold Sidebottom played 20 times for Manchester United, without scoring, from 1972-75, and played for Yorkshire County Cricket Club. He was born in Barnsley, Yorkshire, and played in one Test Match for England in 1985. Arnie was a right-handed batsman and a right-arm fast-medium bowler. Andy Goram played two games for Manchester United in season 2000-01, on loan from Motherwell Football Club, a 4-2 home win over Coventry City and a 2-1 loss way to Southampton, both games in the Premier League.

He played cricket for Scotland four times between 1989-91 as a wicket-keeper, a left-handed batsman and a right-arm medium-pace bowler, and remains the only person to have represented Scotland in a first-class cricket match and in a full international football match. However, his manager at Glasgow Rangers at the time, Walter Smith was unhappy with his goalkeeper's interest in cricket and ordered his No.1 to concentrate on his football career. In May 2016, Goram (born on 13 April 1964 in Bury, England) played for a Scotland Over-50s team against a Lancashire Over-50s side. Sadly, Andy passed away on 2 July 2022.

Did You Know That?

ANDY GORAM WON five Scottish Premier League titles, three Scottish Cups and two Scottish League Cups during his Glasgow Rangers career (1991-98). When Manchester United won the inaugural Premier League title in season 1992-93, Goram was named the Scottish Professional Footballers' Association Players' Player of the Year and the Scottish Football Writers' Association Player of the Year. In 2010 he was inducted to the Scottish Football Hall of Fame.

TOP 10 MANCHESTER UNITED MARKSMEN IN A LEAGUE CAMPAIGN

Manchester United's Top 10 goalscorers in a single season during their Old Trafford careers.

1. Dennis Viollet – 32 goals, 36 games (1959-60)
2. Cristiano Ronaldo – 31 goals, 34 games (2007-08)
3. Denis Law – 30 goals, 30 games (1963-64)
4. Jack Rowley – 30 goals, 40 games (1951-52)
5. Bobby Charlton – 29 goals, 38 games (1958-59)
6. George Best – 28 goals, 41 games (1967-68)
7. Wayne Rooney – 27 goals, 34 games (2011-12)
8. Wayne Rooney – 26 goals, 32 games (2009-10)
9. Jack Rowley – 26 goals, 37 games (1946-47)
10. Robin van Persie – 26 goals, 38 games (2012-13)

Did You Know That?

 JACK ROWLEY SCORED 42 league goals in season 1941-42 for Manchester United. However, it was not an official record as War

Time goals counted as friendlies despite United winning the Football League Northern Section (First Championship).

NEVER LOST FOR WORDS

On 18 May 2021, Manchester United icon Eric Cantona was inducted to the inaugural Premier League Hall of Fame. King Eric was one of six players from a 23-man shortlist to join inductees Thierry Henry and Alan Shearer, after United's French Maestro received the most combined votes from the public and the Premier League panel.

Cantona famously joined United from bitter Yorkshire rivals, Leeds United, on 27 November 1992, and became a talismanic figure at Old Trafford, helping Alex Ferguson's side to win four of the first five Premier League titles, as well as the FA Cup in 1994 and 1996, thereby making United the first English club to win the Double twice. Always a man of his own, King Eric retired from football at the end of the 1996-97 season at the age of only 30 and when still at the peak of his powers, yet his achievements will never be forgotten.

Speaking to PremierLeague.com, the iconic Frenchman typically commented, *'I am very happy and very proud but, at the same time, I am not surprised. I would've been surprised not to be elected! I played football, I loved football, I dreamed about football as a kid. Of course, to play in England was a dream, it was a dream for everybody, playing for the Premier League. I have been lucky to play in this team, with wonderful players, a wonderful manager and wonderful fans. We won and we really enjoyed (it), and it was the football I dreamed about because Manchester United, it's a club where they want to win things but in a good way. It was like this in the time of Matt Busby, it's the identity of this club and the philosophy of this club'.*

Ending his interview with the Premier League in style, King Eric added, *'I think you have maybe nearly 30 players who could be elected. Me, it's different. If you have to elect one, it's me. But the other ones are all great. Me? I'm exceptional!'*

Did You Know That?

 ALONG WITH ERIC, David Beckham, Dennis Bergkamp, Steven Gerrard, Roy Keane and Frank Lampard were also inducted.

ELEVEN FAMOUS FREE EXITS FROM OLD TRAFFORD

1. George Best (released) August 1974
2. Denis Law (Manchester City) July 1973
3. Bryan Robson (Middlesbrough as player/manager) May 1994
4. Martin Buchan (Oldham Athletic) July 1983
5. Denis Irwin (Wolverhampton Wanderers) July 2002
6. Kevin Moran (Sporting Gijon (Spain) August 1988
7. Steve Bruce (Birmingham City) June 1996
8. Brian McClair (Motherwell) June 1998
9. Tony Dunne (Bolton Wanderers) August 1973

10. Paul Parker (released) June 1996
11. Peter Schmeichel (Sporting Lisbon) June 1999

Did You Know That?

PETER SCHMEICHEL PLAYED 398 times for Manchester United, keeping 180 clean sheets, scoring one goal in a 2-2 draw at Old Trafford on 26 September 1995 versus Rotor Voldograd (Russia) in a Round 1, second leg tie of the 1995-96 UEFA Cup. Paul Scholes also scored. United's Great Dane was the first, and to date, only goalkeeping Red to score a goal from open play and the second No.1 to score for the club in a competitive game after Alex Stepney, who scored twice from the penalty spot in season 1973-74.

NONE SHALL PASS

Only 11 goalkeepers have kept 50 or more clean sheets for Newton Heath/Manchester United.

1. David de Gea (2011-2023) - 190 in 545 games
2. Peter Schmeichel (1991-99) – 180 in 398 games
3. Alex Stepney (1966-78) – 174 in 539 games
4. Gary Bailey (1978-87) – 161 in 375 games
5. Edwin van der Sar (2005-11) – 135 in 266 games
6. Alfred Steward (1920-32) – 96 in 326 games
7. Harry Moger (1903-12) – 92 in 266 games
8. Jack Crompton (1945-56) – 67 in 212 games
9. Ray Wood (1949-59) – 55 in 208 games
10. Frank Barrett (1896-1900) – 54 in 136 games

11. Fabien Barthez (2000-04) – 50 in 139 games

Of the 11, Edwin van der Sar holds the best games to goals conceded ratio with an impressive 0.508 goals conceded to the number of appearances he made.

Did You Know That?

MANCHESTER UNITED PLAYED Tottenham Hotspur in the 1967 FA Charity Shield final. At the time the English First Division champions played host to the FA Cup winners. Spurs beat Chelsea 2-1 at Wembley Stadium in the first ever all-London FA Cup final. United won the 1966-67 First Division Championship by four points over runners-up, Nottingham Forest. The game, the traditional curtain raiser to a season, was played at Old Trafford on 12 August 1967 and ended 3-3; Bobby Charlton scored twice for United and Denis Law also scored. Jimmy Robertson and Frank Saul scored for Spurs but their other goal came from a very unusual source. Pat Jennings, Tottenham Hotspur's Northern Ireland international goalkeeper, punted a ball up into the air from a goal kick in the eighth minute of the game, six minutes after his teammate, Robertson, put the visitors 1-0 ahead, and as Stepney moved towards the area where he thought the ball would land, it hit the turf and took an unexpected bounce over his head and into the net. The result meant that the two clubs jointly shared the Charity Shield, holding it for six months each.

ANGLO-SCOTTISH FA CUP WINNERS

When Manchester United defeated Crystal Palace 1-0 in the

1990 FA Cup final replay at Wembley Stadium (scorer: Lee Martin), following a 3-3 draw in the first game (scorers: Mark Hughes 2 and Bryan Robson) it was the first trophy which Alex Ferguson had guided the club to since taking over from Ron Atkinson as manager of the club on 6 November 1986. However, the FA Cup win held much more significance in football history, as Ferguson became the first manager to guide a club to FA Cup success in England and Scotland. The United manager had previously managed Aberdeen to Scottish FA Cup glory in 1982, 1983, 1984 and 1986. He went on to steer Manchester United to further FA Cup wins in 1994 (Double winners), 1996 (Double winners), 1999 (Treble winners) and 2004.

On 15 May 2021, Leicester City defeated Chelsea 1-0 at Wembley Stadium in the 2021 FA Cup final. The Foxes were managed by ex-Glasgow Celtic manager from 2016-19, Brendan Rodgers, who had previously managed the Glasgow giants to two Scottish FA Cup victories in 2017 and 2018. Rodgers, born in Carnlough, Northern Ireland on 26 January 1973, left Celtic for Leicester City in February 2019, and became only the second manager to guide a club to FA Cup glory north and south of the border, when his side beat the London Blues.

Rodgers wrote his name into the history books of Leicester City Football Club by finally breaking The Foxes' FA Cup final hoodoo. In their previous four appearances in the final (1949, 1961, 1963 and 1969), they had lost on each occasion, including a 3-1 defeat by Manchester United in the 1963 FA Cup final (scorers: David Herd two and Denis Law). Quite ironically, in the semi-finals of the 1962-63 FA Cup, Leicester City beat Liverpool 1-0 and Manchester United defeated Southampton

1-0. In the 1976 FA Cup final, Southampton caused an FA Cup shock and beat the overwhelming favourites, beating Manchester United, 1-0, but just 12 months later, United beat the red hot favourites, Liverpool, who were chasing the Treble, 2-1 (scorers: Stuart Pearson and Jimmy Greenhoff).

Did You Know That?

WHEN MANCHESTER UNITED lifted the first of their 12 FA Cup successes in 1909, they beat Bristol City 1-0 at the Crystal Palace. Sandy Turnbull scored the only goal of the game in the 22nd minute of the final. Arsenal have won the most number of English FA Cups, 14, and have been runners-up seven times. United have been runners-up on eight occasions. Celtic have lifted the Scottish FA Cup 41 times, whilst their 'Old Firm' rivals are seven trophies behind them with 34 wins.

LIKE FATHER, LIKE SON

In the history of the Premier League (1992-present) only 13 father and son partnerships have played in the Premier League. Four of the dads played for Manchester United, with all of them except Gordon Strachan playing in the Premier League for United. The Scottish international played for United in the First Division during his five years at Old Trafford and for Leeds United in both the First Division and the Premier League.

Steve (United 1988-96) and Alex Bruce (Birmingham City and Hull City).

Paul (United 1989-95) and Tom Ince (Huddersfield Town, Crystal Palace and Hull City).

Peter (United 1991-99) and Kasper Schmeichel (Manchester City, Leicester City).

Gordon (United 1984-89) and Gavin Strachan (Coventry City).

The remaining eight are: Kevin and Tyrese Campbell; Alan and Jack Cork; Paul and Darnell Furlong; Alfie and Erling Haaland; Rob and Elliot Lee; Steve and Dan Potts; Gus and Diego Poyet; Ian Wright and Bradley Wright-Phillips and Ian Wright and Shaun Wright-Phillips.

Kasper Schmeichel won the Premier League with Leicester City in season 2015-16, whilst his dad, a United Legend, won five Premier League crowns during his Old Trafford career – 1992-93, 1993-94, 1995-96, 1996-97 and 1998-99.

Did You Know That?

DURING THE 1930S, Alec Herd won the FA Cup with Manchester City (1934, Matt Busby was a teammate of his in the final) and the First Division Championship (1936-37). In 1948. Herd left City after spending 15 years at Maine Road and signed for Stockport County. On the final day of the 1950-51 season, Alec, aged 39, played alongside his son up front for Stockport County in the Football League Third Division North. The Herds helped their side to a 2-0 victory. David played for Stockport County from 1951-54 and for Arsenal from 1954-61. In July 1961, United signed Herd from The Gunners for £35,000 and he went on to win the FA Cup (1963, scored twice in the final), two First Division Championships (1964-65 and 1966-67), the FA Charity Shield (1965) and the European Cup (1968).

In 2013, aged 42, Henrik Larsson made a romantic return to the club where his football career all began, Hogaborgs BK, Sweden and re-joined them as a player and coaching assistant. Having been born in Helsingborg on 20 September 1971, it was the Swedish striker's hometown club whom he joined aged seven. In one game Henrik played alongside his 15-year-old son, Jordan, and although all of the media centred around the senior Larsson, it was Jordan who scored in the game.

On 14 November 2015, Old Trafford played host to a charity match arranged by UNICEF Ambassador David Beckham with the proceeds going to UNICEF Children. Beckham captained a Great Britain and Ireland XI, managed by Sir Alex Ferguson, and beat a Rest of the World XI skippered by Luis Figo and managed by Carlo Ancelotti, 3-1 (scorers: Michael Owen two and Paul Scholes, with Dwight Yorke scoring for the Rest of the World XI). Fifteen minutes before the end of the game, Beckham was replaced by Beckham when his 15-year-old son Brooklyn came on as a substitute for his dad. However, David then came back on again, much to the delight of the packed house of 75,381 fans and passed the ball to his son.

I HEAR YOU KNOCKING

On 8 June 1971, Frank O'Farrell answered Manchester United's call to take charge of the club after the legendary Sir Matt Busby retired as manager for the second time. In doing so, O'Farrell became the first, and only Irish-born manager, in the club's history. He left Leicester City and signed a five-year contract with Manchester United worth £15,000 per year.

Did You Know That?

WHEN O'FARRELL ACCEPTED United's offer, the No.1 song in the UK Singles Charts was Knock Three Times, performed by the group, Dawn. The song was the 300th No.1 hit in the UK Singles Charts. A chorus from the song is:

Oh, my darling
Knock three times
On the ceiling if you want me
Mmm, hmm, twice on the pipe
If the answer is no

The Manchester United Board of Directors nearly brought the ceiling down to get their preferred choice to replace Sir Matt.

MIKI

Henrikh Mkhitaryan, nicknamed 'Miki' by his teammates is the only Armenian-born player to have played for Manchester United, 63 games and 13 goals (2016-18). United signed him from Borussia Dortmund on 6 July 2016 for £26 million. He holds the record for the most number of Armenian Footballer of the Year awards, having won it on 10 occasions (2009, 2011-17 and 2019-20). Prior to moving to Germany to play for Borussia Dortmund in 2013, who were managed by Jurgen Klopp at the time of his arrival, he played for Shakhtar Donetsk from 2010-13. He is Armenia's all-time leading international goalscorer and on 29 May 2014, he became the first Armenian international to score a hat-trick for his country in a 7-1 friendly win versus Guatemala in Los Angeles.

Did You Know That?

HENRIKH MKHITARYAN WAS also named the Commonwealth of Independent States (CIS) Footballer of the Year in 2012 and 2013, thereby becoming the first Armenian footballer to be named the best player from post-Soviet countries.

NEVER ON THE SCORESHEET

More than 330 outfield Manchester United players never scored a goal for the club during their Old Trafford career including:

Charlie Moore	328 games, 1919-21 & 1922-31
Thomas Jones	200 games, 1924-37
Jack Mellor	122 games, 1930-37
Mal Donaghy	119 games, 1988-92
Richard Holden	117 games, 1904-14
Thomas Gibson	115 games, 1950-55
George Perkins	102 games, 1892-96
Darren Ferguson	30 games, 1990-94
Walter Winterbottom	27 games, 1936-38
Jonathan Greening	27 games, 1998-2002

Did You Know That?

THE IDEA OF having one person in charge of the England national football team was first mooted by Stanley Rous, the Football Association secretary, on 20 October 1945. Rous, and the FA, appointed Walter Winterbottom national director of coaching on 8 July 1946 with responsibility for the national team. There was no specific appointment as England's team manager after this point, he just merged into the role. The ex-Manchester United player took charge of Team Great Britain in the 1952 Olympic Games in Helsinki, Finland, and was in sole charge of the Football League Inter-League matches from October 1956 to July 1960.

From September 1960, the Football League Inter-League matches would be managed in an honorary capacity by the previous season's Football League champions. Harry Potts of Burnley (First Division Champions 1959-60), was first, then Stan Cullis, Wolverhampton Wanderers (English First Division champions 1957-58 and 1958-59), had a stint six months later. From July 1961, with the 1962 FIFA World Cup looming, Winterbottom was invited again to take charge of the League XI. Each inter-League match was considered an international Preparation Match. Winterbottom announced his resignation on 1 August 1962, effective on appointment of a successor manager and left the post in November 1962.

Under his stewardship, England reached the World Cup group stage in 1950 (Brazil), the quarter-finals in 1954 (Switzerland), the group play-off in 1958 (Sweden) and the quarter-final stages again in 1962 (Chile). Alf Ramsey's position as England manager was confirmed in October 1962, and he formally took charge in May 1963. Winterbottom took charge of England in 139 internationals with a record of 78 wins, 33 draws and 28 losses, 383 goals for and 196 against, a win ratio of 68%. No players received a yellow or red card during his tenure.

BEHIND CLOSED DOORS

On 12 March 2020, Manchester United played in a game which created club history. The team were in Austria at a time when the world was dealing with the pandemic COVID-19. United were playing LASK Linz in a Europa League Round of 16 first leg tie. UEFA ordered all clubs to play behind closed doors and United beat their Austrian opponents 5-0 without any fans inside the Linzer Stadion, Linz. It was United's first ever competitive fixture in any competition to be played behind closed doors. The scorers were: Odion Ighalo, Daniel James, Juan Mata, Mason Greenwood and Andreas Pereira.

Did You Know That?

ON 31 JANUARY 2020, the former Watford and Nigerian international striker, Odion Ighalo, joined Manchester United on loan until the end of the 2019-20 season from the Chinese club, Shanghai Greenland Shenhua. He made an immediate impact at Old Trafford, scoring twice against Derby County in the FA Cup and scoring Europa League goals versus Club Brugge and LASK Linz, before the COVID-19 pandemic resulted in the suspension of all football in March 2020. On 4 February 2021, Ighalo joined Al Shabab in the Saudi Arabia professional league. He played 23 times for Manchester United and scored five goals.

PLEASE RELEASE ME (LET ME GO)

Some 58 years before Englebert Humperdinck enjoyed his first No.1 in the UK music singles charts with the song *Please Release Me (Let Me Go)* on 2 March 1967, a Manchester United player was effectively singing the opening lines of the song:

> *Please release me, let me go*
> *For I don't love you anymore*
> *To waste our lives would be a sin*
> *Release me and let me love again*

In May 1909, United signed goalkeeper Elijah Round from Charlton Athletic. United were recently crowned FA Cup winners for the first time in the history of the club, and acquired Round as an understudy to Harry Moger. On 9 October 1909, Round made his debut in a 3-2 loss away to Liverpool at Anfield in the First Division (scorer: Sandy Turnbull two). He played his second and last game in a United shirt on 26 February 1910, losing 7-1 away to Aston Villa in the league, with Billy Meredith scoring United's only goal in the game. Ernest Mangnall, the Manchester United manager, decided Round was not the back-up goalkeeper he initially thought he would prove to be and placed him on the transfer list. United rated him at £25.00 but Round objected to the transfer fee and unsuccessfully tried twice to get the club to drop it and release him from his Old Trafford nightmare by giving him a free transfer. He was eventually released by the club and joined Barnsley, but the transfer fee was not recorded.

Did You Know That?

MANCHESTER UNITED PAID £7.8 million to AS Monaco in May 2000 to sign their French international 1998 FIFA World Cup winning goalkeeper, Fabien Barthez. On 30 June 2004, having played 139 times for the club, his contract was cancelled by mutual consent and he was permitted to leave Old Trafford. Barthez, who won the Premier League title with United in 2000-01 and 2002-03, rejoined one of his former clubs, Olympique de Marseille (1992-95).

OUT OF AFRICA

In the history of Newton Heath Football Club (1878-1902) and Manchester United Football Club (1902-present), only 10 players who were born in Africa have pulled on the famous jersey for the club. Gary Bailey, United goalkeeper from 1978-87, was signed by the club from Wits University, Johannesburg, but Bailey was born in Ipswich, England on 9 August 1958.

Quinton Fortune (South Africa): 126 games, 11 goals (1999-2006).

Eric Djemba Djemba (Cameroon) 39 games, 2 goals (2003-05).

Mateus Alberto Contreiras Goncalves (Manucho) (Angola): 3 games, 0 goals (2008-09).

Mame Biran Diouf (Senegal): 9 games, one goal (2009-12).

Wilfried Zaha (Ivory Coast): 4 games, 0 goals (2013-15).
Eric Bailly (Ivory Coast): 2016-present
Odion Ighalo (Nigeria): 23 games, five goals (2020-21).
Amad Diallo(Ivory Coast): 2021-present.
Hannibal Mejbri (Tunisia) 2021-present
André Onana (Cameroon) 2023-present

Did You Know That?

IN 1985, THE movie *Out of Africa*, starring Robert Redford and Meryl Streep, directed and produced by Sydney Pollack, was released. Gary Bailey was in goal for United when they beat Everton 1-0 after extra-time in the 1985 FA Cup final. Norman Whiteside scored the only goal of the final, a superb curler in the 110th minute when United were down to 10 men after Kevin Moran was sent off in the 78th minute of play. *Out of Africa* won seven Academy Awards including Best Picture and Best Director.

MATT BUSBY RETURNS AFTER MUNICH

On 23 August 1958, Matt Busby took charge of his beloved Manchester United team for the first time since his Busby Babes drew 3-3 with Red Star Belgrade in Belgrade, the capital city of Yugoslavia on 5 February 1958. The game against the reigning Yugoslavian First League Champions, was a European Cup quarter-final, second leg tie. In the first leg, played at Old Trafford on 14 January 1958, United won 2-1 thanks to goals from Bobby Charlton and Eddie Colman. Having earned a hard fought 3-3 draw on a snow covered pitch (scorers: Charlton two and Dennis Viollet), in the Yugoslav capital, Busby's young and exciting side had progressed to the semi-finals of the most prestigious European club competition despite only being in its third season.

The Busby Babes were on the brink of winning the European Cup in only their second attempt with the champions of Italy, AC Milan, next-up for them in the semi-finals. The other semi-finalists were the champions of Hungary, Vasas SC, and the reigning Spanish champions, and winners of the inaugural European Cup in season 1955-56 and holders of the European Cup having successfully defended it in season 1956-57, Real Madrid. Despite Real Madrid beating United 5-3 over two legs in the semi-finals of the 1956-57 European Cup, the Spanish aristocrats knew that Busby's side had not only learned from this defeat but had become a better team because of it. Busby's young side quickly found out just how sour losing tasted. Manchester United look destined to be crowned champions of Europe in season 1957-58 until the cruel hand of fate intervened and dealt the club the bitterest blow it had ever, and will ever, suffer.

The day after the Red Star Belgrade game the United players and officials were in buoyant mood. The night before their hosts treated them to a Gala Dinner in a five-star hotel in Belgrade and bestowed gifts on them as well as wishing them good luck versus AC Milan and a safe trip home. But, the combination of a slush covered runway at Munich Airport, where United's chartered flight home had to stop off to re-fuel for the home journey to Manchester, and ice on the wings of their British

European Airways Elizabethan Class jet named 'Lord Burleigh', brought about the blackest day in the history of Manchester United Football Club.

The game on 23 August 1958, was Manchester United's opening game of the 1958-59 First Division Championship season. It was just 189 days since Busby last took charge of his most beloved United. During that time as he gradually recovered from his injuries, which included a period of recuperation in the fresh mountain air of the Swiss Alps, things were no longer the same at the club both on and off the pitch. Not only had Busby lost eight of his team in Munich, he also lost two members of his other team, his backroom staff, Trainer Tom Curry and Chief Scout Bert Whalley. And, Busby's close friend and club Secretary, Walter Crickmer, was no longer there to welcome him back to Old Trafford at the start of the new season.

There were times when Busby was so down he contemplated retiring. The demons in his head tortured him as he blamed himself for the loss of 23 lives in the crash. It was Busby who convinced Crickmer and the club's Chairman, Harold Hardman, to enter the European Cup in season 1956-57 and again in 1957-58, despite the fact that the Football League strongly opposed their participation.

But Busby somehow managed to make a deal with his broken heart and returned as manager of Manchester United thanks mainly to Murphy reminding him that it would be what their lost boys would want him to do, and the encouragement and support he received from his wife, Jean, who never left his side during his period of convalescing. She was his rock, and like Murphy, she told her husband that he owed it to everyone who lost their lives in the air disaster to rebuild his team and make it rise like a Phoenix from the ashes.

The side he selected to play Chelsea in the First Division Championship on 23 August 1958, only contained five of the last Manchester United side he sent out for a game, the 3-3 draw in Belgrade: Harry Gregg, Bill Foulkes, Bobby Charlton, Dennis Viollet and Albert Scanlon (Ian Greaves, Freddie Goodwin, Ronald Cope, Wilf McGuinness, Ernie Taylor and Alex Dawson also played in the game). As he gave the players their pre-match team talk in the home dressing-room at Old Trafford, his mind must have cast him back to that freezing cold afternoon inside the visitors' dressing-room at the JNA Stadium, Belgrade when he addressed his Babes for what turned out to be the last time before their game against Red Star Belgrade.

The Match programme for the Chelsea game, *United Review*, carried the following message on Page Three.

A MESSAGE FROM THE CHAIRMAN

My dear friends,

To-day Manchester United stands at the crossroads.

Many of our finest players together with some of the most experienced members of our staff are no longer with us. Matt Busby regains his strength, but the team you cheer to-day is about to start one of the most testing seasons in the history of the club.

What has the future in store for us? From last season's tragedy there sprang the realization that great team work can bring success. Supported by only two first team players and fine new club men, a team of reserves and juniors began the road to Wembley and the Semi-Final stages of the European Cup Competition.

Were these boys inspired? Inspired yes, not only by the memory of their comrades but by the inspiration they derived from our supporters. In asking once more for your cheers in victory we ask also for your tolerance in defeat. Give us your loyalty and United will be great again.

Yours sincerely,

H. P. Hardman,
Chairman,
MANCHESTER UNITED
FOOTBALL CLUB LTD.

Harold Hardman's promise to the fans that 'United would be great again', was borne out when Matt Busby built his third great team which went on to win the FA Cup in 1963, the First Division Championship in seasons 1964-65 and 1966-67, and what can only be described as Busby's and the club's Holy Grail, winning the European Cup in 1968.

Charlton welcomed his manager back to his spiritual home by scoring a hat-trick in United's 5-2 victory over Chelsea at Old Trafford. Alex Dawson also scored twice in United's opening game of the new season (Jimmy Greaves scored both goals for the visitors).

Did You Know That?

ONE OF THE TOP Box Office attractions at the movie theatres in 1958 was a war film called *The Young Lions*. At the end of the movie one of the leading characters, Noah, played by Montgomery Clift, is discharged from the United States army at the end of the Second World War. He emerges from a subway station and walks home. His wife, Hope, played by Hope Lange, is at the window of their home and when she sees him approaching, she holds up their baby daughter who he sees for the first time. He ascends the stairs quickly to embrace his family. Matt Busby lost eight Young Lions in the Munich Air Disaster and when he returned to Old Trafford on 23 August 1958, he was warmly welcomed by a new set of cubs which Jimmy Murphy had assembled for him to commence building a new great Manchester United team.

PART 3

KING ERIC SLIPS THROUGH OUR FINGERS

THREE LIONS ON A SHIRT

UNITED NOT SUCH JOLLY GOOD FELLOWS

WHAT'S UP, DOC?

BATTLE OF THE CROISSANTS

KNIGHTS OF OLD TRAFFORD

WHEN UNITED MISSED OUT ON SIGNING KING ERIC

On the day of Eric Cantona's 55th birthday, 24 May 2021, Sir Alex Ferguson admitted he was close to signing Eric Cantona for Manchester United earlier in the Frenchman's career. Eric the King was available for transfer in 1991 after falling out of favour in his homeland, and the Manchester United boss consulted those in the know to back up his instincts about the player. Although the response was positive, Cantona underwent a trial with Sheffield Wednesday before ending up with Leeds United, helping Howard Wilkinson's team win the First Division Championship title in season 1991-92, just before the advent of the Premier League.

The missed opportunity only ended up delaying the perfect union at Old Trafford as the Reds pulled off one of the all-time transfer coups in persuading Leeds United to part with their enigmatic centre-forward on 27 November 1992. Eric's arrival at Manchester United proved the catalyst in sparking a period of domestic dominance for the club, and he was a key part of the Double winning teams of 1994 and 1996, scoring in both FA

Cup triumphs: two goals versus Chelsea in a 4-0 victory in 1994, and the only goal of the 1996 final, a 1-0 win over Liverpool.

'I was at a game in Paris, sitting next to Michel Platini and Gerard Houllier,' recalled Sir Alex. 'Platini says to me – it was the time he (Cantona) was suspended from French football – he says, "You should go and sign Cantona". I say, "Is he not a problem?" He says, "If you recognise him and bring him into the fold, I tell you he's a great player." Gerrard Houllier endorsed that exactly. I was going home the next day, I go into training and he's signed for Sheffield Wednesday on loan/trial. Trevor Francis was the manager. They were training indoors, because the weather was bad. He's very friendly with Howard Wilkinson, so when his loan was up, Trevor tried to further it and he said no chance. So, he phoned Howard and Howard signed him. And they won the League. He won the League for them. There's no question in my mind.'

Gordon Strachan was the captain of Leeds United when they won the First Division Championship title in season 1991-92, Manchester United finishing in runners-up position. Strachan played for Alex Ferguson at Aberdeen from 1977-84, and he was a Manchester United player on 6 November 1986, when Ferguson left the Scottish club to replace Ron Atkinson as the new manager of United. Strachan was a part of Ferguson's United team until the diminutive Scottish international midfielder left Old Trafford on 23 March 1989, and signed for Leeds United in a £300,000 transfer.

Did You Know That?

ERIC CANTONA COULD have become a Liverpool player. There is a line in the famous song *My Way* sung by Frank Sinatra which is, '*Regrets, I've had a few*'. Graeme Souness was the manager of Liverpool from 1991-94 and he most definitely enjoyed his share of regrets. On 15 April 1992, *The Sun* newspaper published a story about Souness convalescing after recently having heart surgery and showed a photograph of him kissing his girlfriend. The headline was *LOVERPOOL*, and the strap line *Kiss seals Graeme's double joy*. It was pure mature cheddar cheese material. The reference to a double was Souness' clean bill of health and Liverpool reaching the 1992 FA Cup final versus Sunderland. The problem with the Liverpool fans wasn't Souness's smooch with his girlfriend. On the day the paper was published Liverpool were holding a memorial service at Anfield to commemorate the third anniversary of the Hillsborough Disaster which occurred on 15 April 1989 when 96 Liverpool fans lost their lives before their team's FA Cup semi-final versus Nottingham Forest at Hillsborough Stadium.

The newspaper was despised in Liverpool and the Merseyside people rejected it so much that shops in the city stopped stocking it. In the aftermath of the disaster, the newspaper published a story on 19 April 1989, under the headline *THE TRUTH*. It was a full front page spread claiming to tell the true story of what happened on that fateful day at Hillsborough Stadium. The sub headlines read *Some fans picked pockets of victims, Some fans urinated on brave cops*, and *Some fans beat up brave cop giving kiss of life*. But as history, and more importantly, the truth has shown, *The Sun* lied. Nonetheless, Souness regretted his decision to do the interview.

However, Souness's biggest regret must surely have occurred on 6 November 1991, almost one year to the day before Eric Cantona pulled on the famous red shirt of Manchester United for the first time and not the red jersey of their greatest rivals, Liverpool.

Liverpool played AJ Auxerre from France in a UEFA Cup, Round 2, second leg tie at home. Liverpool were playing their first season of European football since the fateful Heysel Disaster at the 1985 European Cup final. Liverpool were handed a 6-year ban from European competition. Two weeks before the French outfit flew into Liverpool, they won the first leg 2-0 at their Stade de l'Abbe-Deschamps home. After Liverpool beat their French opposition 3-0, Souness received a visit in his office from the manager of the French national side at the time, Michel Platini. And, in a strange twist of fate, it was Platini who scored the only goal of the game for Juventus when they beat Liverpool 1-0 in the 1985 European Cup final at Stade du Heysel, Brussels.

In Souness' own words, 'We had played Auxerre at home (in November 1991) and Michel Platini came to see me. He said he had a player – a problem boy but a proper player. Cantona. I said the last thing I needed was another problem player. I had 30-pluses that I was trying to get out so I didn't need more hassle. I said I was looking for something else. I said no thanks.'

Thankfully, Alex Ferguson said, 'Oui,' when Leeds United decided to offload their 'Problem Boy'. Merci Beaucoup, Monsieur Souness.

THREE LIONS ON A SHIRT

A total of 70 Manchester United players have been capped at full international level by England whilst they were at the club (to the end of the 2021-23 season). The first was a captain of United. His name is Charlie Roberts, who had joined United from Grimsby Town on 22 April 1904 in a £600 transfer. The fee was a record for United, but it would prove to be money spent very wisely. Roberts was a talismanic captain, skippering the club to their first ever major trophy successes, the First Division Championship in seasons 1907-08 and 1910-11, as well as their first FA Cup final win in 1909. He was a no-nonsense player, as hard as granite and took no prisoners on the field of play. He was a Man's Man of his generation and in many ways Roy Keane's style of play could well have been developed from the DNA of Roberts' all out winning mentality.

Charlie Roberts was born on 6 April 1883, in Rise Carr, Darlington, County Durham. According to the 1901 Census, Roberts was a furnaceman's labourer in the Albert Hill Iron Works, Springfield, Darlington and was living with his parents at 7 Low Boyne Street in the Harrowgate area of Darlington. His father was listed as a labourer in the scrapyard at the Ironworks owned by the Darlington Iron Company. Roberts began his early career playing with his local side, Darlington St. Augustine's FC and joined the local amateur side, Bishop Auckland FC.

He joined Grimsby Town FC in May 1903, and after making 31 league appearances and scoring four goals, he moved to Manchester United. At the start of the 1906-07 season, Ernest Mangnall, the manager of United, had no hesitation in making him the club captain. In the summer of 1912, Manchester City attempted to sign Roberts but their offer of £1,500 was refused. However, Oldham Athletic signed him as their captain on 24 August 1913 for another club record selling fee for a player, £1,500. Roberts did not want to leave Old Trafford, his spiritual home, but after United refused to guarantee him a second benefit match, he was reluctantly allowed to leave. At Oldham Athletic he made 72 league appearances and scored twice. He missed the early part of the 1916-17 season because of pneumonia. He then played in a game against Stoke City in 1918 and *'received such severe injuries,'* that he never played again. He retired in the early part of the 1920-21 season, although he had been on the sick list for some time, having undergone a variety of operations.

On 24 June 1921, he was appointed the manager of Oldham Athletic and resigned on 15 December 1922. Roberts made 302 appearances for Newton Heath/Manchester United from 1904-13, scoring 23 goals. He played under three Secretaries (Manager) at the club: Ernest Mangnall 275 times, J. J. Bentley 21 times and T.J. Wallworth on six occasions. On 25 February 1905, he won the first of his three caps for England in a British Home International Championship match versus Ireland at Ayresome Park, Middlesbrough. The game ended 1-1. His other two caps came against Scotland and Wales in the 1905 British Home International Championship which was won by England.

Did You Know That?

DURING HIS PLAYING days, he was a Sunday School teacher, and was the owner of stationery and newsagents' shops in the Manchester area. During his recuperation Roberts gave lectures to Scottish players, in hope of setting up a union in the Scottish field.

NEWTON HEATH – THE NICKNAMES

Newton Heath Lancashire and Yorkshire Railway Football Club, 1878-1902, were known by various nicknames:
The Heathens
The Newtonians
The Coachbuilders

Did You Know That?

WHEN THE WORKERS from the Carriage and Wagon Works of Newton Heath Lancashire and Yorkshire Railway Company formed a football club in the summer of 1878, they partnered with the already existing Cricket Club the Railway had, and which was formed in 1850. In the early years, the two clubs shared one name, Newton Heath Lancashire and Yorkshire Railway Cricket and Football Club, before 'Cricket' was subsequently removed by the football section of the club and the two sports departments went their separate ways.

IN AFFECTIONATE REMEMBRANCE OF MANCHESTER UNITED

Burnley Football Club beat Manchester United 2-0 at Turf Moor on 15 January 1910 in Round 1 of the 1909-10 FA Cup competition. United were the reigning FA Cup holders, but exited the 1909-10 FA Cup with a whimper. A company produced a Memoriam Card to glorify Burnley's victory. This form of card was very popular at the time to embarrass English football's top teams when a smaller club defeated a so called 'Bigger' club in the league or in the FA Cup. This particular postcard read:

IN AFFECTIONATE REMEMBRANCE OF
MANCHESTER UNITED
WHO FELL A PREY TO BURNLEY SKILL
ON JANUARY 15th 1910
AND WERE INTERRED AT TURF MOOR SAME DAY

And the following line was included at the foot of the postcard:
No flowers, no wreaths, just let them rest.
They've played the game and done their best.

Did You Know That?

MANCHESTER UNITED (then Newton Heath) first met their Lancashire opponents, Burnley, separated by just 35 miles, on 1 February 1901; a 0-0 home draw in Round 1 of the 1900-01 FA Cup. The Heathens lost the replay 7-1 at Turf Moor on 13 February 1901 (scorer: Alf Schofield).

NOT SO JOLLY GOOD FELLOWS

On 7 January 1975, Walsall, a Third Division side, dumped Manchester United out of the 1974-75 FA Cup in the Third

Round. United, a Second Division team at the time, drew 0-0 with Walsall at Old Trafford on 4 January 1975, but lost the replay 3-2 after extra-time at Fellows Park, Walsall three days later. Gerry Daly scored a penalty for United with Sammy McIlroy also scoring.

Did You Know That?

WALSALL FOOTBALL CLUB was founded in 1888 as Walsall Town Swifts, an amalgamation of Walsall Town and Walsall Swifts. They are nicknamed 'The Saddlers,' which reflects the West Midlands' town's status as a traditional centre for saddle manufacturing.

WHAT'S UP, DOC?

In 1972, the movie *What's Up, Doc?* was the second biggest selling movie of the year with revenue from the Box Office amounting to $57,142,740. *The Poseidon Adventure* was the biggest movie viewers' attraction bringing in receipts of $93,300,000. But in 1972, Old Trafford had its very own Box Office attractions, and although Bobby Charlton, Denis Law and George Best were still Manchester United players, the leading stories on the back pages of all the British newspapers were mainly centred around Best's activities off the pitch. However, in December 1972, the back pages were dominated with the managerial change at Manchester United. Frank O'Farrell was sacked by United on 19 December 1972, and three days later they called for 'The Doc' and appointed Tommy Docherty as the 17th different person to take charge of team selection.

Did You Know That?

THE MOVIE *What's Up, Doc?* is about an accidental mix-up of four identical plaid overnight bags which led to a series of numerous wacky and wild situations. A definition of plaid means chequered or tartan twilled cloth, typically made of wool. In many ways, Docherty had four very different plaid bags in the shape of Law, Best, Charlton and himself. Within 13 months of Docherty's arrival at Old Trafford, Law, Best and Charlton had all packed their bags and left Manchester United.

The Poseidon Adventure is about the fictional aging luxury cruise liner, SS Poseidon, on her final voyage from New York City to Athens, before it is scrapped. On New Year's Eve the ship is overturned by a tsunami. Ironically, George Best played his last ever game for Manchester United on New Year's Day 1974, a 3-0 loss to Queens Park Rangers in the First Division Championship. However, United's ship had already been floundering before Best's exit. Ex-Red, Don Givens (Manchester United 1969-70, eight games and one goal) scored for QPR in the game.

BATTLE OF THE CROISSANTS

On 5 October 1977, Manchester United, managed by Dave Sexton, met AS Saint-Étienne in a Round 1, second leg, European Cup Winners' Cup tie having drawn the away game 1-1 (scorer: Gordon Hill) three weeks earlier in France. However, although United were at home in the return leg, the game was not played at Old Trafford. AS Saint-Étienne was founded in 1919 by employees of a grocery store chain based in Saint-Étienne called Groupe Casino, under the name Amicale des Employés de la Société des Magasins Casino (ASC). The football club adopted green as its primary colour as it was the principal colour of Groupe Casino. In 1920, the French Football Federation (FFF) prohibited the use of trademarks in sports club forcing the club to drop 'Casino' from its name and they then changed their name to simply Amical Sporting Club to retain the ASC acronym. In 1927, Pierre Guichard was appointed President of the club and, after it merged with a local club, Stade Forézien Universitaire, they changed their name to Association Sportive Stéphanoise. Three years later, July 1930, the National Council of the FFF voted 128–20 in support of professionalism in French football and in 1933, Association Sportive Stéphanoise turned professional and changed their name to AS Saint-Étienne.

UEFA actually kicked United, the reigning FA Cup holders having beaten Liverpool 2-1 in the 1977 Silver Jubilee cup final, out of the European Cup Winners' Cup competition on 22 September 1977, following crowd trouble by United fans in the first leg in France at Stade Geoffroy-Guichard on 21 September 1977. The stadium is nicknamed '*le Chaudron*' (the Cauldron), or '*l'enfer vert*' (the Green Hell), a testimony to the green kit worn by AS Saint-Étienne.

During the first leg against the reigning French cup holders (Coupe de France), who were beaten 1-0 by FC Bayern Munich in the 1976 European Cup final, a large number of French fans threw bread at the United fans at a time when there was a bread shortage in England as a result of a strike by bakery workers. One English newspaper carried the headline *Breadlam! The Great Loaf Rush*. The home fans taunted United's travelling Red Army by throwing stale baguettes and croissants at them, which the United fans did not take too kindly to, resulting in the Red Army going on the rampage on the unsegregated terraces inside Stade Geoffroy-Guichard and in the town after the game. The game was quickly dubbed 'The Battle of the Croissants'.

However, following an appeal, UEFA allowed United back into the competition two days later on the condition that they staged the fixture more than 200 miles from Old Trafford as a punishment for the behaviour of their fans. Home Park, Plymouth was chosen to stage the tie, which was quite ironic as it was the home of the only team in English football whose home kit was green, Plymouth Argyle. Arthur Albiston, United's left back, later recalled the decision, 'The first idea was to play it in Glasgow but UEFA kiboshed that one. I suppose Plymouth was nearer France!' Meanwhile, Merlin (Gordon Hill's nickname) said, 'All the boys were saying we better get our trunks on to play as, if we went north, 200 miles would have been in the North Sea, east would have put us in the English Channel and west would have put us in the Irish Sea'.

The Manchester United squad actually travelled to Home Park on the Plymouth Argyle coach. The Plymouth players were used to long haul travels to away games up the M5 and beyond to clubs such as Blackburn Rovers, Blackpool, Bolton Wanderers, Burnley, Carlisle United, Hull City and Sheffield United. And so, to make their journeys as comfortable as possible, their coach was fitted out with first-class reclining seats from an airliner. 'I don't think anyone in our party was able to resist the temptation to play with the controls on the way to our hotel!' said Martin Buchan, the United captain.

Tens of thousands of United fans descended on the south coast, a distance of 281 miles from Manchester. 'Home Park was packed to the rafters. I don't think their players were used to having fans so close to the pitch like we were in England. The United fans made it a little bit unsettling for them and that helped us,' recalled Albiston. It was, and remains, the only European game played at Home Park. Manchester United progressed to Round 2 with a 2-0 victory (3-1 on aggregate) thanks to goals from Steve Coppell and Stuart 'Pancho' Pearson, who scored in the 1977 FA Cup final. A crowd of 31,634 poured into the ground whilst back in Manchester, 27,245 Reds went to Old Trafford to watch the match on a closed-circuit television relay, no doubt with flasks of tea and sandwiches, as the strike by the bakery workers had been settled by then!

'It was a bad time for crowd trouble but the fans followed us down to Home Park and made it a home tie. Although it was strange playing at Plymouth, the crowd was fantastic. We went through and I think United will go through again this time. They're playing very well,' said ex-United striker, Jimmy Greenhoff, who like Pancho scored in the 1977 FA Cup final to deprive Liverpool of winning The Treble some 22 years before Manchester United achieved this remarkable feat in season 1998-99. Jimmy's younger brother, Brian, played alongside him that night and quite ironically, 40 years later United faced AS Saint-Étienne in the Europa League in season 2016-17, which saw United's Paul Pogba play against his older brother, Florentin.

'UEFA had to take a stand and do something and it was better for us to travel to Plymouth than being kicked out, which would have been a travesty for the players who had got that great result in Saint-Etienne. Even though we felt a little bit aggrieved, we were still just glad to be in the competition. We thought, our fans travelled all that way, we didn't want to let them down,' said Sammy McIlroy.

However, although eventful, United's run in the competition proved to be short. They lost the first leg of the Second Round tie 4-0 away to FC Porto, the holders of Taça de Portugal (cup of Portugal), on 19 October 1977. Two weeks later United almost pulled off 'The Great Escape', winning the home tie 5-2 (scorers: Steve Coppell two, Jimmy Nicholl and two own goals by Alfredo Murça), but exiting the competition with a 6-5 aggregate defeat.

Did You Know That?

SOME 37 YEARS after the 'Battle of the Croissants', Arsenal players threw slices of pizza at Sir Alex Ferguson and the Manchester United players during a fracas in the tunnel at Old Trafford on 24 October 2004 following United's tempestuous 2-0 Premier League victory over The Gunners, a result that ended their 49-match unbeaten run. Ruud van Nistelrooy scored a penalty in the 73rd minute and Wayne Rooney sealed victory in the 90th minute in a game later dubbed 'Battle of the Buffet'.

BRIDGE OVER TROUBLED WATER

On 28 March 1970, the song *Bridge Over Troubled Water* went to No.1 in the UK singles charts. It was Simon & Garfunkel's only UK No.1 hit single despite recording many other iconic hits including *The Boxer*, *Mrs Robinson* and *The Sound of Silence*. The same day, the song went to the top of the music charts, Manchester United lost 2-1 to local rivals, Manchester City, in the First Division at Old Trafford. United were managed by ex-player, Wilf McGuinness at the time, and the writing was on the wall for him as he failed to steer United out of troubled waters. United, English First Division champions just three years earlier, 1966-67, and Champions of Europe in 1968, under Sir Matt Busby's leadership, were a team in decline and ended the 1969-70 season, McGuinness's first in charge of the club, eighth in the league table although they did reach the FA Cup semi-finals.

By December 1970, the waters at Old Trafford got even more choppy as the United players, which included Bobby Charlton, Denis Law and the mercurial George Best, could not reproduce the form or the goals which made Manchester United the most feared club side in England and Europe during the 1960s. On 29 December 1970, Dave Edmunds was occupying the No.1 spot in the UK Singles Charts with *I Hear You Knockin'*, his first and only No.1 hit song. That same day, Louis Edwards, the chairman of Manchester United, knocked on the door of Wilf's manager's office at Old Trafford, sat down and told McGuinness his time was up, and fired him. Wilf had been in charge of the club on 88 occasions with a record of 32 wins, 33 draws, 23 losses, goals for 131, goals against 115, and a win ratio of 36.36%. He had led United to the semi-final of the League Cup in seasons 1969-70 and 1970-71, as well as the semi-finals of the FA Cup.

Did You Know That?

WILF MCGUINNESS WAS a Busby Babe who made his debut for the club on 8 October 1955 aged just 17, in a 4-3 win over Wolverhampton Wanderers in the First Division at Old Trafford (scorers: Tommy Taylor two, John Doherty and David Pegg). He was a prodigious talent which was fully recognised by Matt Busby and his assistant manager, Jimmy Murphy, who was in charge of the club's Youth team. The young McGuinness was the captain of the Manchester, Lancashire and England Schoolboys before signing apprentice forms with Manchester United in June 1953, turning professional in November 1954.

He went on to play a further 84 times (two goals) for the club he supported as a young boy, having been born in Collyhurst, Manchester on 25 October 1937. During the 1959-60 season, he suffered a broken leg in a reserve game which brought the curtain down on his playing career aged just 22. He made two appearances for England before he was forced to hang-up his boots. With United he won the FA Youth Cup final in 1953-54, 1954-55 and 1955-56; First Division Championship winners' medals in 1955-56 and 1956-57, plus the FA Charity Shield in 1956 and 1957.

THE POPE'S FAVOURITE MANCHESTER UNITED MANAGER

The *Pontifical Equestrian Order of St. Gregory the Great* (Latin: *Ordo Sancti Gregorii Magni*; Italian: *Ordine di San Gregorio Magno*) was established on 1 September 1831, by Pope Gregory XVI, just seven months after his election as Pope. The order is one of the five Orders of the Knighthood of the Holy See. This prestigious honour is bestowed upon Roman Catholic men and women in recognition of their personal service to the Holy See and to the Roman Catholic Church, through their unusual labours, their support of the Holy See, and the examples they set in their communities and their countries. In 1972, Sir Matt Busby was bestowed with the *Pontifical Equestrian Order of St. Gregory the Great.*

Did You Know That?

SIR MATT BUSBY was a devout Roman Catholic and when Tommy Docherty's affair with the wife of the club physio became public knowledge in the summer of 1977, despite winning the FA Cup only 44 days previously, a 2-1 win over Liverpool on 21 May 1977, at Wembley Stadium, Docherty was sacked on 4 July 1977. Busby was the club President at the time.

ORCHESTRAL MANOEUVRES IN RED

When Tommy Docherty was appointed the manager of Manchester United on 22 December 1972, his fellow Scotsman, Martin Buchan was already at the club having been signed by Frank O'Farrell, Docherty's predecessor, from Aberdeen on 29 February 1972 in a £125,000 club record transfer deal. Following the retirement of Bobby Charlton at the end of the 1972-73 season, Docherty had no hesitation in calling the stylish 24-year-old Buchan into the manager's office at Old Trafford and informed his young centre-half that he was the club's new captain. Buchan skippered United to the Second Division title in season 1974-75, FA Cup runners-up in 1976 and FA Cup winners in 1977. During an interview, Tommy Docherty, United's manager in the 1977 FA Cup final, summed Buchan up perfectly when he said, 'Martin Buchan has that much class, the Royal Philharmonic Orchestra should be playing in the stands at Old Trafford accompanying him'. Martin Buchan played 456 times for United and scored four times, from season 1971-72 to 1982-83. His goals came against Bolton Wanderers (six games against them), Derby County (14 games against them), Everton (16 games against them) and City (20 games against them).

Did You Know That?

JUST OVER A month after Tommy Docherty took charge of Manchester United, Sweet went to No.1 in the UK Singles Charts with their first, and only No.1 hit Blockbuster. Two of the lines from the song are:

Does anyone know the way? Did we hear someone say?
(We just haven't got a clue what to do!)
Does anyone know the way? There's got to be a way
(To Blockbuster)

Tommy Docherty knew the way and he helped transform United from being a sleeping lion cub, a side whose best years were behind them, to becoming a roaring lion once again.

THE KNIGHTS OF OLD TRAFFORD

Two former Manchester United players and two former Manchester United managers have received Knighthoods.

Sir Walter Winterbottom (player, 1936-38, 27 games, 0 goals)
Sir Bobby Charlton (player, 1956-73, 758 games, 249 goals)
Sir Matt Busby (manager, 1945-69 & 1970-71, 1,140 games)
Sir Alex Ferguson (manager, 1986-2013, 1,500 games)

Did You Know That?

OF UNITED'S FOUR Knights, only Sir Bobby Charlton did not manage the country of his birth. Walter Winterbottom managed England from 1946-62, Matt Busby managed Scotland in 1958 and Alex Ferguson was the manager of Scotland at the 1986 FIFA World Cup finals hosted by Mexico following the death of Jock Stein on 10 September 1985.

11 MANCHESTER UNITED PLAYERS WHO PLAYED FOR SIR ALEX FERGUSON WHO BECAME MANAGERS

1. Roy Keane – Sunderland AFC and Ipswich Town
2. Ryan Giggs – Wales and Manchester United (caretaker)
3. Jaap Stam – PEC Zwolle (Holland, caretaker), Jong Ajax (Holland), Reading, Feyenoord (Holland) and FC Cincinnati (USA)
4. Ole Gunnar Solskjaer – Molde FK, Cardiff City and Manchester United
5. Mark Hughes – Wales, Blackburn Rovers, Bradford City, Manchester City, Fulham, Queens Park Rangers, Stoke City and Southampton
6. Gordon Strachan – Coventry City, Southampton, Glasgow Celtic, Middlesbrough and Scotland
7. Steve Bruce – Sheffield United, Huddersfield Town, Wigan Athletic (twice), Crystal Palace, Birmingham City, Sunderland AFC, Hull City, Aston Villa, Sheffield Wednesday and Newcastle United
8. Teddy Sheringham – Stevenage, ATK (India)
9. Lauren Blanc – Bordeaux France, Paris Saint-Germain and Al-Rayyan (Qatar)
10. Bryan Robson – Middlesbrough (player/manager), Bradford City, West Bromwich Albion, Sheffield United and Thailand
11. Michael Carrick - Middlesbrough

Did You Know That?

GARY NEVILLE WAS appointed the manager of Valencia CF in December 2015, after leaving his role as a pundit for SKY Sports. The older of the two United Legends – Gary was born on 18 February 1975 and Phil on 21 January 1977 – was in charge of the Spanish club for just 28 games, which included a 7-0 drubbing by Barcelona, and he swiftly returned to the safe comfort of the SKY Sports studio. 'I never should have said yes to the job. I wasn't qualified for the job and didn't wake up every morning and think about coaching. There was already far too much going on with the SKY stuff, writing articles for a newspaper and doing all the stuff in Manchester with Salford,' said Gary Neville in 2019. Phil Neville was the head coach of Inter Miami from 2021-23.

EL MATADOR

Edinson Cavani's nickname is '*El Matador*', which is quite fitting as it means Bull Fighter. He was born in Salto, Uruguay on 14 February 1987, just three weeks after his fellow Uruguayan international striker, Luis Suarez, was born in the same city on 24 January 1987. Cavani began his youth career with Danubio based in Montevideo in 2000, where former Red, Diego Forlan (Manchester United, 2002-04) spent three years of his playing career. On 26 May 2021, Cavani played for United versus Villarreal CF in the 2021 Europa League final and scored in the 1-1 draw after extra-time (United lost the penalty shootout 11-10, with David De Gea the only player to miss from the spot). Forlan left Old Trafford on 21 August 2004 to join Villarreal and played for the Spanish side until the end of the 2006-07 season. In his first season with the La Liga club he scored 25 League goals to win the coveted Pichichi Trophy as the Spanish league's top goal scorer. Michael Owen (Real Madrid) finished joint 10th with 13 La Liga goals. In season 2008-09, Forlan won the Pichichi Trophy again, this time scoring 32 times in La Liga for Atlético Madrid who he played for from 2007-11.

Did You Know That?

THE INAUGURAL FIFA World Cup finals were held in 1930 and were hosted by Uruguay. The final was played at the Estadio Centenario in the capital city, Montevideo, on 30 July 1930. Uruguay reached the final to face Argentina for the honour of becoming the first country to be crowned World champions and lift the gold trophy aloft. It was a repeat of the Gold Medal Match at the 1928 Summer Olympic Games in Holland. Uruguay beat their South American rivals 2-1 in a replay of the Olympic football final played at the Olympic Stadium, Amsterdam on 13 June 1928, having drawn the first game 1-1 three days earlier at the same venue. On the day of the 1930 World Cup final, the stadium gates were opened at 8.00am and six hours before kick-off the stadium was full, with 93,000 fans.

Amazingly, the game was in danger of being called off due to an argument over the match ball; as to which country would provide it. These were long before the days of the competition's first ever sponsored ball, the '*Adidas Telestar*' at the 1970 finals in Mexico. The agreement was that Argentina would provide the ball for the first-half and Uruguay would provide the ball for the second-half. Uruguay won the 1930 World Cup final 4-2 and Jules

Rimet, the President of FIFA, presented the trophy to the Uruguayan captain, Jose Nasazzi. The following day was declared a national holiday in Uruguay, but in the Argentinian capital, Buenos Aires a mob threw stones at the Uruguayan consulate in the city.

THE SPANISH INQUISITION

The Tribunal of the Holy Office of the Inquisition (Spanish: *Tribunal del Santo Oficio de la Inquisición)*, commonly known as the *Spanish Inquisition* was established in 1478 by Roman Catholic Monarchs, King Ferdinand II of Aragon and Queen Isabella I of Castile.

The Inquisition was originally intended primarily to identify heretics among those who converted from Judaism and Islam to Catholicism. According to modern estimates, around 150,000 people were prosecuted for various offences during the three-century duration of the Spanish Inquisition, of which between 3,000 and 5,000 were executed.

When Manchester United lost the 2021 Europa League final to Villarreal CF on 26 May 2021, they faced their own Spanish Inquisition. The Spanish side, who finished in seventh place in La Liga in season 2020-21 (28 points behind champions Atletico Madrid) beat United 11-10 in a penalty shootout after the game ended 1-1 following extra-time in Gdańsk, Poland (scorer: Edinson Cavani). United were firm favourites to win their sixth major European trophy, having won the European Cup in 1968, European Cup Winners' Cup in 1991, UEFA

Champions League in 1999 and 2008 and the Europa League in 2017. In the end, they lost their third European final and as in the previous two, they succumbed to a Spanish club having lost the 2009 and 2011 UEFA Champions League finals to their European nemesis at the time, FC Barcelona.

The 2021 Europa League final was the fifth time United had faced Villarreal CF, with each of the previous four meetings finishing 0-0 in the UEFA Champions League in seasons 2005-06 and 2008-09.

United had faced Villarreal CF more times without ever scoring against them than they have against any other opponent in the history of the club. It was United's eighth major European final, the second-most of any English club after Liverpool (14). Villarreal CF reached their first major European final in their history after being formed on 10 March 1923, as *Club Deportivo Villarreal*, and they became the eleventh different Spanish side to do so.

The previous two Spanish sides to reach a major European final for the first time also faced English opposition: Alavés lost 5-4 after extra-time to Liverpool in the 2001 UEFA Cup final and Sevilla FC beat Middlesbrough 4-0 in the 2006 UEFA Cup final. Steve McClaren, Alex Ferguson's assistant manager during their triumphant 1998-99 Treble winning season, was the manager of Middlesbrough.

The 2021 Europa League final was Manchester United manager Ole Gunnar Solskjaer's second final in his managerial career, having won the 2013 Norwegian Cup with Molde FK, a 4-2 win against Rosenborg. Solskjaer missed out on becoming the first Norwegian manager to win a major European trophy.

Did You Know That?

ON EACH OF the last nine occasions when a Spanish side has met English opponents in the final of a European competition (including UEFA Super Cup finals), the La Liga club has triumphed. The last Spanish team to lose to an English club was Alavés versus Liverpool in the 2001 UEFA Cup final.

I FOUGHT THE LAW AND THE LAW WON

In 1966, the song *I Fought The Law And The Law Won*, written by Sonny Curtis of the band, The Crickets, was a Top 10 hit in the UK singles charts for the Bobby Fuller Four. Their version of the song is ranked No.175 on the 2004 Rolling Stone magazine list of The 500 Greatest Songs of all Time. In 1979, The Clash recorded their version of the song. Two of the lines from the song are:

Breakin' rocks in the hot sun
I fought the law and the law won

On 15 December 1962, just seven months after he signed for Manchester United in a British record transfer fee of £115,000 from AS Torino, Denis Law played for United in a 3-0 defeat away to West Bromwich Albion in the First Division. When the 22-year-old Law moved back to Manchester, he played for

Manchester City from 1960-61 before moving to Italy for a year, he stayed with the same Landlady with whom he had lived during his time as a Manchester City player. Four days before the trip to The Hawthorns, he married Diana who he had met in a dance hall in Aberdeen (the place of his birth on 24 February 1940) when they were both teenagers. Denis was not his usual menacing self in the game against The Baggies, but it had nothing whatsoever to do with Honeymoon Blues. After the game Denis, who was as hard as nails on the pitch for club, and especially for country, made a startling confession to his manager, Matt Busby. He told his Boss that throughout the game the referee, Mr Gilbert Pullin, was constantly abusive towards him and for no apparent reason. Busby, ever the protector of his players, reported what Denis had told him to the Football Association (FA). The FA then held an enquiry into the alleged incident and found in favour of The Lawman, a nickname given to Denis by United fans before they referred to him as 'The King'. Mr Pullin refuted Denis's record of events but the FA found in favour of the United forward; though Mr Pullin refused to accept and subsequently tendered his resignation as a Football League referee.

Denis later claimed that, 'In the eyes of some referees, I was a marked man' and blamed the incident for the 'staggeringly heavy punishments' that he received later in his career. Needless to say, Pullin fought the law and The Law won.

Did You Know That?

 ON 15 APRIL 1967, England faced Scotland at Wembley Stadium in the British Home International Championships. England were the

reigning World champions after defeating West Germany 4-2 after extra-time in the 1966 FIFA World Cup final at the same venue. Bobby Charlton was the current European Footballer of the Year, the winner of the Ballon d'Or, whilst Law was the first Manchester United player to be accorded the game's most prestigious individual accolade in 1964. George Best made-up United's Trinity when he won the honour in 1968.

Law was in the Scotland side to face the Auld Enemy and lined-up in the tunnel opposite Charlton, and another Manchester United teammate, Nobby Stiles. Charlton and Law acknowledged each other as teammates should, but Nobby never even looked at Law, with or without his glasses on. For Stiles this was a war, England versus Scotland, not quite on the same scale as *The Battle of Bannockburn*, but a war nonetheless in which he had to be victorious for his country. The Scots won the game 3-2, which was made all the sweeter for Law as he scored for his beloved nation, as did a future Manchester United player, Jim McCalliog (Sheffield Wednesday). It was England's first defeat since their captain, Bobby Moore, held aloft the famous and iconic gold Jules Rimet trophy following their win over West Germany on 30 July 1966. It ended England's unbeaten run of eleven games at the Empire Stadium (Wembley) which began in 1962.

Nobby Stiles, Denis Law's Manchester United teammate, said later, 'I knew the Scots were taking it very seriously when Denis came on to the pitch wearing shinpads. I had never seen him wear them before'. Four of the Scottish team helped Glasgow Celtic become the first British club to win the European Cup the following month, defeating Inter Milan 2-1 in the final in Lisbon. The newly Knighted England coach, Sir Alf Ramsey, said, 'Scotland deserved their victory, but I hope they will accept it as a fact rather than an excuse when I say we were heavily handicapped by injuries'.

After the game the Scots hailed themselves as the new World champions as it was England's first defeat since being crowned World Champions. On this occasion, the Lawman fought the law (the FA are the game's governing body in England) and The Law won.

THE PRAWN SANDWICH BRIGADE

On 8 November 2000, Manchester United beat Dynamo Kiev 1-0 at Old Trafford in a Matchday 6, UEFA Champions League Group G game (scorer: Teddy Sheringham 18 minutes). The game is enshrined in the history of the club for what happened after it rather than during the 90 minutes of play. What is probably overlooked by many Reds is that had George Demetradze not missed a sitter from only five yards out in the 85th minute of the game, United would have been eliminated from the competition. RSC Anderlecht (Belgium) won the Group with 12 points from runners-up United who had 10 points. However, PSV Eindhoven (Netherlands) finished third on nine points and if Dynamo Kiev had drawn 1-1 with United at Old Trafford, the Dutch side would have progressed to the Second Group Stage in place of United. As it turned out, it was PSV Eindhoven who had to settle for UEFA Cup football.

After the game the United captain, Roy Keane, was interviewed. Keano was furious with the reaction of some sections of the Old Trafford crowd during the game. The atmosphere was nothing short of dire and he was not happy with some of the booing directed at his teammate, Mikael Silvestre. Keano typically did not hold back his feelings with the BBC Radio Five Live listeners, 'Sometimes you wonder, do they understand the game of football? We're 1-0 up, then there are one or two stray passes and they're getting on players' backs. It's just not on. At the end of the day, they need to get behind the team. Away from home our fans are fantastic, I'd call them the hardcore fans. But at home they have a few drinks and probably the prawn sandwiches, and they don't realise what's going on out on the pitch. I don't think some of the people who come to Old Trafford can spell 'football', never mind understand it,' said United's fiery and talismanic Irish skipper.

Danny Baker, a journalist, summed up Keano's comment really well when he was asked why he thought Roy said what he did. Baker said, 'For these outsiders to come, to pay to watch football through glass, they can't even smell the grass, to hear the players grunting and groaning, to hear the crowd, and then to top it all, they are not even eating a meat pie. Where he grabbed that phrase from, I'll never know. But, let's not kid ourselves, if Dickens had written it, Oh My God, get that man an award.'

It was the coining of the phrase, *Prawn Sandwich Brigade* (PSB).

However, if you attended a game at most Premier League clubs today as a corporate guest, the sight of a prawn sandwich sitting on a platter would probably be a distant memory for the club's catering staff. Prawn sandwiches are just so yesterday. Today's corporate guests are more used to finger food, artisan vegetables and of course, countless glasses of bubbly prosecco. Even Kylie Minogue (yes, the singer) has endorsed her own prosecco wine. In 2020, Kylie released a single entitled *Say Something*. Maybe the Australian actress and singer had a prawn sandwich during the recording rehearsals and remembered that Roy Keane most definitely said something after United's 1-0 victory versus

Dynamo Kiev some 20 years earlier.

The third and fourth lines of Kylie's song are:

Baby, you could light up the dark
Like a solar scape

In many people's eyes, Roy Keane could start a fight in an empty room or with his shadow. He could light a fire in a storm. That's his make-up, his DNA, and that is why he is a Manchester United Legend. Keano comes across as being arrogant, and outspoken, but he wears his heart on his sleeve and the colour of that shirt is red, Manchester United red. A solar scape is an artificial object leaving the Solar System. Roy Keane helped Manchester United become the Masters of the Universe. During his 12 years with United, he helped the club win seven Premier League titles, four FA Cups, four FA Community Shields, the UEFA Champions League title in 1999 and the Intercontinental Cup in 1999.

Did You Know That?

THE PRAWN SANDWICH was 'invented' in 1981, by *Marks & Spencer*, as part of their lunchtime sandwich meal offer, something different to a Ploughman's lunch. In season 1900-01, one year before Newton Heath Football Club faced bankruptcy, but were subsequently saved, and were then reborn as Manchester United Football Club, the club's financial plight was so bad that the fans had to hold whip-rounds to pay for the team's railway fares to away fixtures. Travelling to an away game, the players' pre-match meal consisted of bread and cheese and a bottle of beer, a far cry from today's choreographed meals which ensure the players consume the right balance of nutrients, protein and vitamins. And, the players' wages were still based around the takings at the gate, which to say the very least, were not a King's ransom. Historically, the catching of prawns has been carried out in Southport, England since 1113 in the Parish of North Meols.

BUSBY BABES LOSE FA YOUTH CUP FOR THE FIRST TIME

On 8 April 1957, Manchester United's Youth team, famously dubbed *The Busby Babes*, lost their first ever FA Youth Cup game since the inaugural edition of the competition was held in season 1952-53. The Babes won the 1953 FA Youth Cup final, a 9-3 aggregate victory over two legs against Wolverhampton Wanderers. They retained the trophy the following season beating Wolves again, this time with a 5-4 aggregate win, and they made it three in-a-row when they defeated West Bromwich Albion 7-1 over two legs in the 1955 FA Youth Cup final. Their fourth consecutive win in the final arrived in 1956 with a 4-3 victory versus Chesterfield, again over two legs.

However, despite losing 3-2 to Southampton at Old Trafford in the second leg of the 1956-57 competition, the team coached by Matt Busby's right-hand man, Jimmy Murphy, reached their fifth FA Youth Cup final in succession having beaten The Saints' junior team 3-1 at The Dell in the first leg. In the 1957 final, the best Youth team in the history of the FA Youth Cup, turned on the style and hammered West Ham United 8-2; a 3-2 first leg win at The Boleyn Ground, London and a 5-0 drubbing of their southern opponents at Old Trafford.

The Busby Babes were by far the best Youth side in England

and during the 1950s they could have gone toe to toe against most of the big clubs at the time. When they took to the pitch, their opponents were already staring the inevitable in the face, a loss, but the only question was, by what scoreline?

The players may well have been aged 18 and under, but the tenderness of age of Murphy's young charges was not a barrier to their self-belief or to their immense talent. On the contrary it was their strength. It was what gave them solidarity, some 28 years before the birth of Solidarity, the first independent Trade Union recognised by a Warsaw Pact country, Poland. Solidarity was formed in August 1980, at the Lenin Shipyard, Gdańsk, Poland, not too far from Stadion Miejski in the Polish city where Manchester United lost the 2021 Europa League final to Spain's Villarreal CF.

Manchester United's Youth team simply steamrolled every team that stood in their path. In every FA Youth Cup game, Murphy, the genial Welshman who doubled-up his role as the assistant manager of Manchester United (1955-71), with his part-time role as the coach/manager of the Welsh international football team from 1956-64, knew his Boys were just quite simply too good for their rivals. But, perhaps with the exception of a few of his FA Youth Cup winning players during the 1950s (namely Bobby Charlton, Eddie Colman, Duncan Edwards, Mark Jones, Wilf McGuinness, David Pegg and Liam Whelan), Jimmy would not tell a player just how good he believed he was.

Murphy never let any of his team become too carried away with themselves or get too big for their boots. Complacency was not a word in the Welshman's dictionary, but humility was. Murphy was not only Matt Busby's assistant manager, he was the one man at the club that Busby relied upon to produce a player from the Manchester United Junior Athletic Club to the level whereby that teenager was good enough to be told by Busby on the Friday before a First Division game, 'Son. You are making your first team debut on Saturday. Now go home and rest. Get to bed early tonight. Get up early tomorrow morning and get on your bike or get the bus to Old Trafford five hours before kick-off. I'll be waiting for you'.

These words were like manna from heaven to a Busby Babe. It was their Greek Mount Olympus moment, an acknowledgement by Murphy and Busby that not only were they ready to make the next step in their young career to the senior team, but the ultimate reward for all of the hours they spent running up and down the steps of the Stretford End at Old Trafford during an arduous, and intensive, training session. Not to mention the countless number of pairs of football boots they had to clean for the senior players and cleaning the First Team dressing-room. This was their *One Moment In Time*, which is the name of a song recorded by Whitney Houston. And they did not fail their audition.

The opening lines of Whitney's song are:

Each day I live
I want to be
A day to give
The best of me
I'm only one
But not alone
My finest day
Is yet unknown

When Murphy told Busby about a 'very special' player he had in the Youth team, their one moment in time had arrived. Their debut for United was not only their one moment in time, it was their finest day because they pulled on the jersey of the world's most famous Football Club, Manchester United.

The loss of these young players crushed the heart of their mentor, their father figure, Jimmy Murphy. Jimmy loved every player who came under his charge. His ultimate goal was that if a kid wanted to join the Manchester United Junior Athletic Club, then it was his duty, if not responsibility, to coach that young player as best he could in the hope that one day, Matt Busby would accept Murphy's recommendation that the teenager was ready to progress to the first team.

Six years after the Munich Air Disaster, the Manchester United Youth Team won the FA Youth Cup for a sixth time. Jimmy Murphy guided his young stars to the 1964 final versus Swindon Town and, once again, the Welshman had carefully crafted a team packed with potential. Duncan Edwards may well have been Murphy's crown jewel in his 1952-53, 1953-54 and 1954-55 FA Youth Cup winning teams but in season 1963-64, a young Irishman was his priceless pearl. Seventeen-year-old George Best had already announced himself to football fans having made his senior debut for Manchester United on 14 September 1963, in a 1-0 win against West Bromwich Albion at Old Trafford in the First Division. The mercurial Best tore the Swindon Town back four to pieces and scored United's goal in the first leg of the 1964 final, a 1-1 draw at The County Ground, Swindon. In the second leg at Old Trafford, Best tortured the visitors once more and although he did not score, he helped his teammate, David Sadler, grab a hat-trick. John Aston Jr also scored in the 4-1 victory over The Robins. Ironically, when Best made his first team debut it was Sadler, who made the step up to the first team in a 3-3 draw away to Sheffield Wednesday in the league on 24 August 1963, who scored the only goal of the game.

Did You Know That?

DURING THE 1960S, Jock Stein the legendary manager of Glasgow Celtic, the first British Club to win the European Cup in 1967 adopted the Busby/Murphy model and set-up his own Youth team. Stein set out to attract the best young talent in Scotland to Parkhead, Glasgow in the hope that one day they would be good enough to pull on the iconic green and white hooped jersey of the Scottish giants. Indeed, so prodigious was the young talent at Stein's disposal that in 1968 he contemplated playing them as the club's second team and asked the Scottish Football Association for permission to let them join the Scottish Second Division. However, the clubs already in the division were fearful that this group of teenagers would quite simply just be too good for them and the permission was never granted.

Stein saw these young men as the heirs apparent to his famous 1967 Lisbon Lions and dubbed them 'The Quality Street Gang'. In 1968, the Glasgow Rangers reserves side looked set to be crowned Reserve League Cup winners as the Celtic Boys needed to beat Partick Thistle by at least seven goals to win the trophy. They won 12-0 with a future Manchester United striker scoring four times, Lou Macari. On 7 October 1968, Bobby Brown, the manager of the Scotland international football team, asked Stein to play his kids against the national side as a warm-up for Scotland's encounter versus Denmark nine days later. The Quality Street Gang outclassed a full international Scotland team which included Ronnie Simpson (Glasgow Celtic goalkeeper), Colin Stein (Glasgow Rangers) and the Leeds United pair of Eddie Gray and club captain, Billy Bremner, and ran-out 5-2 winners. Scotland went on to beat Denmark 1-0 away and were captained by Bremner.

PART 4

UNITED'S ORIGINAL WELSH WIZARD

HAT-TRICKS ON THE DOUBLE

STAR SPANGLED REDS

THE CHARLTON BROS.

£2 SEASON TICKETS

LOU AND BRUNO SHOW

UNITED'S ORIGINAL WELSH WIZARD

On 2 December 1907, Charlie Roberts, the captain of Manchester United, and his mercurial teammate, Billy Meredith, held a meeting in the Imperial Hotel, Manchester with a view to forming a union for footballers. The United pair were founder members of the Association Footballers' Union (AFU) in 1898 but it was dissolved within three years. Following the meeting the Association of Football Players' and Trainers' Union (AFPTU) was formed which still exists today although it is now called the Professional Footballers' Association. The principal reason why the AFU was successful was because the Football Association (FA) had finally ratified the maximum wage for a footballer in 1901 at £4 per week.

In the summer of 1909, the AFPTU was attempting to affiliate to the Federation of Trade Unions but the FA was worried that the players might become embroiled in other unions' strikes which could disrupt league and FA Cup games. The FA decreed that any player who would not leave the union would have their wages frozen by the club and would be banned from playing in the Football League. Led by Billy Meredith, the Manchester

United players refused to relinquish their union membership and called themselves 'The Outcasts F.C.' When they were not permitted to train at Clayton, the players found a pitch at nearby Fallowfield where they prepared for the start of the 1909-10 season. Thankfully, on 31 August 1909, just a day before the 1909-10 season began, the FA backed down, recognised the union, lifted the suspensions and agreed to the clubs paying out any back pay that was owing to players.

In October 1906, Ernest Mangnall, the Manchester United manager, made one of the most important signings in the history of Manchester United when he persuaded the Welsh international outside-right, Billy Meredith, to join the club. Meredith was a household name in Manchester long before he arrived at Bank Street, Clayton, having played for local rivals, Manchester City, since 1894. William Henry 'Billy' Meredith was born in a small coal mining village near Chirk in North Wales on 30 July 1874. Aged just 12, he packed up his school books and packed a sandwich instead and went off to work at the Black Park Colliery close to his home. His first job down the mine was to unhook the tubs at the bottom of the main shaft. After spending four years in near total darkness down at the foot of a shaft, Billy put his feet to work and joined his local football club, Chirk Football Club, as an amateur player in 1890. The team was primarily made-up of fellow miners but in 1892, the 18-year-old Meredith was forced to leave his local side when a strike by the miners forced the club to leave their Football League. During his schooldays, the young Billy showed enormous potential as a footballer, but his mother persuaded him to seek a career as a miner. However, rather than return to the Black Park Colliery full-time in 1892, Meredith put his faith in his talent and ability with a football and signed for Northwich Victoria.

After playing just 11 League games for Northwich Victoria from 1892-94, scoring five times, Billy attracted the attention of several Football League clubs, including Bolton Wanderers. Di Jones, who was also born in Chirk, was a full-back with Bolton Wanderers and he recommended Billy to J.J. Bentley, the Secretary of Bolton Wanderers Football Club. But, much to his regret some time later, Bentley passed-up on signing the young Welsh winger, claiming that he was too inexperienced and his frame was too slight. Meredith signed for Ardwick Football Club in early 1894. However, as a result of his mother's influence – she did not regard playing football as a way to make a living – Meredith played for Ardwick but commuted back and forth from Manchester to Chirk and continued working down the pits for a further year. Despite his young age, Billy was a strong believer that footballers should also have proper jobs, and advocated that clubs should allow their players to seek employment outside of football. In April 1894, Ardwick changed their name to Manchester City Football Club.

Meredith won League Division Two winners' medals with City in 1899 and 1903, and an FA Cup winners' medal with The Citizens in 1904 when he captained the club. However, 'Old Skinny' as he was nicknamed, due to his wiry frame, was involved in a bribery scandal in April 1905 when he was accused by the Aston Villa captain, Alec Leake, of offering him £10 to throw a match prior to kick-off. It was the final league game of the 1904-05 season and City needed to beat Aston Villa to stand a chance of winning the Division One title. Villa won the game

3-1 and finished fourth in the league, four points behind City who in turn finished a single point shy of runners-up, Everton and two points adrift of the champions, Newcastle United. Meredith always maintained that he was innocent of the charges but the FA threw the book at him by suspending him and fining him. When Manchester City refused to pay his wages during the suspension, Meredith retaliated and opted to tell the public exactly what was going on at Manchester City.

In an interview with a sports journalist, Meredith said, 'What was the secret of the success of the Manchester City team? In my opinion, the fact that the club put aside the rule that no player should receive more than £4 a week. The team delivered the goods, the club paid for the goods delivered and both sides were satisfied'. His statement caused shockwaves at the FA which had imposed a £4 per week maximum wage on all clubs in 1901. The FA acted immediately and carried out a thorough investigation at City and discovered that the club had made payments over and above the £4 ceiling to every player on their books. The club was fined £250, manager Tom Maley (the older brother of Glasgow Celtic manager Willie Maley) was handed a life suspension from the game (lifted by the FA in 1910) and 16 other players along with Meredith were fined and suspended until 31 December 1906. In order to pay the numerous fines imposed, City were forced to sell their best players in an auction held at the Queen's Hotel, Manchester. United manager Ernest Mangnall attended and signed Meredith after agreeing to pay his £500 signing-on fee, in addition to signing three of his former City teammates, Jimmy Bannister, Herbert Burgess and Alexander 'Sandy' Turnbull. Manchester United also paid Meredith's £100 fine but their investment in him reaped riches the club had never enjoyed before. With these four players trading the blue of City for the red of United, the first golden era of Manchester City had come to an end and United's first golden era was just about to begin. Shortly after joining United, Chairman John H. Davies set Meredith up in business until he could resume his playing career and provided him with the funds to open a sports shop in St. Peter's Square, Manchester.

On New Year's Day 1907, a huge crowd of 40,000 fans poured into Bank Street to see the new quadruplet of players make their debuts for Manchester United in a First Division match versus Aston Villa. After the match the *Manchester Guardian* reported the welcome Meredith received from suspension: *It was a scene of wonderful enthusiasm, an amazing tumult of waving arms and handkerchiefs.* The vast majority of the fans turned out to see Meredith and he did not disappoint them as he made his trademark winding runs down the wing – with a toothpick hanging from the corner of his mouth – followed by a perfect delivery into the opponents' box. Meredith claimed that the toothpick aided his concentration and that he preferred chewing tobacco but opted for the toothpick after the cleaning ladies refused to try and remove the stains from his jersey after games. Sandy Turnbull scored the only goal of the game to give the new recruits and United a 1-0 win after Meredith skipped past the Villa defence to deliver the killer pass. United's brand of stylish attacking football was the talk of the Division and they ended the campaign in a respectable 8th place.

Within two years of winning promotion from the Second Division after finishing runners-up in it at the end of the 1905-

06 season, United were crowned champions of England in season 1907-08 for the first time in the club's history, thanks to their famous half-back line, Meredith's outstanding displays on the wing, and Turnbull's goals. The team played some wonderful attacking football throughout the season, thrilling fans up and down the country with their skills, a style of play United fans would become accustomed to over the next century and beyond. The team also collected the Manchester F.A. Senior Cup by beating Bury 1-0 in the final. As newly crowned League Champions, United played in the inaugural Charity Shield in 1908. They won the trophy after beating the champions of the Southern League, Queens Park Rangers, after a replay. The first game was played on 27 April 1908 and ended 1-1 at Stamford Bridge, London with Meredith scoring for United The replay took place at the same venue on 29 August 1908 with United winning 4-0, thanks to a hat-trick from Sandy's namesake, Jimmy Turnbull, and a fourth from George Wall.

Meredith, also dubbed 'The Welsh Wizard', helped Manchester United to FA Cup final glory in 1909 and a second First Division title in season 1910-11 as well as a second Charity Shield in 1911. He returned to Manchester City in 1921 at the age of 47 and played a further 32 games before retiring in 1924, making him the oldest ever player for City, United (aged 46 years and 281 days, on 7 May 1921) and Wales (aged 45 years and 229 days). He later ran the Stretford Road Hotel and helped to coach the short-lived Manchester Central Football Club. He made 48 appearances for his country from 1895-1920, scoring 11 goals.

Billy Meredith was able to play football at the top level in his late forties due to his strict fitness regime and abstinence from alcohol. Sir Stanley Matthews was the oldest player ever to play in the First Division, aged 50 years and 5 days, and is the oldest player ever to win an international football cap for England, aged 42 years and 104 days.

Meredith was always willing to capitalise on his huge popularity and he invested in numerous local businesses which included him buying a cinema. In 1909, he used his £500 signing-on fee to set up a sports outfitter's shop opposite the Manchester Town Hall, which then supplied United with their kit for the 1909 FA Cup final. And yet, despite being one of the most famous and popular players of the Edwardian heyday of Mancunian football, and as well as being an actor, Meredith was close to poverty when he died on 19 April 1958 aged 73.

He was without question, football's first Superstar, some 60 years before George Best was officially credited with this iconic status.

Did You Know That?

J.J. BENTLEY MANAGED Manchester United from 1912-14 and must have rued the day he failed to sign Billy Meredith. However, Bentley was not the first or last club official to miss out on acquiring a genius because he thought the player lacked experience or the physicality to make it in the game. In the early 60s, George Best was playing for the Cregagh Boys Club, quite close to the Cregagh Estate in east Belfast where the young Belfast Boy was born on 22 May 1946, when his hopes of becoming a professional footballer were almost dashed. His local team were Glentoran Football Club, whose home ground, The Oval, is situated quite close to the world famous Harland and Wolff shipyard in Belfast, but they thought George was 'too small and too light' to make it as a footballer and did not sign him.

As George himself once said, 'There was more fat on a chip than on me'. Thankfully, Manchester United's Chief Scout in Northern Ireland, Bob Bishop, disagreed and after seeing the young, skinny 15-year-old play in a junior game, he immediately rushed to a nearby post office and sent a telegram to the Manchester United manager, Matt Busby. The telegram simply read... *I think I've found you a genius.* How true these words proved to be.

SEVEN GOALS, TWO HAT-TRICKS

Christopher Taylor played 30 times for Manchester United from 1926-30, and scored seven goals. In season 1925-26, he scored six times in the First Division and remarkably, both were hat-tricks for the club.

Taylor joined United from Redditch United in February 1924. On 21 April 1926, he scored his first hat-trick for United versus Sunderland at Old Trafford with Thomas Smith and Harry Thomas also finding the back of The Black Cats' net in a 5-1 victory. Then in United's final league game of the campaign he scored another hat-trick, again in front of the Old Trafford crowd, this time in a 3-2 victory over West Bromwich Albion. Taylor's seventh and final goal for the club came in an FA Cup Third Round tie. On 12 January 1929, he scored in United's 3-0 win over Port Vale at The Old Recreation Ground, Hanley, Stoke-on-Trent (James Hanson and Joe Spence also scored in the game). In September 1931, he left Old Trafford and moved to nearby Hyde United.

Did You Know That?

PORT VALE, NICKNAMED 'The Valiants', played their home games at The Old Recreation Ground from 1913-40, which was the club's sixth home ground. In 1950, the club moved to their present home, Vale Park, Stoke-on-Trent.

STAR SPANGLED REDS

On 15 November 2018, Wayne Rooney became only the second player to win a full international cap for England whilst playing for a Major League Soccer (MLS) team when England beat the USA 3-0 at Wembley Stadium. On 11 July 2007, David Beckham joined LA Galaxy from Real Madrid and six weeks later, 22 August 2007, he captained England in their 2-1 loss to Germany in a friendly at the new Wembley Stadium. Not only did the game mark the first time a player from the MLS captained England, but Becks also became the first MLS player to be capped by England.

When Rooney came on for his former Manchester United teammate, Jesse Lingard, in the 58th minute of the game, it was his 120th senior cap and when he came on to the pitch, he was handed the captain's armband. His record in his 120 international appearances (2003-18) is: a record 53 goals (seven penalties), 72 wins, 29 draws, 19 losses, for 195 goals, against 80 goals (a win ratio of 72.0%).

Rooney captained England 22 times and was first given the armband by Fabio Capello on 14 November 2009 when England lost a friendly 1-0 to Brazil at the International Stadium, ad-Dawha, Qatar in a game played to celebrate six years of the Al Jazeera sports channel. He received 12 yellow cards and was sent off twice – versus Portugal at the 2006 World Cup and versus Montenegro in a Euro 2012 qualifier in Podgorica. Gareth Southgate was the sixth England manager to cap him: Sven Goran Eriksson 33 caps (17 Everton, 16 United, 2003-06, 11 goals); Steve McClaren seven caps (2006-07, three goals); Fabio Capello 33 caps (2008-11, 14 goals, one captaincy); Roy Hodgson 42 caps (2012-16, 25 goals, 18 captaincy); Sam Allardyce one cap (2016, one captaincy); Gareth Southgate three caps (2016, two captaincy). He never played when Stuart Pearce took caretaker charge of England for their friendly against The Netherlands at Wembley Stadium on 29 February 2012, a game England lost 3-2.

When Rooney packed his bags and moved his family across the *Big Pond* in June 2018, to begin a new chapter in his football career with D.C. United in Washington, he became yet another ex–Red to ply his trade in the MLS. However, long before Rooney took the decision to go transatlantic, a number of other former United players, some notable stars in their day, had trail blazed their way around the North American Soccer League (NASL 1968-84) and later Major League Soccer.

- **Gerry Daly** -New England Tea Men 1972 (on loan) & 1973 (on loan)
- **Gordon Hill** – Chicago Sting 1972 (on loan) and 1982-83, Montreal Manic 1981-82
- **David Sadler** – Miami Toros 1973 (on loan)
- **Ian Storey-Moore** – Chicago Sting 1975
- **George Best** – Los Angeles Aztecs 1976 and 1977-

78, Fort Lauderdale Strikers 1978-79, San Jose Earthquakes 1980-81
- **Jimmy Ryan** – Dallas Tornado 1976-79 and Wichita Wings 1979-82 (indoor)
- **Jim McCalliog** – Chicago Sting 1977
- **Alan Brazil** – Detroit Express 1978 (on loan)
- **Colin Waldron** – Tulsa Roughnecks 1978, Philadelphia Fury 1978 and Atlanta Chiefs 1979
- **Tony Dunne** – Detroit Express 1979
- **Ted MacDougall** – Detroit Express 1979 (on loan)
- **Alex Stepney** – Dallas Tornado 1979-80
- **Jimmy Greenhoff** – Toronto Blizzard 1981
- **Brian Kidd** – Atlanta Chiefs 1981 (on loan), Fort Lauderdale Strikers 1982-83 and Minnesota Strikers 1984
- **David McCreery** – Tulsa Roughnecks 1981-82 & 1989
- **Chris McGrath** - Tulsa Roughnecks 1981-82
- **Jimmy Nicholl** – Toronto Blizzard 1982 and 1983-84
- **Terry Cooke** – Colorado Rapids 2005-09
- **David Beckham** – LA Galaxy 2007-12
- **Mikael Silvestre** - Portland Timbers 2013-14
- **Kleberson** – Philadelphia Union 2013 (on loan), Indy Eleven 2014-15 and Fort Lauderdale Strikers 2016
- **Tim Howard** – North Jersey Imperials 1997, Metro Stars 1998-2003, Colorado Rapids 2016-19, Memphis 901 (2020)
- **Bastian Schweinsteiger** – Chicago Fire 2017-19
- **Zlatan Ibrahimović** – LA Galaxy 2018-19
- **Wayne Rooney** – D.C. United 2018-20

Martin Buchan, United's stylish 1977 FA Cup winning captain, played eight games as a guest player for the Washington Whips in 1967 and scored one goal. The Washington Whips were a football club based in Washington D.C. and played in the United Soccer Association. The League was made up of teams imported from foreign Leagues. The Washington Whips were actually Aberdeen Football Club. Buchan remains the only player to captain a Scottish FA Cup winning side (Aberdeen 1970) and an English FA Cup winning side.

The USA final 1967 was the United States Soccer Association's first, and only, post-season championship game. Buchan and his Washington Whips teammates faced Los Angeles Wolves (Wolverhampton Wanderers) in the final at the Los Angeles Memorial Coliseum on 14 July 1967 in front of 18,000 fans. Northern Ireland legend, Derek Dougan, led his American club to a 6-5 win after extra-time with 'The Doug' scoring one of the goals. Ray Wood, who won two First Division Championship winners' medals with Manchester United in 1954-55 and 1956-57, was a goalkeeper/coach for Los Angeles Wolves in the 1967 tournament.

Tommy Jackson, Manchester United 1975-78, played 12 times as a guest player for the Detroit Cougars in 1967, who were actually Glentoran FC from Belfast. One infamous match played by the Detroit Cougars took place on 14 June 1967 at their Tigers Stadium home against the Houston Stars. The match had to be abandoned after 73 minutes following a mass brawl between the players. Players from the visiting side, who were actually Bangu Atletico Club from Rio de Janeiro, Brazil, launched two-footed drop kicks into the backs of the Belfast men and even used the corner flags as weapons. The Detroit Police and private security had to come out on to the pitch to restore order. The Cougars were trailing 2-0 when the referee ended the game, but the result stood.

Mickey Thomas, Manchester United 1978-81, played for Wichita Wings from 1976-78. The Wichita Wings were a professional indoor soccer franchise and are based in Wichita, Kansas. On 21 August 1979, they were admitted to the Major Indoor Soccer League as an expansion club.

Bill Foulkes, Manchester United 1951-70, managed three teams in the USA: Chicago Sting 1975-77, Tulsa Roughnecks 1978-79 and San Jose Earthquakes 1980.

Jimmy Ryan, Sir Alex Ferguson's assistant 1998-99 and 1999-2000, played for Dallas Tornado from 1976 to 1979.

Nobby Stiles, Manchester United 1960-71, managed Vancouver Whitecaps from 1981 to 1984.

Jaap Stam, Manchester United 1998-2001, managed FC Cincinnati from 2020-21.

Phil Neville, Manchester United 1994-2005, managed Inter Miami from 2021-23.

Did You Know That?

GERMANY'S 2-1 WIN on 22 August 2007 meant that they became the first team to beat England at the new Wembley Stadium. Playing alongside Beckham that day were United's Michael Carrick and Rio Ferdinand. Michael Owen and Alan Smith also played but they were at Newcastle United at the time. The Germans were also the last team to beat England at the old Wembley Stadium – 1-0 on 7 October 2000 in a World Cup 2002 UEFA Group Nine qualification game which marked the end of

Kevin Keegan's reign as England manager. The England side contained four United players: Beckham who captained the side, Gary Neville, Paul Scholes and Andy Cole. Future United star, Michael Owen, also played in the game but he was playing for Liverpool then. Phil Neville (Everton) was an unused substitute. Beckham won 115 caps for his country and captained them on 59 occasions, the first occasion being when Peter Taylor took charge of England for the only game of his managerial career with England, a 1-0 friendly loss against Italy at Stadio delle Alpi, Turin on 15 November 2000. Beckham made his final appearance for England on 14 October 2009, a 3-0 over Belarus at Wembley Stadium in a FIFA 2010 World Cup, UEFA Group 6 qualifying match. He came on as a substitute in the 58th minute for Aaron Lennon.

CHARLTON BROTHERS IN RED

'Some people are on the pitch. They think it is all over. It is now.' The famous words of Kenneth Wolstenholme after Geoff Hurst scored England's fourth goal in the 1966 FIFA World Cup final.

Bobby Charlton and his older brother, Jack, won the 1966 World Cup final with England when they defeated West Germany 4-2 after extra-time at Wembley Stadium on 30 July 1966. In the final, played before 100,000 fans, England wore their away kit of red shirt, white shorts and red socks, whilst the Germans were the designated home team and wore their traditional colours of white shirts, black shorts and white socks.

Jack was at Leeds United having joined the Yorkshire club as an apprentice in the summer of 1952, aged 17. Bobby signed for Manchester United as a trainee in January 1953, aged 15, a Busby Babe. Major Frank Buckley was in charge of Leeds United when Jack left his home in Ashington, a rural coal mining village in Northumberland, England. When he left school at the age of 15, he was offered a trial at Leeds United, where his uncle Jim Milburn was a left back. However, he turned down the opportunity to become a footballer and chose to join his father, Robert, down the mines. His father had no interest at all in football, but his mother, Cissie, played football with her children and later coached the local school's team. The legendary Newcastle United and England international striker, Jackie Milburn, was his mother's cousin. Jack, Bobby and their two brothers, Gordon and Tommy, got their football gene from their mum. But life wasn't easy for the four boys in a village where men had to become men before they became a teenager. The four brothers shared the same bed in their modest home.

Life underground did not suit Jack and he decided to apply for a job as a policeman, his 6 feet, 1.5 inches stature more than met the Metropolitan Police Force's entry criteria. He also reconsidered his Uncle Jim's offer and was offered another trial for the Elland Road club. The date of his trial game fell on the same day he was invited for an interview to join the Northumbria Police Force. Jack opted for the trial game and as the saying goes, the rest is history. He impressed in the game and was offered a contract to join Leeds United which he gratefully accepted. After playing for the club's Reserve side for two years, in 1952 aged 17, he was offered a professional contract. He made his debut on 25 April 1953, versus Doncaster Rovers at Elland Road on the final day of the club's Second Division Championship season which ended 1-1. Jack replaced a Leeds United and Wales legend at centre-half in the game, John Charles, when Major Frank Buckley decided to move Charles to the centre forward position. It proved to be an inspired decision which reaped dividends for Charles, Leeds United and Wales.

In the summer of 1960, Matt Busby was in search of a new centre-half. Jack's contract with Leeds United had come to an end and he was negotiating a renewal contract with his employer. Busby heard about this impasse and approached the older Charlton brother about the possibility of him teaming-up with his kid brother at Old Trafford. However, in the summer of 1957, Busby signed Frank Haydock, a 17-year-old, born in Eccles, Salford, Manchester, and in December 1959, Haydock agreed professional terms with Manchester United. Busby intended to blood the 19-year-old Busby Babe into his first team in season 1960-61, and reportedly told Charlton senior that his appearances for Manchester United would very much depend on the progress of Haydock. Jack was having none of it and declined the opportunity to sign for Manchester United. In his mind, he was second best to no player and signed a new contract with Leeds United.

As a Leeds United player, Jack went on to win the Second Division Championship title in 1963-64, the First Division Championship title in 1968-69, the League Cup in 1968, the FA Charity Shield in 1969, the FA Cup in 1972 and the Inter-Cities Fairs Cup in seasons 1967-68 and 1970-71. As for individual awards, Big Jack was named the Football Writers' Association Footballer of the Year in 1967, was inducted into the English Football Hall of Fame in 2005. With England he also won the British Home International Championship in seasons 1964-65, 1965-66, 1967-68 and 1968-69. As for Frank, he played only six times for United from 1960-63, and moved to Charlton Athletic in August 1963, in a £10,000 transfer.

Did You Know That?

BOBBY MADE HIS debut for England on 19 April 1958, Scotland 0 England 4, a British Home International Championship match played at Hampden Park, Mount Florida, Glasgow, aged 20 years and 190 days. He scored on his debut and went on to score a total of 49 international goals in 106 appearances for his country from 1958-70. Jack made his England debut on 10 April 1965, England 2 Scotland 2, a British Home International Championship match at Empire Stadium, Wembley, London aged 29 years and 37 days. He won 35 caps and scored 6 goals, 1965-70.

A £2 SEASON TICKET AT OLD TRAFFORD

On 15 September 1923, Manchester United welcomed Bury to Old Trafford for a Second Division game. Money was tight at the club and the Board of Directors came up with all sorts of ideas to attract fans to home games. One such idea was printed in the match programme for the visit of Bury, and carried the title: *CROWD ESTIMATE COMPETITION*

The prize on offer was £2 cash or a season ticket for the following season.

A cut-out section was in the programme for fans to tear out, write their guess on and include their name and address. Home telephone numbers, mobile numbers and email addresses were more than half a century away. The fan's guess had to arrive at Old Trafford by 10.00am on the morning of the game.

Underneath *CUT HERE* it read: *I estimate that the attendance at the match with SOUTH SHIELDS on September 29 will be –*

The fan who guessed the closest home gate, which was 22,250 in United's 1-1 draw versus South Shields (scorer: Arthur Lochhead), could take the £2 cash prize, the equivalent to £120 today, or accept a season ticket for another Second Division campaign as United ended season 1923-24 in 14th place.

With money being so tight in the early 1920's, perhaps the fan opted for the cash prize. To put the cash prize into perspective, the cost of a pint of beer in 1923 was 10d, which in 2023 equates to 4.5 pence.

Did You Know That?

THE 1923–24 SEASON was Manchester United's 28th season in the Football League and their second consecutive season in League Division Two, having narrowly missing out on promotion the previous season when they finished in fourth place.

THE LOU & BRUNO SHOW

When Bruno Fernandes scored a hat-trick in Manchester United's pulsating 5-1 (Mason Greenwood and Fred also scored) victory over Leeds United on 14 August 2021, he scored the club's first opening day hat-trick since Lou Macari took the match ball home after netting a treble of goals against Birmingham City at St Andrews, Birmingham on 20 August 1977 in the First Division Championship (Gordon Hill also scored in a 4-1 win).

There have been other notable hat-tricks from Manchester United players in previous clashes with rivals Leeds United. Andy Ritchie netted the perfect hat-trick (header, right foot and left foot) as an 18-year-old in a dominant 4-1 victory at Old Trafford in the First Division on 24 March 1979 (Mickey Thomas also scored). Stan Pearson and Dennis Viollet, two Manchester United legends, also bagged hat-tricks against their Yorkshire rivals. On 27 January 1951, Stan took a rain soaked, heavy and mud covered ball home after bagging a treble in a 4-1 FA Cup Round 4 home win (Jack Rowley also scored). Eight years later, 21 March 1959, Viollet scored his War of the Roses hat-trick when United won their League encounter 4-1 at Old Trafford with Bobby Charlton also scoring in the game.

Did You Know That?

ANDY RITCHIE PLAYED 42 games for Manchester United from 1977-80, scoring 13 times. He played 159 league games for Leeds United from 1983-87, scoring 47 times.

A STAR IS BORN

In 1976, the movie *A Star is Born*, featuring Kris Kristofferson and Barbra Streisand, was a huge hit in the cinemas up and down the country. In 1976, Manchester United had their very own star, Steve Coppell. Season 1975-76 saw United play First Division football once again after a one year sabbatical in the Second Division. Tommy Docherty's exciting young side were a breath of fresh air and they continued to play the free flowing, attacking style of football which helped them clinch the Second Division Championship just four months earlier.

Perhaps it was the exuberance of youth in the side and lack of top flight football experience, or maybe it was down to their manager, Tommy Docherty's swagger which reflected on the players performances, but United settled in seamlessly among the big boys of English football. They were undefeated in their opening six games which produced five wins, one draw, 14 goals for, four goals against and, against all odds, they sat on top of the table. However, with the combination of a dip in form which saw them fall off the top of the table after a dismal February (won one, drew three and lost one of their five league games, scoring seven and conceding four – they beat West Ham United 4-0 at home) coupled with some injuries to key players, they simply just could not sustain their title challenge despite not having been outside the Top 5 all season. United eventually finished in a respectable third place in their first year back, behind Queens Park Rangers and champions, Liverpool. It was United's highest place finish since season 1967-68 when they so narrowly missed out on winning a very unique Double of First Division Championship and European Cup. United were crowned champions of Europe, the first English club to win European club football's most coveted and prestigious trophy. The League title that season left Old Trafford and made the short trip across the city to Maine

Road to give Manchester City their second title (1936-37). City won the league with 58 points to United's 56.

But it was in the FA Cup when Docherty's young charges, captained by the inspirational Martin Buchan, with seasoned strikers, Lou Macari and Stuart 'Pancho' Pearson, really shone.

In Round 3 of the 1975-76 FA Cup, United's inexperienced, but hugely ambitious side, beat Oxford United 2-1 at Old Trafford with both goals scored by United's classy Republic of Ireland midfielder, Gerry Daly. There were very few players who were as calm taking a penalty as Daly. He was coolness personified and seemed to have the knack of sending the goalkeeper the wrong way. In the next Round United's name was drawn from the hat with another home tie, Peterborough United. Goals from Alex Forsyth, Sammy McIlroy and Gordon Hill eased them past The Posh into Round 5 with a 3-1 victory. Round 5 brought about a trip to Filbert Street to face Leicester City, a rematch of the 1963 FA Cup final which United won 3-1 (scorers: David Herd two and Denis Law). On this occasion United defeated The Foxes 2-1, Macari and Daly were the goal scorers.

The Sixth Round produced another home tie. Wolverhampton Wanderers were the visitors and left Old Trafford earning a home replay following a 1-1 draw (scorer: Daly). Three days later, United beat Wolves 3-2 after extra-time at Molineux Stadium with goals from Pancho, Brian Greenhoff and Sammy McIlroy.

Along with United, Crystal Palace, Derby County and Southampton were in the hat for the semi-final draw. Crystal Palace were a Third Division side (finished fifth), Southampton were in Division Two (finished sixth), whilst Derby County ended the season in fourth place in the First Division, one place and three points behind United. The two top flight sides were drawn together and all of the money was on whoever won this game would see off lower Division opposition in the showpiece final. Odds on.

On 3 April 1976, Tommy Docherty's Tartan Army of Reds travelled to Hillsborough Stadium, the home of Sheffield Wednesday, to see if United could reach their first FA Cup final since their victory at Wembley Stadium in 1963. The Brotherhood of Man were at No.1 in the UK chart with their 1976 Eurovision Contest winning song, *Save Your Kisses For Me*. But the question on the fans' lips was, 'Who would be kissing goodbye to their dreams of lifting the FA Cup?' Well, 90 minutes, 120 minutes, or a replay would provide the answer.

It was a bright sunny afternoon in South Yorkshire and three-quarters of the ground was steeped in red. Hillsborough Stadium, along with Villa Park, home to Aston Villa, were among the favoured venues to host FA Cup semi-final games. In many ways it proved to be a hoodoo for both clubs as Villa had not reached the last four of the competition since 1959-60 when they won the Second Division Championship and were beaten 1-0 in the semi-finals by Wolverhampton Wanderers at The Hawthorns, West Bromwich, who went on to beat Blackburn Rovers in the final. Sheffield Wednesday made it all of the way to the final in 1966 but lost 3-2 to Everton after being 2-0 up after 57 minutes.

The United side that day was: Alex Stepney, Alex Forsyth, Stewart Houston, Martin Buchan (Capt), Brian Greenhoff, Steve Coppell, Gerry Daly, David McCreery, Gordon Hill, Sammy McIlroy, Stuart Pearson.

Derby County, managed by Dave Mackay, were the reigning First Division champions (they were also champions in 1971-72 when Brian Clough was in charge). Their strong side included Roy McFarland, David Nish, Colin Todd, Archie Gemmell, Kevin Hector, Bruce Rioch, ex-Manchester City forward, and totally loathed by United fans, Francis Lee, and the player whose goal in extra-time of the 1971 FA Cup final gave Arsenal the Double, Charlie George.

On the day United were too good for The Rams. Their defence were never given a moment's rest with the two Northern Ireland internationals, McCreery and McIlroy, a Green Dynamic Duo, bossing the midfield. McCreery in particular was a constant thorn in their side with his ferocious, no prisoners taken style of tackling.

Pancho never allowed a defender to take his time on the ball, Coppell and Hill made non-stop raids on both wings all afternoon whilst Buchan did what Buchan did best, marshalled his defence and led his team like a Field Marshall commanding his troops.

The mercurial Gordon Hill, who always looked like he had the ball tied to the tip of his left boot with an invisible piece of string, was the game's outstanding player. Hill, quite appropriately nicknamed 'Merlin', was a magical player and scored a goal in each half, 12th and 83rd minutes, to give United a 2-0 victory. But more importantly the win booked United's place in the FA Cup final versus Southampton who that same afternoon beat Crystal Palace by the same score at Stamford Bridge, London.

The Doc brought Hill to Old Trafford in November 1975, a £70,000 bargain purchase from Millwall. Hill was born in Surrey, England on 1 April 1954 but contrary to folklore, he was nobody's fool. His wizardry skills made fools out of defenders up and down the length and breadth of England. He left United in April 1978, a £250,000 move to Derby County where he once again played for Tommy Docherty who was appointed the manager of Derby County after he was sacked by United on 4 July 1977. Hill made 134 appearances for United and scored 51 goals, a more than decent return from a left winger. Gordon produced some spellbinding performances for United and there is no doubt that his magic wand most definitely worked.

Alas, there was no pot of gold for United at Wembley Stadium in the final, losing 1-0 to Southampton. After the game the Doc promised the United fans that they would be back in the final the following May and win the FA Cup. He was true to his word as United won the FA Cup in season 1976-77.

Did You Know That?

AT THE END of the 1976-77 season, Gerry Daly left United and teamed-up with his old boss, Tommy Docherty. Not long after his arrival at The Baseball Ground, Daly scored a penalty versus Manchester City in a home First Division game. But the referee made him take the spot kick again following complaints from the City players, who claimed that the ball was not on the penalty spot! In fact, no one knew where the penalty spot was as the box was a mud bath. So, the referee had the penalty spot repainted and Daly placed the ball on it. Daly retook the penalty and scored again sending Joe Corrigan the wrong way.

BELT-UP

The *United Review*, Manchester United's official matchday programme, for the Arsenal game on Saturday 14 May 1977, included an advertisement for a Red Devils Souvenir Belt Offer.

The United fans were tempted to pay £2 for, *Individual photo-slides of all your first team players on a fabulous black belt with chromium buckle. Each slide shows player in coloured team strip with an individually printed autograph. Slides can be arranged in any order and the belt fits any waist size.* United won the First Division game 3-2 (scorers: Jimmy Greenhoff, Gordon Hill and Lou Macari). United finished in sixth place in the First Division Championship in season 1976-77 and defeated Liverpool 2-1 (scorers: Stuart Pearson and Jimmy Greenhoff) in the 1977 FA Cup final.

During the season, David Soul went to No.1 in the UK singles charts with *Don't Give Up On Us*. It was Soul's, one half of the hugely popular *Starsky* (played by Paul Michael Glaser) *and Hutch* (played by David Soul) TV cop show, first No.1 hit. The TV heartthrob went on to hit the top spot a second time in the UK with *Silver Lady*. Despite being relegated to Division Two at the end of the 1973-74 season, United fans never gave up on their team and supported them with their unequivocal loyalty. The team repaid their allegiance and dedication by winning the Second Division Championship in season 1974-75 to regain a place at the top table of English football.

Did You Know That?

ON 14 MAY 1977, the Manchester United Development Association (MUDA) was established to help generate funds for the payment of building works to upgrade Old Trafford. The *United Review* for the Arsenal match also advertised the formation of MUDA.

PART 5

TOMMY DOCHERTY'S TARTAN ARMY

CASINO ROYALE

LILYWHITES TURN RED

BEST VALUE FOR MONEY

ONE MANCUNIAN HEART

LEGEND OF JOSEPH WALTON

CASINO ROYALE

On 27 November 2006, the Ulster Bank in Northern Ireland produced a new £5 bank note. Exactly one year and two days after the death of George Best, 25 November 2005 aged 59, the bank immortalised the Manchester United and Northern Ireland international, on a banknote. A limited edition of 1 million £5 George Best bank notes were printed and they were all snapped up by fans and collectors within 24 hours. The colourful banknote came with a commemorative folder but for the vast majority of those who acquired one, they had no intention of ever spending it. The folder simply said: "*Celebrating the LEGEND, a commemorative banknote.*"

The £5 banknote which was printed in honour of *The Belfast Boy* was not the first time money played a part of his rollercoaster of a career. A few months after he took the decision to retire aged just 27, George was in a Spanish casino in mid-1974, and for a change he enjoyed a quite successful evening at the gambling tables. At the end of a night's gambling he took great pleasure in scooping up his casino chips up and placing them on to a waiter's tray before making his way to the casino's cash desk. When the cashier saw the iconic footballer, and world superstar, approach her kiosk she must have been thinking how much more money George wanted to spend on chips, yet only to be surprised to discover that Bestie was actually cashing out. George was calling it a night, or rather an early morning, and was in the mood for celebrating having won around £50,000.

Ray Stevens was at No.1 in the UK charts with *The Streak*, but George's winning streak was a world away from the theme of Stevens' song which was about an individual who liked to take all of his clothes off and streak in various public places. At the time, George, who quite amazingly was a very shy young teenager when he made his debut for Manchester United aged 17, was the world's most attractive single male. He looked like a movie star and enjoyed a lifestyle that only a lottery win today could bankroll.

There wasn't a girl who didn't want to date him, let alone marry him; mums adored him, whilst most husbands would have gladly tucked Bestie and his wife into bed at night. And, long before the world embraced LGBT, many males also loved George.

Having collected his winnings, George went to his bedroom accompanied by his latest girlfriend at the time, Marjorie Wallace. George, being George, did not want the night to end. Why would he after such a successful evening at a time when he won as much money as his yearly salary as a Manchester United player. So, Bestie, in typical fashion, ordered room service. It was the early hours of the morning but the time of day was irrelevant to the United player and most definitely was not going to put him off celebrating a successful night. Bestie ordered champagne, of course, a selection of caviar, and what he always ordered regardless of where he was at the time, the English newspapers.

When the hotel waiter opened the door and entered George's hotel suite, he saw the United legend lying on the bed beside Marjorie, the reigning Miss World winner and first American to claim the title, with banknotes on top of them, around them and lying scattered everywhere on the bedroom floor. He parked his catering trolley close to the king-size bed, which included an ice bucket with the hotel's most expensive bottle of champagne inside it, plates of Russian caviar and a selection of newspapers. George lifted a handful of money off the bed and gave it to the waiter as a tip. It was more than the hotel employee earned in a week delivering room service.

However, the waiter had a question on his mind which he just wanted to ask George before saying goodnight. He looked at the United star, Miss World 1973, and all of the cash lying all over the room and just said, 'Mr Best. Where did it all go wrong?'

In 1967, *Casino Royale* was a huge hit in the cinemas around the world. It was a spy parody comedy film loosely based on Ian Fleming's first James Bond novel. The film stars David Niven as the 'original' Bond, Sir James Bond 007. But in 1967, the words 'The name is Bond, James Bond' did not quite carry the same meaning as 'The name is Best, George Best'. But then again, nobody had to ask the name of the mercurial handsome young Irishman who wore the No.11 shirt of Manchester United as he was already a household name having just helped the club to win the English First Division Championship title in season 1966-67, his second league winners' medal in three seasons (1964-65).

Did You Know That?

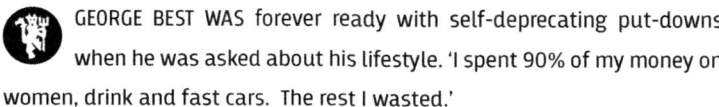
GEORGE BEST WAS forever ready with self-deprecating put-downs when he was asked about his lifestyle. 'I spent 90% of my money on women, drink and fast cars. The rest I wasted.'

TWO LILYWHITES WHO MANAGED THE RED DEVILS

On 5 April 1958, Manchester United Football Club welcomed Preston North End to Old Trafford for a First Division Championship game. The club were still trying to come to terms with the loss of eight Busby Babes, as well as the Secretary of Manchester United, Walter Crickmer, trainer Tom Curry and coach Bert Whalley, following the fateful Munich Air Disaster on 6 February 1958. Although the funerals of all 23 people who perished in the crash had been held, the city of Manchester was still in mourning. Reds and Blues from every part of the city were 'united' in their grief. The Busby Babes may have been worshipped by Manchester United fans but Manchester City fans also felt the grief their rivals were experiencing, as three of the players who died were Manchester-born lads: club captain Roger Byrne (Gorton, Manchester), Geoff Bent (Salford, England) and Eddie 'Snakehips' Colman (Ordsall, Salford, Manchester).

The city of Manchester was passionate about their own boys regardless of their affiliation to either club and this was never more evident when a dad brought his son up as a Blue or as a Red, only to see his child fulfil his dreams of becoming a professional footballer by having to change colours. It had to be a heart-wrenching moment for any dad to see his son move over to his club's greatest rivals, but also coupled with a sense of pride that finally after all of the evenings and Saturday afternoons he spent as a part-time taxi driver, standing in the rain supporting his flesh and blood in countless junior and youth games, his son had gone from kicking a football on the street to becoming a professional footballer. The badge on the shirt may well not have been to the dad's choice but that was irrelevant because nothing could take away the bursting pride he had in his heart for his son. These were the days when parents did what was right for their son and ignored any promises of riches offered by other clubs in return for persuading their child to join their club.

When the Preston North End coach parked outside Old Trafford before the game, their players entered the stadium which was still more like a morgue to home fans than a stadium where they could celebrate performances out on the pitch. Indeed, when the bodies of Geoff Bent, Roger Byrne, Eddie Colman, Mark Jones, David Pegg, Tommy Taylor and Liam Whelan were returned to Manchester, they were laid out in coffins side-by-side in the gymnasium at Old Trafford, the last time seven of the most iconic players in the illustrious history of Manchester United were together. Their fellow Busby Babe, perhaps the most famous of all, Duncan Edwards, was still battling for his life in the Rechts der Isar Hospital in Munich, West Germany. He still had no idea that his teammates had died and he was more concerned about playing for United in the next game rather than trying to recover from his injuries.

But whereas the football world could mourn the loss of a team, eerily 58 days previously, only the Manchester United fans could celebrate the lives of Geoff Bent, Roger Byrne, Eddie Colman, Duncan Edwards, Mark Jones, David Pegg, Tommy Taylor and Liam Whelan.

Meanwhile, Matt Busby was still fighting an uphill battle to save his own life, and had even been given the Last Rites as he was a devout Roman Catholic, in the German hospital when Jimmy Murphy, Busby's right-hand man and the assistant manager of the club, unwillingly took temporary charge of the side to play Preston North End.

Murphy selected his team: Harry Gregg, Bill Foulkes, Ian Greaves, Ronald Cope, Stan Crowther, Frederick Goodwin, Ernie Taylor, Bobby Charlton, Colin Webster, Kenny Morgans, Thomas Heron.

The Preston North End side were led by the legendary England forward, Tom Finney, and a former Manchester United left-back, Joseph Walton. Walton played 23 games for Manchester United from 1945-48, but never scored. He made his debut for United against Preston North End on 26 January 1946 in a 1-0 'home' win at Maine Road in an FA Cup Fourth Round, first leg tie. United were using their neighbours' ground as Old Trafford had been badly damaged during a German bombing raid on the Salford area of Manchester during the Second World War.

Heron made his club debut. Crowther and Taylor were making their 10th appearance, whilst Morgans was making his 11th, and Cope his 14th. Goodwin was pulling on a United shirt for the 37th time. Just 24 earlier, Charlton and Alex Dawson scored for United in a 2-2 draw at Old Trafford in the league. The match programme for the visit of Preston North End actually listed Alex Dawson and Shay Brennan as starting players but they were replaced by Thomas Heron and Kenny Morgans after it had been printed.

Gregg, Foulkes and Morgans were passengers on the Munich flight. When they were sitting beside each other in the dressing-room just half an hour before kick-off versus Preston North End, they looked around the room and saw the familiar 10 red jerseys and a green jersey that they were used to seeing before every home game. However, the hairstyles and voices of their teammates had changed since the opening league game of the 1957-58 season when United beat Leicester City 3-0 at Filbert Street. Liam 'Billy' Whelan scored a hat-trick. For Gregg, it must have been particularly difficult, as the young Busby Babes looked upon the tall 25-year-old Irishman as their father figure on the pitch.

Gregg had no hesitation in coming to the edge of his 18-yard box and giving any member of his back four a right bollicking if United had just conceded a goal, and Gregg had homed in on the player he thought was at fault for the ball ending up in his net. Gregg was a different character to what goalkeepers should have been, a custodian who was supposed to stay on his goal-line unless a ball was crossed into the box. Harry's game (the name of his autobiography is *Harry's Game*) was to dominate the box. He was like a bouncer at a night club who said who could and could not gain admission to his domain. And, if a centre forward was brave enough, or stupid enough, to go one on one against Northern Ireland's international goalkeeper, who went on to win the Best Goalkeeper Award at the 1958 FIFA World Cup finals, there was only one winner and he was wearing a green jersey. But no United midfielder or forward, including Bobby Charlton, or later Denis Law and George Best, escaped Gregg's wrath.

Under the rules of the game, Harry may well have only been permitted to approach the perimeter of his area, but when he wanted to make his feelings known, and he had no hesitation in doing so on countless occasions, his rough Irish brogue voice could be heard in the stand behind the opposition's goalkeeper. None of his teammates, including the legendary Tottenham Hotspur and Northern Ireland captain, Danny Blanchflower, were safe if you were not playing Harry's game.

Harry, in particular, must have shed a tear or more for Matt Busby's eight lost Babes, because as much as they respected Matt Busby, who signed their apprenticeship contract for Manchester United, and Jimmy Murphy who was like a second father figure to them, then unquestionably United's big soft-spoken Irishman was their Godfather. A Godfather's role – and we are not talking about Marlon Brando's role in the 1972 iconic movie *The Godfather*, which earned Brando the Oscar for Best Male Actor – is to look after a child in the event that the child becomes parentless. The father figure of the Busby Babes was unquestionably Jimmy Murphy, but with Matt Busby still recovering from his injuries, the young players at Manchester United were also looked after by Harry. An excellent choice for any young Red, because you could bet your house on it that if any opposing player hurt or even ruffled up a United player, then when the opportunity arose Harry would ensure the aggressor had an early bath. A car crash on the pitch would have occurred and Harry would have been the first person to help the St. John's Ambulance crew which were on duty to place the injured player on a stretcher.

Harry was as hard as nails and he most definitely took no prisoners when it came to claiming a ball which had the audacity to enter his house, the United 18-yard box. When Harry pulled on a United jersey it was most definitely a case of 'No Visitors Welcome'. The shop was closed and if you dared to venture in then he treated you like a burglar. It was a 'No Go Area', many years before No Go Areas became a regular occurrence during The Troubles in Northern Ireland.

The game versus The Lilywhites, the nickname of Preston North End, ended 0-0 but two of the opposing players went on to become the manager of Manchester United. Preston North End's two inside-halves were Tommy Docherty and Frank O'Farrell. Both of these talented players would go on to become the manager of Manchester United Football Club, O'Farrell from 8 June 1971 to 19 December 1972, and Docherty who succeeded his Republic of Ireland counterpart, from 22 December 1972 to 4 July 1977.

Did You Know That?

JOSEPH WALTON JOINED Manchester United as a trainee in April 1940, just two months shy of his 15th birthday, born on 5 June 1925 in Manchester, England. He was an outstanding player for Manchester and Lancashire Schoolboys and in October 1943 he turned professional. During the war he became a regular for United in the emergency Football League North competition and he was selected three times to represent the Football Association. Matt Busby knew he had an exceptional talent in Walton and did not want to sell him to one of the club's biggest Lancashire rivals, Preston North End, when they enquired about his availability in March 1948. Several other clubs were also keen on signing him but he opted to join Preston.

When Busby drove his diminutive left-back to Deepdale, the home of Preston North End to finalise the move, Busby tried to persuade him to stay at United. But, the wavy haired 22-year-old Mancunian was tired of playing second fiddle to his manager's preferred full-back partnership of John Aston and club captain, Johnny Carey. The Lilywhites paid Manchester United £12,000 for his services which was a British record transfer fee for a full-back at the time.

He played 435 times for Preston North End before leaving them in February 1961 to sign for Accrington Stanley in a £1,590 transfer deal, paid in four instalments. Accrington Stanley were struggling in the Fourth Division at the time and in March 1962 the club went bankrupt and were forced to tender their resignation from the Football League. Remarkably, Walton was never capped at full international level by England. On 9 March 1946, a human crush happened during an FA Cup match between Bolton Wanderers and Stoke City at Burnden Park, Bolton. The crush resulted in the deaths of 33 people and injuries to hundreds of Bolton fans. It was the deadliest stadium-related disaster in British history until the Ibrox Park Disaster in Glasgow, Scotland on 2 January 1971. On 24 August 1946, Walton was called-up by England to play against Scotland in an unofficial international match. England and Scotland drew 2-2 at Maine Road before a packed house with all of the gate receipts amounting to £12,000 donated to the Burnden Park Disaster Fund.

TOMMY DOCHERTY'S TARTAN ARMY

Following Manchester United's 5-0 loss against Crystal Palace at Selhurst Park, London in the First Division on 16 December

1972, the Old Trafford Board of Directors sacked Frank O'Farrell as the manager of the club. The genial Irishman had only been in charge for 18 months having succeeded Sir Matt Busby as manager on 8 June 1971. His record during his time in charge of United was: played 81 games, won 30, drew 24, lost 27, goals for 115, goals against 111 (win average of 37.04%).

The manager of the Scotland international side, Tommy Docherty, was in attendance at the game, no doubt casting his eye over the four Scots whom O'Farrell had included in his team for the visit to the capital. Martin Buchan, Ted MacDougall and Willie Morgan all started in the game whilst the club's greatest ever Scottish player, Denis 'The King' Law replaced full-back, Tony Dunne, in the 25th minute. Palace led 2-0 at half-time and Docherty made his way to the Boardroom at Selhurst Park for a cup of tea and a sandwich. Sir Matt, who had also managed Scotland during his managerial career, was also a half-time guest in the ground's executive area and the two Scots had a chat. Sir Matt and The Doc then returned to their executive seats to watch the second-half but before the final whistle was blown, a deal was done which would see Docherty resign as the manager of the Scottish international side and accept the offer to become the new manager of Manchester United on an initial three-year contract.

Bert Head was the manager of Crystal Palace at the time when O'Farrell's head was placed on the chopping block. Three days after the defeat, Docherty was announced as the new manager of Manchester United. He became only the fourth man from north of the border to take charge of Manchester United, following John Chapman (1921-26), Scott Duncan (1932-37) and the man widely regarded as the 'Father of Manchester United', Sir

Matt Busby (1945-69 and 1970-71). A new, more outspoken, fervent, passionate and hugely more successful Scot, and like Sir Matt a future Knight of the Realm, would become the fifth Tartan warrior at Old Trafford in the following decade.

The Doc took charge of United for the first time on 23 December 1972, a 1-1 draw versus Leeds United at Old Trafford in the First Division with MacDougall scoring for United. Within weeks of Docherty taking-up his new managerial role, the music industry in the United Kingdom was in the grip of *Glam Slam*. On 27 January 1973, The Sweet went to the top of the UK singles charts with their smash hit *Blockbuster*, which spent five weeks in the No.1 slot. Then, Slade knocked The Sweet off the top perch with their fourth No.1 hit, Cum On Feel The Noize, which enjoyed four weeks over the airwaves as the nation's favourite song. Docherty included four Scots in the team which drew with their Yorkshire rivals, the same four Scottish international players who played against Crystal Palace.

Tommy Docherty was capped 25 times by Scotland (scored one goal) from 1951-59, and coached the national team as caretaker manager in 1971 before getting the role full-time in season 1971-72. In Docherty's first season in charge of United he could not halt the slide the club were on and they were relegated to the Second Division. United's opening Second Division game of the 1974-75 season was an away trip to play Orient at Brisbane Road, Leyton, East London on 17 August 1974. Docherty, as passionate a Scot as any man, picked seven Scottish internationals to get the club's season off to a good start in their pursuit of making an immediate return to the top flight of the English game. The players were: No.2 Alex Forsyth, No.3

Stewart Houston, No.5 Jim Holton, No. 6 Martin Buchan, No.7 Willie Morgan, No.8 Lou Macari, No.10 Jim McCalliog (No.1 Alex Stepney, No.4 Brian Greenhoff, No.9 Stuart Pearson and No.11 Gerry Daly also played, with Sammy McIlroy replacing Macari as a substitute in the game). United won the game 2-0 with both goals scored by Scots, Willie Morgan and Stewart Houston. The No.1 song in the UK singles charts on 17 August 1974, when United beat Orient was *When Will I See You Again*, sung by The Three Degrees.

No doubt, United's travelling Red and White Army were thinking when they would see First Division football again. Only the team's performances during the 1974-75 season would determine the club's future which could even result in them slipping further into obscurity, and becoming a fallen giant never to rise again. The 1974 Eurovision Song Contest was won by the Swedish group, ABBA, with their song *Waterloo*. Manchester United faced their own Waterloo, not quite the same as the Battle of Waterloo which was fought in The Netherlands on 18 June 1815 (the town of Waterloo later became part of Belgium), but a battle nonetheless to prove they were good enough to compete in the top tier of English football. Rival clubs would have loved nothing better than for Manchester United to suffer yet another fall from grace and be relegated to the Third Division, a fate Manchester City endured after being relegated to Division Two (the third tier after the Premier League and Division One) at the end of the 1997-98 season.

But, Docherty's confidence and enthusiasm, coupled with his 'It's us against them', (them being United's 21 opponents in the league) galvanised his team which was a mixture of raw youth and experience but full of zest. However, when United kicked off the 1974-75 season, it was not only his third season in charge of Manchester United, but more importantly, it was his first campaign without being able to call upon one of United's most hallowed three players, the United Trinity, George Best, Denis Law and Bobby Charlton.

On 21 September 1974, Karl Douglas was No.1 in the UK singles charts with *Kung-Fu Fighting*. The Manchester United fans were always ready to rumble some 18 years before Michael Buffer trademarked the saying, 'Let's Get Ready To Rumble' in 1992, although he first uttered his iconic introduction to a boxing world title fight in 1984. The same day Douglas went to the top spot, United beat Bristol Rovers 2-0 in the league (scorers: Brian Greenhoff and an own goal), to stay top of Division Two having won six and drawing two of their opening eight games.

The UK music charts during 1975 seemed to reflect Manchester United's past and future and the fans. On 18 January 1975, Status Quo were No.1 with *Down Down*, which incredibly was the rock band's only No.1 hit, but United were doing the opposite and heading *Up Up* to the First Division. At the time United had played 27 league games, winning 17, drawing six and losing just four. On 1 February 1975, Pilot took their song *January* to No.1, a month (January 1975) which saw United unbeaten in the league and in the FA Cup. At the end of January 1975, United were top of the league table with 40 points from their 27 games (the two points for a win system was in place) with Sunderland in second place on 35 points, Norwich City 31 points and Aston Villa fourth on 30 points but having only played 26 games.

On 22 February 1975, Steve Harley & Cockney Rebel went

to No.1 in the hit parade with *Make Me Smile (Come Up And See Me)*, and that same day United lost 2-0 away to Aston Villa in the league. Despite the defeat, Tommy Docherty's Red and White Army boarded their coaches and made their way back from Birmingham to Manchester after the game singing away to Harley's song as United were still top of the Second Division, a four-point cushion over Sunderland. And, fans up and down the country, including the fans of First Division clubs, all wanted to see their team play against Manchester United. Bob Stokoe's Sunderland team, which included many of the side which so famously beat Leeds United 1-0 in the 1973 FA Cup final, looked to be the biggest threat to United winning the title, although Norwich City (38 points) and Villa (37 points with a game in hand) were not giving up the chase.

Two weeks later, Telly Savalas who played the New York Police Department Lieutenant Theodore *Kojak* in the hit TV series Kojak, was No.1 in the charts with If. Kojak's famous line in the show was 'Who Loves Ya, Baby?' The United fans were loving Docherty's swashbuckling style of play, with Stepney in nets keeping his back four in line, captain Martin Buchan passing the ball to his midfielders like Church-goers passed the money platter around during a Sunday service, effortlessly. And up front Docherty had a potent Anglo-Scottish striking partnership with the diminutive, but tigerish, Luigi 'Lou' Macari who snapped at the ankles of defenders like a Jack Russell dog gnawing on a bone, and Stuart 'Pancho' Pearson who would not have looked out of place playing *Robin Hood* as he constantly stole the ball from the opposition with his aggressive and forceful style of play to give it to Macari or slot it into the back of the net.

On 22 March 1975, United played Nottingham Forest away and beat Brian Clough's team 1-0 with a goal from Gerry Daly. The Irish midfielder was such an underestimated player, all left foot, but with a deft touch that a master pickpocket would envy. United were now seven points clear of Villa, 49 vs 42, although United had played 35 games, one more than the team who had now become their biggest challengers for top spot. This time on the coaches home the United fans had a new song to sing because a Scottish boy band had just achieved their first No.1 hit, *Bye Bye Baby* sung by The Bay City Rollers. The song was still at No.1 in the charts when United returned to Nottingham on 19 April 1975 to play their penultimate league game of the season. A draw with Notts County would be good enough to see United crowned champions of the Second Division and thousands of United fans travelled to the game.

This time the United faithful had a new brand of clothing to wear as the latest fashion rage was jeans, shirts and jackets adorned with tartan stripes similar to the clothing items worn by The Bay City Rollers. *Tommy Docherty's Red Army* had suddenly become *Tommy Docherty's Tartan Army*. Stuart Houston and Brian Greenhoff scored for United in a 2-2 draw to earn them the point they needed. United were crowned champions on 61 points and it was *Bye Bye Baby* to Division Two football after spending a one-year sabbatical away from the top flight. Aston Villa finished runners-up (58 points) and also won the League Cup, whilst Norwich City finished third (53 points).

Manchester United rounded their season off in style, as champions should do, and put on a master class display of attacking football defeating Blackpool 4-0 at Old Trafford on the final day of the season before a bumper crowd of 58,769 fans (scorers: Pearson two, Macari and Brian Greenhoff). *The Rollers* were still flying high at the top of the music charts as *Rollermania* swept Britain and the loudspeakers around the Theatre of Dreams belted out the hit for the fans to enjoy. There was no need for the DJ to dig out his copy of *When Will I See You Again*, because not before long *Tommy Docherty's Tartan Army* would be visiting your town or city very soon. A more fitting choice of song was '*Welcome Home*' by Peters and Lee which was No.1 on 21 July 1973. United had returned to their First Division home.

And, it would not have come as a surprise to any United fan had the team taken to the Old Trafford pitch with a tartan collar and tartan cuffs on their red shirts in place of their white ones. When the final whistle went the fans invaded the pitch, a sea of red, white and tartan poured out of the four stands to join the players when club captain, Martin Buchan was presented with the Second Division Championship trophy.

The Rollers spent six weeks at the top of the charts and were replaced on 8 May by Mud with *Oh Boy*, their third and final UK No.1 single. And, Oh Boy, *Tommy Docherty's Tartan Army* certainly had a new season to look forward to.

Docherty guided United to third place in the First Division in season 1975-76, behind runners-up Queens Park Rangers and Liverpool, who claimed their ninth crown as Kings of England. He also took his team all the way to Wembley where they lost 1-0 to Second Division Southampton in the 1976 FA Cup final. The following campaign, 1976-77, United finished in sixth place in the First Division and once again The Doc steered Manchester United to play under Wembley's famous Twin Towers in the 1977

FA Cup final. Whereas Docherty's side were red hot favourites to beat Southampton in the 1976 showpiece, Liverpool were odds-on with the bookmakers to beat United in the 1977 final having retained their League Championship crown and also reached their first European Cup final.

Liverpool were on the brink of winning the Treble but as the headline on the back page of the Sunday Post newspaper which was published on Sunday 22 May 1977, famously read: *Doc's Tigers Tear Up Liverpool's Treble Dream*, when United beat them 2-1 thanks to goals from Pancho and Jimmy Greenhoff, the older brother of Brian who played alongside him in the game. Liverpool beat Borussia Monchengladbach 3-1 at Stadio Olimpico, Rome, Italy on 25 May 1977 to become the second English club to hold aloft European football's most prestigious trophy, nine years after Matt Busby's iconic side became the first to do so in 1968.

A short while after Martin Buchan held aloft the FA Cup trophy at Wembley following United's 2-1 win over Liverpool, a song which went to No.1 in the UK singles charts that evening was played over the stadium's tannoy system. The United fans who had stayed behind to see the players parade the trophy around the pitch were entertained with Rod Stewart's double-A side hit, *I Don't Wanna Talk About It/First Cut Is The Deepest*. The Liverpool fans who scurried their way down the tunnels certainly did not want to talk about the match as United had just inflicted the first cut in their Treble dreams.

But little did the 50,000 jubilant United fans who left Wembley that afternoon know, The Doc would not be in charge of the team for the 1977-78 season, which would see them return to

European competition for the first time since season 1968-69, when they exited the European Cup as holders to AC Milan in the semi-final stage. On 4 July 1977, just 44 days after he danced with joy with his players at Wembley Stadium, and pictured with Pancho and Macari holding the trophy above their manager's head, he was sacked by the club. Two days before his sacking Hot Chocolate enjoyed their only No.1 hit single with *So You Win Again*. However, *Tommy Docherty's Tartan Army* no longer felt like winners having just lost the manager they idolised.

Did You Know That?

EXACTLY 18 YEARS after Manchester United won the Second Division Championship in season 1974-75, they lifted their next championship title. In season 1992-93, Alex Ferguson guided Manchester United to the inaugural Premier League title. In a strange coincidence to when United won the Second Division under Tommy Docherty in 1974-75, Aston Villa finished runners-up to Ferguson's side in 1992-93 and Norwich City finished third.

PART 6

COLE THE GOAL

THE MAN WHO SAVED MAN UNITED

RECORD SCORE CHALKED OFF

FA SUSPEND THE BOSS

UNITED'S SILVER FOX

CAVANAGH'S NEW TV

COLE THE GOAL

Andy Cole's first four full England caps were awarded by four different England managers: Terry Venables (England 0-0 Uruguay, 29 March 1995, one cap), Glenn Hoddle (England 2-0 Italy, 4 June 1997, one cap), Howard Wilkinson (England 0-2 France, 10 February 1999, two caps) and Kevin Keegan (England 3-1 Poland, 27 March 1999, six caps). Cole was also capped five times by Sven-Goran Eriksson. His goal against Albania in a 3-1 away win on 28 March 2001, under Eriksson, ended his England goal drought at the 13th attempt. In total he was capped 15 times and scored once. Howard Wilkinson had two spells as the manager of England, either side of Keegan.

Cole's career in the white of England was a world away from what he did on the pitch in the red of United. It was as though they were two different players, football's equivalent of *Dr Jekyll and Mr Hyde*. They just looked like two different players, one full of confidence in front of goal and the other who just did not want to fail in front of goal. Andy could not stop scoring for United – 121 goals in 275 appearances from 1994-95 to 2001-02 – and he was the provider of numerous assists for his fellow strikers, including the prolific Dwight Yorke and one of the players who kept him out of the England squad on many occasions, his Old Trafford teammate, Teddy Sheringham. The United fans nicknamed Andy 'Cole the Goal', but England head coach Glenn Hoddle never really rated him and did not select Andy for his 1998 FIFA World Cup finals squad despite the fact that Cole netted 25 times in 45 games for Manchester United in season 1997-98, a ratio of better than a goal every two games. When asked why Andy was not in his 1998 squad for France, quite incredibly Hoddle said, 'He needs seven or eight chances to score one goal'. Andy was clearly rattled with Hoddle's remark because when he was later asked about his England exclusion for France '98, he said, 'My record speaks for itself and when I have finished it will all be down there in black and white for people to see'.

When Andy retired from playing, he had amassed 229 goals in 509 games for a variety of clubs. And, one of those clubs has echoes of Black and White, because Andy scored 68 goals in just 84 matches for Newcastle United which ensured he was inducted into the Magpies' Hall of Fame, despite the acrimonious nature of his departure.

Did You Know That?

ON 10 JANUARY 1995, the Newcastle United manager, Kevin Keegan, agreed for his club to sell their crown jewel, Andy Cole, to Manchester United for £6 million plus Keith Gillespie, one of Manchester United's leading young players, who was valued at £1 million. The fee was a new British record transfer.

JAMES W. GIBSON – THE MAN WHO SAVED MANCHESTER UNITED

James W. Gibson, was the Chairman of Manchester United from 19 December 1931 until his death in September 1951 and his son, Alan, was elected to the club's Board of Directors in 1948 which was the beginning of a lifetime of serving Manchester United. There is a red plaque on the bridge over the train track at Old Trafford marking the impact James W. Gibson had on the club over the years. It is a most fitting and poignant location for this tribute as it was Gibson who in 1934 negotiated with the Midlands Railway Authorities for steps to be built from the existing platform just outside the ground so that fans no longer had to walk miles to attend matches. The services ran out of the old Manchester Central Terminus to make a stop at Old Trafford on matchdays and the United fans still use the station on match days. There is also a plaque in his honour in the Old Trafford players' tunnel alongside another saviour of the club, John Henry Davies, and a display in the club's museum.

Manchester United is world famous for nurturing young talent and developing youth team players to be good enough to play in the first team, from Busby's Babes to Fergie's Fledglings. Quite remarkably for the past 85 years, since season 1937-38, United have had a homegrown player in their first team squad. In season 1936-37, James W. Gibson and Walter Crickmer established the Manchester United Junior Athletic Club (MUJAC), the club's first ever Youth team. At the time Gibson said he would like to 'have a first team made entirely of home grown youngsters all from the Manchester area'. However, the promising young prospects who joined MUJAC were not forced to sign for United, on the contrary they were asked merely 'to consider playing for the first team one day,' Louis Rocca was appointed as the Chief Scout of MUJAC and through his connections to the Manchester Catholic Sportsman's Club, he appointed a network of scouts from the Catholic Church. James W. Gibson purchased the lease from his own pocket for the Old Broughton Rangers Rugby Ground for the MUJAC players to train on, which later became United's famous Cliff training ground, where the young United stars of the future were put through their paces. The MUJAC team played under the name 'United Colts'. Consequently, had it not been for James W. Gibson, many United legends, Best, Hughes, the Class of '92 et al, as well as Season 2023-24 players Scott McTominay and Marcus Rashford, would never have played for Manchester United.

But how did James W. Gibson become involved with the club? United were in difficulty on and off the pitch. Indeed, in December 1931, Manchester United almost folded as the club was heavily in debt with a £25,000 mortgage and they could not even find the money to pay the players' wages. The impact of the Great Depression following the Wall Street Stock Market Crash on 29 October 1929, known as 'Black Tuesday', was felt worldwide and hit United particularly hard. Home attendances were particularly poor with a meagre 6,396 turning up to see a 2-0 win over Millwall on 5 December 1931, and a fortnight later only 4,697 were in attendance to watch United lose 1-0 to Bristol City. Stacey Lintott, a local sportswriter met James

Gibson at a dinner in Manchester, and he told James about the situation at United. It was agreed that Walter Crickmer would visit James at his home in Hale Barns to discuss the situation. James was the sole owner of Briggs, Jones & Gibson (he had some years earlier bought out his two partners) which was a thriving military uniform manufacturing company.

Herbert Bamlett resigned as manager on 9 November 1930 after United lost 13 of their opening 14 First Division games of the 1930-31 season. Crickmer was appointed as the club's temporary manager and remained in the post until Scott Duncan was appointed manager on 13 July 1932. So Crickmer, with cap-in-hand, told James W. Gibson about the club's plight and dire financial position. Gibson agreed to help and gave a gift of £2,000 (£118,000 today) to pay the backlog of players' wages and the wages of the club's officials until mid-January 1932. He also bought all of the players and staff a turkey for Christmas. That night the *Manchester Evening News* reported the news: *Mr J. Gibson, a Manchester businessman with no previous record in big football, has taken over Manchester United for a month, and he has paid the players' wages for this week. He has undertaken to be responsible for the Club's expenditure from December 16 until January 9. If during that time sufficient support is forthcoming at Old Trafford then he is prepared to consider securing a new manager, four first-class players, and he construction of covered accommodation on the popular side of the ground.*

James W. Gibson's plan was to raise monies for the club with a view to getting it back to a sound financial footing. He proposed a new issue of 'Patron's Tickets' but the response from the United fans was not what he had hoped for due to the recession. James was moved as he did receive a letter from a man who said he could not attend matches as he worked on Saturdays but enclosed a Postal Order for 6d. (2½ pence), and hoped it would help as he couldn't afford more. This helped set James' resolve even further to aid United for the long term having seen what the club meant to the supporters.

James Gibson, together with his sister and younger brother, were orphaned when they were young. James was just 14 years old. Their father had a small business making uniforms but this was closed at the time of his death.

James invested £40,000 (£2.36 million today) of his own money into the club and agreed to be the guarantor for the bank for an overdraft which had reached £17,000. Had United not acquired such a generous benefactor the club would have gone into extinction and would not have gone on to become the world's most famous football club it is today. Not surprisingly James W. Gibson is remembered as 'The Saviour of Manchester United'. In return for his cash injection, Gibson was made the Chairman of Manchester United at a time when City were the most dominant team in Manchester and who went on to win the FA Cup in 1934 (runners-up to Everton in 1933) and the First Division Championship in season 1936-37. Perhaps it was his modest ambition or else he was keeping his future plans for United close to his chest when he said, 'There is sufficient room in Manchester for two good football clubs'.

Duncan remained at the club until 7 November 1937, guiding them to the Second Division Championship in season 1935-36. After United lifted the Second Division Championship, captained by James Brown, the club produced a postcard which was set out to annoy a number of clubs they would face the following season. The postcard proudly boasted that United had now joined a select band of heroes who had won English football's Triple Crown of First Division Championship (1907-08, 1910-11), Second Division Championship (1935-36) and FA Cup (1909). It also stated that Manchester United had now joined the elite of the Football World – Burnley, Everton, Preston North End, Sheffield Wednesday and West Bromwich Albion – who had also won all three trophies. In block capitals the postcard pointed out that the following clubs 'Couldn't do it' – Arsenal, Bolton Wanderers, Derby County, Huddersfield Town, Manchester City, Newcastle United and Sheffield United. It also stated:

MANCHESTER IS PROUD OF –
Mr J W Gibson, the Greatest Sportsman in the Kingdom
Mr Scott Duncan, Football's Greatest Manager
The gallant band of United Supporters not forgetting the Ladies!
And the bravest man was Captain Brown
Who played his Ukulele when they won the Triple Crown!

The triumphant United players toured Manchester on an open top bus on 2 May 1936 after returning home from drawing their final League game of the season 1-1 away to Hull City. However, the boasting was all bravado as United struggled in season 1936-37 and made an immediate return to Division Two having finished second from bottom of the table.

Towards the end of the 1930s, United were in desperate need of a manager to take over from Walter Crickmer who decided that he would relinquish his managerial responsibilities when the atrocities of World War II would eventually come to an end. A board meeting was called at Old Trafford in December 1944 to decide who should be asked to take charge of the team. Rocca had heard that Liverpool had already offered Matt Busby a job as right-hand man to George Kay and it was Rocca who convinced the United board to leave it to him. Rocca wrote a letter to Busby and addressed it to his army regiment. The letter was quite vague, referring only to a job offer just in case it fell into the wrong hands, namely the Board of Directors at Liverpool.

On 1 February 1945, Busby, still in his army uniform, attended a meeting at Cornbrook Cold Storage, Trafford Park, a business unit which was owned by James W. Gibson. Homeless and almost penniless, Manchester United was hardly an appealing prospect to any potential suitor. But Busby was anxious to learn more details of the 'job offer' which Rocca had written to him about. Busby, a former Manchester City (1928-36, FA Cup winner in 1934) and Liverpool (1936-41) player listened to what James W. Gibson had to say and agreed to accept the job to become the new manager of Manchester United, provided James W. Gibson met his conditions. Busby made it clear from the outset that he, and only he, would be in charge of training, selecting the team on matchdays and having the final decision in which players would be bought and sold, and all done so without any interference from the club's directors, who, he believed, did not know the game as well as he did. At the time there wasn't a single club in England who offered their manager such a level of control over the team. It was totally unprecedented in the English game, but James W. Gibson was in no position to argue. Busby was originally offered a three-year contract but the canny Scotsman managed to negotiate himself a five-year deal after explaining to Gibson that it would take at least that long for his football revolution to have a tangible effect.

The two men signed the contract that day but it was not until 1 October 1945, that Busby officially took over the reins at Manchester United, with World War II coming to an end on 2 September 1945. In the interim, Busby returned to the Army Physical Training Corps and in the Spring of 1945, he took their football team to Bari, Italy.

Matt Busby was a football revolutionary and along with Murphy, his right-hand man, the former army buddies changed the history of English football. When Busby accepted Chairman James Gibson's offer to become the new Manchester United manager on 1 February 1945, the club had not won a major trophy in 34 years – the English First Division Championship in season 1910-11 – and were regarded as a yo-yo club. Indeed, in season 1933-34, the unthinkable almost happened, relegation to Division Three for the first time in the club's 56-year history.

On the night of 11 March 1941, Old Trafford's Main Stand was completely destroyed by the Luftwaffe in a German bombing raid on the nearby Trafford Park Industrial Estate. Much of the stadium's terracing was also damaged as was the pitch. Alan Gibson was to later say that he remembered his father learning the news and breaking down in tears – it was the only time he saw his father cry.

The damage meant that future home games that season would have to be played elsewhere and so United turned to their city neighbours and James orchestrated a temporary move for home games to be played at Maine Road whilst Old Trafford was out of commission. City charged United £5,000 a year to use their facilities but they never allowed United use of the home team changing room when the two teams met, even when United were the home team for a wartime Football League.

In the *United Review* for the opening game of the 1946-47 season, Chairman James W. Gibson said a few words:

Dear Friends,

I offer my greetings and a welcome to our Supporters on the return to normal first division football after the interlude of watching teams comprised of strange personnel weary war-workers and travel stained servicemen, who, despite, numerous difficulties, gallantly succeeded in keeping our grand game alive through the darkest days of a world war. Yes, I think you will agree everybody did their best to keep the 'United' flag flying all anxiously waiting and looking forward to this day when we embark on the first post-war season of serious competitive football. It is indeed gratifying to know practically all our service players are with us once more, fully trained and fit to do battle with the best. I was with them on an occasion during training and was really impressed with their activities. Mr Busby, our manager, tells me he is satisfied the team will do well, so we open up full of confidence. A number of the 1939 older players are no longer with us – six years is a long time and changes were imminent, but as you will see, our policy in fostering junior talent is now proving its worth. A lump rises in my throat when I think of our premises at Old Trafford damaged beyond repair by fire and blast in March 1941, and still looking a sorry spectacle owing to the Government policy of issuing only limited licences for building materials whilst the housing problem is so manifest. Against this, we are fortunate that our neighbours, Manchester City, to whom we are greatly indebted, came to the rescue and offered us a temporary home, which we still enjoy. In conclusion I must say how much I appreciate your loyalty during the past war-years and sincerely trust you will be rewarded with real, enterprising football.

Yours faithfully.

After the bombing James W. Gibson spent the war years trying to persuade the Government to grant the club finance to redevelop and rebuild Old Trafford. In November 1944, the club was granted a licence granting permission to demolish the grandstand to allow the reconstruction work to commence. Two years later, with the valuable assistance of Mr Ellis Smith, the local MP of Stoke-on-Trent, James W. Gibson was the main catalyst for a debate in the House of Commons to decide whether or not football clubs which were affected by the war were entitled to financial support. United along with nine other clubs were in need of financial support to rebuild their grounds following damage to them during the war. On 17 November 1944, more than three years after the Luftwaffe raid on the Trafford Park industrial area, the War Damage Commission wrote to the club and stated that they were of the opinion that Old Trafford was not a 'total loss' and awarded United £4,800 to remove the debris and £17,478 to rebuild the stands. Although it cost £90,000 to build Old Trafford in 1909 (it officially opened on 19 February 1910 with a 4-3 First Division loss to Liverpool) the compensation package greatly helped United as the club had a debt of £15,000 at the time. With the building of the stadium now underway, James W. Gibson could now turn his attention to rebuilding the team.

Year after year, and decade after decade, the club's conveyor belt of youth team talent provided players for the first team. In season 1947-48, United's first team included a number of former Youth team players: John Anderson (40 games, two goals, 1947-49), John Aston Snr (284 games, 30 goals, 1945-55), Johnny Carey (344 games, 17 goals, 1937-53), Henry Cockburn (275 games, four goals, 1945-55) and William McGlen (122 games, two goals, 1946-52).

Busby knew he had to replace his ageing side and began a revolution which would see his young side go on to dominate the English game in the latter half of the 1950s. Busby and Murphy took the bold decision to invest in the club's youth set-up and actively set out to recruit the best local talent available by working closely with local schools and promoting Reserve team players. Busby's philosophy was simple, 'If they are good enough, they are old enough'. During their successful 1951-52 First Division Championship-winning campaign, Busby promoted two youth team players into the first team. On 24 November 1951, Busby gave Jackie Blanchflower and Roger Byrne their United debuts versus Liverpool in the white-hot atmosphere at Anfield. The game ended 0-0 with the debutants catching the eye of reporters including Tom Jackson from the *Manchester Evening News* who referred to the United team as 'United Babes' in his match report and later the 'Busby Babes'. Sadly, the one man who had been the catalyst for much of Busby's success, James W. Gibson, did not see United lift the title or witness the revolution of the Busby

Babes later in the decade as he passed away aged 74 in 1951.

James W. Gibson and his wife, Lillian, lost five children to birth complications and illness: a son, twins and two of three triplets. Their son, Alan was born in 1915 and survived childhood pneumonia. Alan went on to serve as a Vice-Chairman and director of the club until his 70th birthday and was Vice-President until his death in 1995. To their immense credit, the Gibson family, unlike other families that followed them, never took any money out of the club, instead they readily parted with their own savings to make the club the institution it is today. James Gibson' original £40,000 loan (*The Gibson Guarantee*) was never repaid to him by the club and nor did he seek reimbursement of same. In September 2016, a piece of art, The Gibson Compass, was unveiled by Trafford Council at Halecroft Park, Hale Barns in Altrincham in recognition of his legacy at the club and the work of his wife, Lillian and Alan.

Ole Gunnar Solskjaer followed the trend set by Matt Busby and later Alex Ferguson, by adopting James W. Gibson's dream and had no hesitation in promoting academy players to his first team squad, including Tahith Chong, James Garner, Angel Gomes, Mason Greenwood, Jesse Lingard, Scott McTominay, Marcus Rashford, Axel Tuanzebe, Brandon Williams, and Paul Pogba who was an Academy player from 2009-11.

Did You Know That?

ALAN GIBSON WAS booked on the chartered flight which the club organised for Manchester United's European Cup quarter-final, 2nd leg tie away to Red Star Belgrade on 5 February 1958. However, a few days before departure, he broke an ankle and had to withdraw from the trip. His place on the trip was taken by the club Secretary, Walter Crickmer, who lost his life in the Munich Air Disaster on 6 February 1958. And in another strange twist of fate, Jimmy Murphy missed the trip to Belgrade as he was in Cardiff at the time coaching the Welsh national team (he was the manager of Wales from 1956-64) for an important FIFA 1958 World Cup play-off game against Israel. The Welsh won the game 2-0 on the same night United drew 3-3 with Red Star Belgrade and Wales progressed to the World Cup finals for the first time in the principality's history having lost the away play-off 2-1 on 15 January 1958 in Ramat Gan, giving the Welsh a 3-2 aggregate victory. Murphy's seat on the ill-fated flight was occupied by United's chief coach Bert Whalley who lost his life in the disaster.

RECORD SCORE CHALKED OFF

On 9 March 1895, Newton Heath welcomed Walsall Town Swifts to Bank Street, Clayton for their Division Two encounter. However, before the game kicked off the manager of the visitors complained to the referee about the state of the pitch which looked like a strange mixture of grass, mud and sand, and very soggy in places. The groundkeeper reacted by spreading several wheel-barrow loads of sand over the pitch. The visitors were still unhappy but the game went ahead and The Heathens won 14-0. However, Walsall Town Swifts registered their complaint about the state of the pitch with the Football League who upheld the complaint and ordered the score to be stricken from the record books and for the game to be replayed. The rearranged fixture took place at Bank Street on 3 April 1895, and this time Newton Heath won 9-0. The club went on to finish third in the league in season 1894-95.

Throughout the history of Newton Heath/Manchester United the club has been quite lucky to have enjoyed the generosity of several benefactors and two of the earliest of these gentlemen were 'Father' Bird and Mr. Sedgwick. Father Bird was a local chimney sweep and a big fan of Newton Heath who would hold post-match dinner parties for the players and club officials at his home. On the evening of the 14-0 victory versus Walsall Town Swifts, a good evening was had by all and following a meal of Lancashire hot-pot the players and guests retired to the drawing-room where they enjoyed drinks and a sing-song. Mr. Sedgwick was the Station Master at Victoria Station, Manchester and was one of the team's most vociferous supporters and a regular attendee at home games. He was very often heard cheering on the players at Bank Street dressed in his frock coat and silk hat. When the team was faced with an away game, Mr. Sedgwick reserved a few first-class carriages on the train for the club directors and players and allowed them to travel up and down the country free of charge.

The terrible condition of the pitch at Bank Street, especially during the winter months, was not the only thing Newton Heath used in their favour against visiting teams. The pitch was situated adjacent to a chemical works which belted out noxious fumes during games much to the annoyance of nearby residents and the visiting players. If The Heathens were struggling in a game, a junior member of the backroom staff was sent to the chemical works and given a specific instruction to inform the foreman to increase the smoke being produced from the chimneys at the plant. The home players were well used to playing in such suffocating conditions as they trained on the pitch regularly and became used to the thick choking smoke. However, their opponents found it difficult to breathe which affected their performance. On many occasions this un-sportsmanship tactic produced the necessary effect enabling Newton Heath to turn around what looked like a home loss into a draw or even better, an unexpected win.

Did You Know That?

WITH THE ASSISTANCE of the chemical works The Heathens' home form for season 1894-95 read: played 15, won 9, drew 6, lost 0 (compared with their away form of six wins, two draws and seven losses) which helped the club to third place in the table and a Test Match encounter with Stoke City, the winner guaranteed Division One football for the 1895-96 season. On 27 April 1895, Newton Heath met Stoke City at Vale Park, Burslem and lost the tie 3-0. Stoke City proved to be the club's nemesis during the season, also knocking them out of the FA Cup in Round 1, winning 3-2 at Bank Street. During the 1894-95 season Newton Heath also participated in the Lancashire and Manchester Senior Cups but were knocked out in the First Round of both competitions. And just as they did in season 1893-94, the club also competed in the County Lancashire Palatine League, along with Bury and Liverpool. They lost home and away to Bury and beat Liverpool at home and drew at Anfield. The season marked their last entry in the Palatine League and produced the first ever league encounter between Newton Heath and Manchester City. The first ever 'Manchester Derby' took place on 3 November 1894 at City's Hyde Road ground with Newton Heath winning the Division Two game 5-2.

MANCHESTER UNITED MANAGER SUSPENDED BY THE FOOTBALL ASSOCIATION

On 31 October 1921, John 'Jack' Robson resigned as the manager of Manchester United due to ill health. The club had won three, drawn five and lost four of their opening 12 games of the 1921-22 First Division season, including a 3-1 win over neighbours Manchester City just two days before Robson left Old Trafford. Joe Spence scored a hat-trick in the Derby match. United were struggling for results and goals having scored just 15 times, but conceded 23. Robson took charge of the club at the end of 1914, and during his time at Old Trafford the team played 121 games with a record of 38 wins, 36 draws, 47 losses, 162 goals for and 175 goals against for a win ratio of 31.40%.

John A. Chapman succeeded Robson as the sixth manager of Manchester United the day after Robson was forced to step down from the job because he just simply wasn't fit enough to fulfil his managerial role. Chapman was born on 14 March 1882 in New Monkland, Lanarkshire, Scotland and aged 22, he began his playing career with Glasgow Rangers. He spent one season with the Old Firm giants before joining Albion Rovers where he played in season 1905-06. However, within a year of joining The Wee Rovers he packed his kit bag again and played for Dumbarton (nicknamed The Sons) in season 1906-07.

In 1910, Chapman began his managerial career and accepted an offer from Airdrieonians, nicknamed The Diamonds, to become their new boss at Broomfield Park, Airdrie. At the end of his first part-season at Old Trafford, 1921-22, he was unable to arrest the halt to United's inconsistent form and they finished rock bottom of the First Division, 22nd place. The players were simply not good enough to keep United in the top flight and in the second half of the season from New Year's Day 1922, the club won only four of their remaining 19 league games. And, they were knocked out of the FA Cup in Round 1, a 4-1 loss to Cardiff City at Old Trafford on 1 January 1922.

In season 1922-23, United finished fourth in the Second Division, followed by 14th place the following season (1923-24) and in season 1924-25, Chapman steered England's most famous club back into the First Division after United finished runners-up to champions, Leicester City. United's first season back among the Big Boys produced a 9th place finish in season 1925-26. The club was finally making progress on and off the pitch under the no-nonsense Scot, a winning team built on a low budget which helped to reduce the club's debt, before his world came crashing down around him. In September 1926, the Football Association appointed a commission to investigate the financial affairs at Manchester United. The outcome sent shockwaves through the other 21 English First Division teams.

On 2 October 1926, Chapman's United side beat Aston Villa 2-1 at Old Trafford in the First Division. But, just five days after goals from Frank Barson and Clatworthy Rennox beat The Villains, John A. Chapman became a villain. The Football Association issued a statement on 7 October 1926, that John A. Chapman, the manager of Manchester United, had been suspended from 'taking part in football or football management' during the remaining games of the 1926-27 season. The sport's governing body in England said that they took the decision to suspend the United manager 'for improper conduct in his position as Secretary-Manager of the Manchester United Football Club'. No further explanation for the suspension was ever given. On 9 October 1926, United had to play a First Division game versus Bolton Wanderers at Burnden Park. But with Chapman suspended, the Manchester United Board of Directors asked one of the club's players, wing-half Clarence 'Lal' Hilditch, to take temporary charge of first team affairs in a player/manager role. It was an unprecedented decision by United's hierarchy and something alien in the game at the time. Lal said yes to becoming the first player/manager in the history of the club.

When his suspension came to an end at the end of the 1926-27 season – the club finished 15th in the First Division – Chapman applied to become the manager of Leeds United. The Yorkshire club had just been relegated to the Second Division and their manager, Arthur Fairclough, resigned. However, Chapman was overlooked in favour of Dick Ray and he turned his attention to a completely different sport and took up the position of General Manager of the Liverpool Greyhound Racing Club in August 1927. Chapman's alleged misdemeanours were never made public.

Did You Know That?

AIRDRIEONIANS FOOTBALL CLUB was founded in 1878, the same year the Carriage & Wagon Workers at the Lancashire and Yorkshire Railway formed Newton Heath Lancashire and Yorkshire Railway Cricket and Football Club. However, the North Lanarkshire club's original name when founded was Excelsior Football Club, changing their name to Airdrieonians in 1881. They were elected to the Scottish Football League for the 1894-95 season, when The Heathens were playing in the English Second Division after finishing bottom of the First Division the previous season. Paul Harvey was born on 28 August 1968 in Glasgow and he began his football career as an apprentice with Manchester United in season 1986-87. However, disillusioned with not been given an opportunity to show off his talent at United under managers Ron Atkinson and Alex Ferguson, he left Old Trafford in May 1987, and joined Clydebank Football Club. He then signed for Airdrieonians in the summer of 1994 in a £150,000 transfer, and in his first year with The Diamonds he won a Scottish FA Cup winners' medal, playing in their 3-2 victory over Dundee at McDiarmid Park, Perth (home to St Johnstone Football Club) in the 1995 Scottish FA Cup final. He scored in the final.

UNITED'S SILVER FOX

Thomas Henry Cavanagh was born in Liverpool on 29 June 1928. He began his football career as an inside forward at Preston North End 1948-50 (0 games) and also played for Stockport County 1950-52 (32 games, two goals), Huddersfield Town 1952-56 (93 games, 29 goals), Doncaster Rovers 1956-59 (119 games, 16 goals), Bristol City 1959-60 (24 games, six goals) and Carlisle United 1960-61 (33 games, four goals).

'Cav' was a colourful character, and in more ways than one. He was player-manager of Cheltenham Town in 1961 but was sacked after only four games in charge when some supporters complained about his constant swearing during matches. Cav told Cheltenham Town that if they did not like his style of management, they could 'f...... find someone else to do the job'. And they did. He then took-up appointments with Brentford and Nottingham Forest, where he was the club's assistant manager to the legendary Manchester United captain, Johnny Carey, before teaming up with future Manchester United manager, Tommy Docherty, at Hull City.

When Tommy Docherty replaced the sacked Frank O'Farrell as the manager of Manchester United, his first signing was not a player despite the fact that the spectre of relegation to the Second Division was already hanging over Old Trafford when the Doc took charge. The league table did not lie. Manchester United had played 22 games, won five, drawn six and lost 11. One of the most important signings the Doc made was his first one, when he appointed Tommy Cavanagh as his assistant manager.

The Doc and Cav first met when Docherty joined Preston North End in 1949. Bill Shankly was also a player at Preston North End at the time. Unlike Docherty, Cav never made it into the first team at Deepdale but the pair struck up a strong and lasting friendship. Shankly was succeeded in the Preston team by Docherty and when the future legendary manager of Liverpool left Deepdale, he told Docherty that all he had to do was just put the No.4 shirt on and let it run round by itself because it knows where to go.

During his Old Trafford career, Cav would run on to the pitch like a whippet when a United player got injured, his silver-white hair flopping around, a beaming reassuring smile on his face as he reached his injured player. And more times than enough all Cav had to do to get the stricken player back on to his feet was to apply his trusty sponge from his bright red bucket to whatever body part the player was complaining about. Those were the days! The Manchester United players and fans all loved him.

Cav's role at United will never be forgotten by Manchester United fans. They all loved the Doc and the swashbuckling style of play he introduced at United. But make no mistake about it, Cav helped the Doc re-shape an ageing side. When the dynamic duo teamed-up at Old Trafford in late December 1972, the United squad included six players who had won the European Cup in 1968: George Best, Bobby Charlton, Tony Dunne, Brian Kidd, Jimmy Rimmer (he was United's only substitute for the game) and David Sadler. The third member of United's famous triumvirate as the recipient of the European Footballer of the Year award, Denis Law, missed the 4-1 win after extra-time over SL Benfica at Wembley Stadium in the 1968 European Cup final, through injury. Law was also, unknown to him, playing his last season with United in 1972-73. After suffering the indignity of relegation to the Second Division at the end of the 1973-74 season, the Doc and Cav guided United to the Second Division title in 1974-75, and third place in the First Division in season 1975-76 when they were also runners-up to Southampton in the 1976 FA Cup final. In season 1976-77, the Doc's last campaign in charge of Manchester United, they finished sixth in the league and beat Liverpool 2-1 in the Jubilee FA Cup final.

When the Doc was sacked by the club on 4 July 1977, just 44 days after he celebrated United's 2-1 win over Liverpool in the FA Cup final on the Wembley pitch with his players, Cav stayed on to become Dave Sexton's right-hand man. Tommy Cavanagh loved United and his 'boys' at the club too much to leave Old

Trafford and team-up with Docherty at his new club, Derby County. He stayed and looked after his boys until Ron Atkinson was appointed manager on 9 June 1981, replacing the sacked Dave Sexton. From 1976-79, Tommy Cavanagh was also the assistant manager of Northern Ireland to Danny Blanchflower. Cav, despite his scouse roots, loved his Reds who wore the green jersey of Northern Ireland. In the summer of 1976, the Manchester United official photographer took a famous pre-season snapshot at Old Trafford of Cav, the Doc, United's legendary Irish scout, Bob Bishop, the man who discovered George Best, and United's Northern Ireland internationals at the time, Tommy Jackson, David McCreery, Sammy McIlroy and Jimmy Nicholl.

In May 1983, Cav was appointed the new coach of the Swedish side, Rosenborg, but was sacked in August of that year. In 1985, he became Martin Buchan's assistant at Burnley. Buchan was one of Tommy's favourite Manchester United players, the club captain and a leader who every player not only looked up to with the utmost admiration, but one day aspired to be. Cav could have counted on one hand the number of times he had to use his magic sponge on Martin.

Buchan rarely got injured because he could time a tackle to perfection, he sensed danger when the opposition were attacking but, like a military general, he positioned his soldiers around him to negate most threats on the United goal. When United's 1977 FA Cup winning captain was sacked by Burnley in late 1985, Cav became their new manager. During his time at Burnley, Cav never hid his feelings for United. He never wanted to leave his United boys, and that was evident during his training sessions with the Burnley players at their Turf Moor ground. Cav never stopped talking about his time at Old Trafford and much to the annoyance of the players he wore his United baseball cap during training sessions. And he infuriated the Burnley fans who attended home games at Turf Moor because he also wore his United baseball cap when he was sitting in the dugout.

In 2018, the book *Wayne Rooney: Always A Blue – The Biography*, was published. The Manchester United legend began his career with Everton but propelled United to trophy success after trophy success during his Old Trafford career. And when he left United on 9 July 2017, he rejoined his boyhood heroes, a case of 'Once A Blue, Always A Blue'. Despite the numerous clubs he played for, and enjoyed a management role at, Tommy Cavanagh most definitely showed his true colour, and it was Red. But it was never the Red of a team from the place of his birth on Merseyside, Cav's Red had a tinge of white and black mixed along with it like a Brighton sticky rock coloured red, white and black with a label stuck on the plastic covering which simply read: *UNITED THROUGH AND THROUGH.*

When Tommy left Burnley in 1986, he worked at the FA School of Excellence at Lilleshall until his retirement. In 2002, Cav was diagnosed with Alzheimer's disease. Sadly, on 14th March 2007, Tommy Cavanagh passed away aged 78.

Upon learning the news that he had died, the Doc remembered his close friend, 'He was excellent at his job. That is why he was my first signing when I came to United in 1972. We made quite a team. Both extroverts, shouting and bawling at everyone. But the players had a lot of respect for Tommy, as he knew what he was doing.'

There are not too many people who were born in Liverpool

who United fans respect but for every Manchester United fan, Tommy Cavanagh tops that particular list.

Did You Know That?

GEORGE BEST ONCE bought Tommy Cavanagh a brand new TV to apologise for being late for training one morning. Can you imagine the many TVs Cav would have had in his house had Bestie bought him one for every morning he turned up late or failed to show up at all? When Tommy was joining in with the celebrations of the team lifting the 1974-75 Second Division title, and the club's 1977 FA Cup final success, snooker was starting to become one of the most watched sports on the BBC. One of the players who featured in many of the World Professional Snooker Championships during the 1970s was a player named David Taylor. The snooker professional was nicknamed 'The Silver Fox', but during the 1970s there was only one silver, and wily, fox, and his name was Thomas Henry Cavanagh.

PART 7

CHURCH GIVES HEATHENS THE BOOT

SOD'S LAW FOR THE LAWMAN

THE CANARY AND THE DRUNKEN GOOSE

DEEPDALE DESTINY

HAT-TRICK OF GOALKEEPERS

CHURCH EVICTS HEATHENS FROM THEIR GROUND

When Newton Heath Lancashire and Yorkshire Cricket and Football Club was formed in 1878 by the workers from the Carriage and Wagon Works of the Newton Heath Lancashire and Yorkshire Railway, they played home games at North Road, Monsall, Newton Heath, Manchester. Their home pitch was owned by the Manchester Cathedral Authorities, part of the Anglican Church, which was the second biggest land owner in England during the Victorian era, 1837-1901. Manchester Cathedral was built in 1421, in a perpendicular Gothic style shortly after the foundation of the collegiate period in the city. Only the Monarch, Queen Victoria, who reigned from 20 June 1837 to her death on 22 January 1901, owned more land in England than the Anglican Church.

Initially, the ground consisted only of the pitch, around which an estimated 12,000 spectators could congregate to cheer on their cricket and football heroes of the day. Both sports were still bathing in their amateur status before their respective histories propelled them into a professional era. The Heathens were founder members of the Football Combination in season 1888-89 and finished runners-up in the Football Alliance in season 1891-92. The Cathedral Authorities recognised their tenant's popularity given their home attendance figures during Newton Heath's football matches and, in 1891, they paid for the construction of a new stand which increased the ground's capacity to 15,000. Perhaps the Church were investing their money in the hope of attracting more followers to their faith than accommodating the working-class men who attended The Heathens' home games.

Despite their nickname, the club's players and fans were far from disbelievers. They were ordinary working men who would religiously attend Sunday service, although many of them went to Mass at their local Roman Catholic Church as opposed to following the faith of the club's landlord. Manchester was a city which had a huge Irish Roman Catholic population and, by 1841, a tenth of Manchester's population was Irish and many lived in the district known as 'Little Ireland', a slum area in the Ancoats area of the city. The vast majority of the men and boys from these Irish families worked at the railway yards in Manchester and on the construction of the Manchester Ship Canal, which commenced in 1887 and was completed in 1893. And at the weekend, they went to see Newton Heath play. The original colours of the club's kit in 1878 was green and yellow half-shirts with white shorts, whilst the first flag of the Irish Republic in 1922 was green, white and orange. The green represented the Roman Catholics in Ireland, the orange represented the Protestants, hence their nickname 'Orangemen', and the white was supposed to be for peace between the two religions which even 100 years later still does not exist.

At the start of the 1886-87 season, Newton Heath Football Club began to break from their sponsoring railway company and signed their first professional player. However, as the years passed the club struggled to afford to pay their landlords, the Manchester Cathedral Authorities, their rent of North Road. Their decision to 'go it alone' in the summer of 1886, without regular cash injections from the Lancashire and Yorkshire Railway, came to an abrupt end during the 1892-93 season. Having finished runners-up in the Football Alliance in season 1891-92, the club applied to join the Football League and their application was successful.

On 14 March 1893, Newton Heath lost 5-0 at home to Sunderland in front of 15,000 paying fans. The game was a sell-out of all 15,000 places at their North Road home. The Heathens fortunes on the pitch were not as successful as their gate receipts and their landlord was having serious reservations about their tenant. The Manchester Cathedral Authorities took the decision that they could no longer permit Newton Heath Football Club to charge spectators to watch football games on their property. The club opposed the Church over their mandate which resulted in the Church's Dean and Canons instructing their solicitors to apply for a 'Notice To Quit' which was served on the club. There was always going to be only one winner of the dispute and it wasn't going to be the blasphemers. God was on one side and The Heathens, later to become 'Devils', were on the other side. It was an unfair match-up despite the fact that no divine intervention was required to settle the dispute. The Anglican Church won this particular contest hands down.

Newton Heath Lancashire and Yorkshire Football Club were

left with no other option but to vacate North Road, Monsall and relocated across the city at Bank Street, Clayton, just in time for the 1893-94 season. In addition to switching grounds, the club also switched their name, and dropped 'Lancashire and Yorkshire Railway'.

Did You Know That?

CHURCHES WERE VERY influential and powerful in the late 19th century and were even responsible for the formation of several football clubs. Prior to the formation of Liverpool in 1892, Anfield was home to Everton Football Club who were crowned First Division champions in season 1890-91. Everton were founded as St Domingo's in 1878, the same year that Newton Heath was formed, and became Everton Football Club in 1879. They moved into Anfield in 1884 when their club President, John Houlding, a local brewery owner, Tory MP and the Mayor of Liverpool, purchased a piece of land at Anfield Road from a fellow local brewer, Mr Orrell. In season 1884-85, Everton FC paid Houlding £100 per year rent for the use of the ground. At the start of the 1889-90 season, Houlding had increased the rent at Anfield to £250 per year. On 12 March 1892, Houlding fell out with his fellow Everton Football Club board members and three days later he formed a new club, Liverpool FC, resulting in Everton having to move across Stanley Park to play at their new home, Goodison Park. Houlding's new club, Liverpool Football Club, became the new tenants of the ground at Anfield Road.

Manchester City Football Club was founded in 1880 as St. Mark's (West Gorton), the club became Ardwick Association Football Club in 1887, and Manchester City in 1894. Southampton Football Club were originally founded at St. Mary's Church in 1885, by members of the St. Mary's Church of England Young Men's Association. The club was originally called St. Mary's Young

Men's Association Football Club and then became St. Mary's Football Club in season 1887-88, before changing their name again to Southampton St. Mary's in 1894 when they became members of the Southern League. After they won the Southern League title in season 1896-97, the club became a limited company and was renamed Southampton Football Club. In 1887, Barnsley Football Club was established by Tiverton Preedy, a clergyman and they played in the Sheffield and District League from 1890 and then in the Midland League from 1895. In 1898, The Tykes joined the Football League. Preedy was very interested in the use of sport within his ministry in the Yorkshire town.

SOD'S LAW FOR THE LAWMAN

During Denis Law's Old Trafford career, 1962-73, he played in 46 FA Cup games for United and scored 34 times, including a goal in United's 3-1 victory over Leicester City in the 1963 FA Cup final at Wembley Stadium. Denis scored a career total of 43 FA Cup goals: he also scored three times in the competition for Huddersfield Town (1956-60) and six times for Manchester City over two spells with the club (1960-61 and 1973-74). Ian Rush holds the modern-day FA Cup goal scoring record with 44 goals (39 for Liverpool, four for Chester City and one for Newcastle United) but he is five short of the competition's record.

The Notts County forward, Harry Cursham, scored 49 goals in just 44 appearances for the club during the late 1800s. His record includes a double hat-trick in an 11-1 win versus Wednesday Strollers in 1881, with his tally coming in 12 FA Cup seasons.

The majority of Cursham's goals came prior to the creation of the Football League in 1888, though he appeared for Notts County in the league's first season, 1888-89, before retiring in the 1890-91 season. Notts County, the oldest professional football club in the world, founded in 1862, never won the FA Cup during Cursham's time with The Magpies, but did win it for the first and only time in 1894, a 4-1 win over Bolton Wanderers in the final played at Goodison Park. In season 1890-91, Notts County were defeated 3-1 by Blackburn Rovers in the 1891 FA Cup final which was played at the Kennington Oval, London.

However, Denis Law's name should be enshrined in the FA Cup History Book as the competition's top goalscorer in the modern era. On 28 January 1961, Denis was a member of the Manchester City side which played Luton Town at Kenilworth Road, Luton in the Fourth Round of the 1960-61 FA Cup. Denis was in a menacing mood and bagged six goals against The Hatters inside an hour giving the visitors a 6-2 lead. The game was effectively over, City guaranteed their name in the hat for the Fifth Round draw which was taking place later that day. But much to the dismay of both sets of players the referee blew his whistle and abandoned the tie during a heavy downpour of incessant rain. According to one local newspaper report of the game: *The Kenilworth Road pitch first resembled a beach with the tide just out, then there was deep mud, then a shallow lake.* Law's double hat-trick was wiped clean from the pages of FA Cup history. The replayed tie took place on 1 February 1961, with Denis finding the back of the net yet again but Sod's law then came into play and City's name were absent from the FA Cup hat for the remainder of the competition, as the home side won the game 3-1. Speaking about the abandoned game some time later, Law said, 'I never did it again. The most I managed in a game that counted was four, which I got a couple of times. But then the heavens opened. Obviously, it wasn't meant to be. The funny thing was when we went for the replay on the Wednesday the pitch was in a worse state than it ever was on Saturday.'

Had Denis's six goals stood, his name would be in the FA Cup book as the joint-holder of the all-time record for scoring the most number of goals in the competition, 49.

Did You Know That?

TED MACDOUGALL JOINED Manchester United from AFC Bournemouth in September 1972 in a £200,000 transfer deal. On 20 November 1971, AFC Bournemouth, a Third Division club at the time, played Margate from the Southern League in an FA Cup First Round tie at Dean Court, Bournemouth. Slade were enjoying their first UK No.1 single with *Coz I Luv You*, and MacDougall, nicknamed 'Supermac' by the fans of the south coast club was adored by fans of The Cherries. Supermac scored nine times in an 11-0 win over Margate but wasn't happy with his triple hat-trick. Speaking to BBC Radio Solent some 40 years later he was asked about his goalscoring feat. 'I was disappointed as I thought I should have got 11. I've gone into training (on the Monday after the game) and manager John Bond has told me he just had a phone call from Geoff Hurst. He was having a testimonial against an All Star World XI at West Ham United's Boleyn Ground on Wednesday and wanted me to play in it. I couldn't believe it, I was a little player in a small team one minute and the next I'm in London. Tommy Docherty was the manager and I was on the bus with Eusebio, Dave Mackay and Jimmy Greaves and all these players I was used to watching on the television. We were then at West

Ham playing in front of a full house with lots of celebrities and I'm in awe of everything that is going on. Anyway, I went on and scored and it was an unbelievable experience. I went from being a Third Division player scoring nine goals, to playing in an All Star World XI for Geoff Hurst pretty much overnight.'

Edward John 'Ted' MacDougall began his career with Liverpool in 1964 when he signed for them as a trainee aged 16. He turned professional at Anfield in 1966, but never made the breakthrough into the first team when Bill Shankly (who was Law's manager at Huddersfield Town from 1956-59) was the manager of Liverpool, and he moved to York City in July 1967 in a £5,000 transfer. MacDougall played 18 times for Manchester United, 1972-73, and scored five times, all five scored in the First Division. He won seven international caps for Scotland and scored three times for his country. Tommy Docherty was the manager of Scotland at the time of Hurst's Testimonial Match and was appointed the manager of Manchester United just a few weeks after MacDougall arrived at Old Trafford. In total, MacDougall scored 256 goals in 535 league games.

THE BANK STREET CANARY AND THE DRUNKEN GOOSE

In season 1897-98, Newton Heath finished fourth in the English Second Division with 38 points from 30 games (won 16, drew six, lost eight). Burnley were crowned champions with 48 points, Newcastle United runners-up on 45 points and Manchester City occupying third place on 39 points. It had been a relatively successful season on the pitch for *The Heathens* but off it, the club were in the red at the bank. Their colour of their bank balance was not yet the same colour as their home shirts, which in season 1897-98, was white shirts, navy blue shorts and navy blue socks.

Home attendances at their Bank Street, Clayton home ground constantly fluctuated during the season with a crowd of 5,000 for their opening fixture of the campaign, a 5-0 victory over Lincoln City on 4 September 1897. Their fourth home league game of the season saw The Heathens welcome The Citizens (Manchester City's nickname) on 16 October 1897. Going into the game, the home side had won four and lost two of their first six league encounters, scoring 13 goals and conceding only four times. The visitors on the other hand were top of the table with seven wins from seven games and were inspired by their Welsh international winger, Billy Meredith (who would go on to inspire Manchester United to trophy successes), scoring freely, 22 goals, and only allowing three past their very strong back four. The Manchester Derby produced Newton Heath's biggest home attendance of the season when 20,000 Mancunians filled Bank Street. In their opening game of the 1897-98 season, Manchester City only attracted 2,000 fans to their Hyde Road home when they beat Gainsborough Trinity 3-0, Meredith was among the goalscorers.

The gate receipts most definitely appeased the club's bank whilst the two sets of fans, undistinguishable of their allegiance to the white (Newton Heath's home jersey was white from 1896-1902) or blue half of Manchester as they were all dressed in weekend suits and hats, went home having seen the spoils shared, a 1-1 draw. Richard 'Dick' Ray, who in 1919 became the first ever manager of Leeds United having played for the club from 1905-08 when they were known as Leeds City, scored for the visiting side, whilst

Matthew Gillespie scored much to the delight of the home crowd.

But, the Secretary of Newton Heath Football Club, who was also the manager of the side, A. H. Albut, knew that the revenue generated from the turnstiles, regardless of the team's results on the field, would not be sufficient to balance the club's Income & Expenditure Account. The financial plight of the club was so perilous that a club director had his house sold over his head to pay the club's debts thereby avoiding bankruptcy and the grasp of the Official Receiver.

The year 1897, was a significant one in the history of England. Queen Victoria was celebrating her Diamond Jubilee, Aston Villa won the Double of First Division Championship and FA Cup (season 1896-97) and left their Wellington Road home ground in Birmingham to move to Villa Park in the city. And on 13 May 1897, Guglielmo Marconi sent the first ever wireless message communication over open sea when the message 'Are you ready' was transmitted across the Bristol Handel from Lavernock Point, South Wales to Flat Holm Island, a Welsh island situated in the Bristol Channel, a distance of 3.7 miles.

But Albut was also a very shrewd businessman and he knew he had to present something else on a matchday to attract the fans to Bank Street other than the game itself. Among his quite entrepreneurial and novel business schemes to attract supporters to home games was to place advertisements in the local press. Albut, was an advertising king some 73 years before Saatchi & Saatchi were founded in London, England in 1970. Albut fully recognised that regardless of the talented footballers he had at his disposal, he needed an added attraction on a matchday to increase the attendance figures.

Albut placed an advertisement in a local newspaper stating that fans who came along to games could hear the Bank Street canary singing before kick-off. However, the canary was in fact a goose which was corralled in a pen in a corner of the ground and was being fattened for Albut's Christmas dinner. The poor goose was adopted as the club's mascot and taken to the pub after home games where it was given ale to drink until it became so drunk that it just collapsed, falling flat down on the floor of the bar.

Did You Know That?

AND ON ANOTHER occasion, when Albut learned that a rival club's star player was complaining to the press that he had not been paid any wages by his club for several weeks, Albut devised a publicity stunt. Newton Heath had recently been served with a writ from one of the club's debtors and Albut persuaded the player to be photographed serving the writ on his club which led to his club releasing him from his contract. Albut then signed the player and when he made his home debut for Newton Heath the following week, an additional £10.00 was added to the gate when the fans turned up to see the new recruit.

FROM OLD TRAFFORD TO DEEPDALE

Manchester United has a close connection with Preston North End. Not only are the two Lancashire Rivals just 27 miles apart, but both clubs share a player and manager association. Six Manchester United players went on to manage *The Lilywhites* after they left The Red Devils:

- **James Vincent Hayes** – Preston North End, July 1919-August 1923
- **Bobby Charlton** – Preston North End, May 1973-August 1975
- **Nobby Stiles** – Preston North End, July 1977-June 1981
- **Brian Kidd** – Preston North End, January 1986-March 1986
- **Sammy McIlroy** – Preston North End, February 1990-July 1991
- **Darren Ferguson** – Preston North End, January 2010-December 2010

Two Manchester United managers have managed Preston North End during their managerial careers: Tommy Docherty managed United from December 1972 to July 1977 and *The Lilywhites* from June – December 1981. David Moyes managed United from July 2013-April 2014 and *The Lilywhites* from January 1998- March 2002.

Vince Hayes played for Newton Heath from 1900-02 and for Manchester United from 1902-05 and won an FA Cup winners' medal with the club during his second spell with them (1908-11) when they defeated Bristol City 1-0 in the 1909 final. He actually left the field injured in the final at the Crystal Palace, but returned a while later to earn his winners' medal. There were no substitutes at the time. Tommy Docherty played for Preston North End from 1949-58, whilst the man who preceded him as the United manager, Frank O'Farrell (June 1971-December 1972) played for Preston North End from 1956-61. Bobby Charlton joined Preston North End after he left Manchester United in the summer of 1973 and was the club's player/manager during the 1974-75 season and Nobby Stiles was a player/coach at the club from 1973-75 alongside his former Manchester United and England teammate, Bobby Charlton.

Alex Ferguson sent a 19-year old David Beckham out on loan to Preston North End in early 1995, after one of his famous Fledglings, a member of The Class of 1992, had already been given his first team debut (as a substitute for Andrei Kanchelskis in the 72nd minute of a 1-1 draw away to Brighton and Hove Albion in the Second Round of the League Cup on 23 September 1992: Danny Wallace scored), and who scored the first of his 85 goals for Manchester United in their 4-0 win over Turkey's, Galatasaray, in a Group A, Matchday 6, UEFA Champions League fixture at Old Trafford on 7 December 1994. Beckham only played five games for Preston North End before United asked him to return. However, he made an instant impression at Deepdale scoring two goals, a free kick and a strike directly from a corner (on his debut versus Doncaster Rovers). On all five occasions he played for Preston North End, Beckham was given a £50 bonus and given his ability to strike a ball, the loanee was instantly placed on set pieces when he arrived at Deepdale by boss Gary Peters.

Did You Know That?

 DAVID HEALY, MANCHESTER United 1999-2001, was sent out on loan to Preston North End by Sir Alex Ferguson during the 2000-01 season and his manager at Deepdale was David Moyes. The young Northern Ireland international striker made his debut for Preston North End on 30 December 2000, and scored after only four minutes in a 3-2 loss to Sheffield United at Bramall Lane, Sheffield in the First Division. After scoring 10 times in 26 games for The Lilywhites in season 2000-01, he signed for them in the summer of 2001 in a £1.5 million transfer.

UNITED'S FIRST DUAL HERITAGE PLAYER AND THE ONLY BUSBY BABE

Dennis Allen Walker was born on 26 October 1944 in Northwich, Cheshire, England to a single mother, Mary Walker. Mary was born in Limerick, Republic of Ireland and was white. Up until a few years ago very little was known about Dennis's father as his name does not appear on the birth certificate, although Dennis always described himself as half-Iranian and half-Argentinian. His father was Afro-Iranian and when he was a young boy, Dennis' mother told him that his father died at sea when he was just a baby. The young Walker learned to speak Arabic and Farsi in order to correspond with his father's family in Iran.

In his second year at secondary school, Manchester United's local scout spotted Dennis and recognising that the young kid had talent in abundance, he recommended him to his manager, Matt Busby. United had the best, and most coveted youth football system in English football and regardless of the city or town of their birth, every schoolboy dreamt of becoming a Busby Babe and following in the football boots of the legendary

Duncan Edwards, Bobby Charlton and many others. Dennis was recruited by United and aged only 15 he left school and signed for the club as a trainee in September 1960. His boyhood dream was fulfilled, he became a Busby Babe, the first and only dual heritage Busby Babe.

Dennis was an outstanding talent at schoolboy level and was on the verge of playing for the England schoolboys Under-15 side before agreeing terms at Old Trafford. When Jimmy Murphy, assistant manager to Matt Busby, and the man in charge of Manchester United's Youth teams, knocked on the front door of the home of the parent/parents of a young boy who he wanted to join his set-up at Old Trafford, it was perhaps one of the most difficult things in the world to do and not invite Jimmy in.

Murphy was a genial Welshman, whose demeanour was so intoxicating, and whose words of comfort and wisdom were so reassuring, that it may have been bordering on a parent committing a sin to refuse him permission to look after their son. Jimmy never promised to take the place of either parent in their son's life but what he did give them was his unequivocal guarantee that he would look after him like he was his own son. Busby knew that Murphy was the patriarch of his Babes and both treated the young boys under their charge as men. Mary Walker, just like the parents of Edwards and Charlton had done in previous years, placed her trust in Manchester United, and in Jimmy in particular, to look after her son and help him become a man. Had Dennis been selected to play for the England schoolboys Under-15 side, he would have been the first dual heritage player to represent England at any level.

A right-sided midfielder or forward, Dennis signed as a full-time professional in November 1961 but had to wait until the end of the 1962-63 season before making his first-team debut.

On 20 May 1963, Busby gave Dennis his chance and selected him in his team which lost 3-2 at the City Ground to Nottingham Forest in the First Division Championship (scorers: Johnny Giles and David Herd). Amazingly, neither Charlton nor Denis Law (Best was still a Youth team player) played in the game which was not only Dennis's first for Manchester United, but also his only ever game for the club.

Busby rested Charlton and played Dennis in his position. Walker's debut was Manchester United's final league game of the 1962-63 season, and five days later, Charlton and Law both played in United's 3-1 win over Leicester City in the 1963 FA Cup final (Best was sitting in the stands at Wembley Stadium watching the game). Law scored in the final as did David Herd, who scored twice for United under the Twin Towers to win the FA Cup for the third time in the history of the club, winners in 1909 and 1948.

After making the breakthrough into the Manchester United first team, Dennis remained on the periphery and when the club embarked on a 1963-64 pre-season tour of Italy, he was not chosen by Busby for any of the matches. But then again, his competition was Charlton and Law and a Manchester United Legend in Genesis, literally waiting in the wings, the iconic, devilish, wizard of the dribble, silky, stylish, mesmeric, iconic, genius of world football, George Best. The 17-year-old Best eventually made his first team debut on 14 September 1963. In April 1964, Dennis left Old Trafford and moved to York City who had just finished third from bottom of the Fourth Division and had to apply for re-election to the league, which was approved.

On 13 June 1964, Dennis married Patricia Cropper in the Parish Church of St Clement, Chorlton-cum-Hardy, and his former United teammate, David Sadler (George Best's best friend at the club) was his best man at his wedding. After 169 appearances for York City, he moved to Cambridge United in 1968 and played for the club in the Southern League and then in the Football League from 1968 until October 1972. In October 1972, he moved to Poole Town Football Club for £1,600, making 74 league appearances for the club and scoring four goals. Poole Town were relegated from the Southern Premier League to the Southern League Division 1 South at the end of the 1972-73 season, and at the start of the 1973-74 season, Dennis was made player/manager. In July 1975, he accepted an offer of a football coaching role in South Africa.

He then returned to the UK to become the Operations Manager at the Arndale Shopping Centre in Manchester. Dennis was on duty on 15 June 1996, when a telephone call came through claiming that a bomb had been planted in the Centre. The Troubles were in their 27th year in Northern Ireland and the Irish Republican Army (IRA) had carried out many bombing campaigns in England during this time. However, hoax calls about bombs being planted at key points in English cities were not uncommon at this time, and any decision to evacuate a major shopping complex or a financial institution would undoubtedly cause a great deal of disruption and financial loss. Thankfully, Dennis decided he would go with his gut feeling he had following the telephone warning and supported the decision to evacuate the Arndale Shopping Centre which was packed with shoppers. Seconds after ensuring everyone was safe a 3,300 lbs IRA bomb was detonated, hurling Dennis across the road and into the window of Debenhams department store. Miraculously he was unhurt, and no one died in the aftermath of the explosion, mainly thanks to Dennis' quick decision making.

Sadly, Dennis suffered a massive stroke and lost the use of the right side of his body. This was difficult for Dennis to endure as he was such a positive outgoing person who loved playing sports, particularly golf. He never fully recovered from the stroke and passed away on 11 August 2003, in Stepping Hill Hospital, Stockport, aged 59.

But Dennis's legacy lives on and thanks to him, the Manchester United team today is a diverse one. Dennis Walker paved the way for those players today to represent the club freely and without the prejudice players like Dennis had to suffer and tolerate during the 1960s and 1970s in order to play the sport they loved.

Did You Know That?

CONSIGLIERE IS A position within the leadership structure of the Calabrian, Sicilian and American Mafia. The word was popularised in English in the 1969 novel, The Godfather, and in the 1972 movie of the same name. In the novel, a consigliere is an advisor or counsellor to the Boss, who also represents the Boss and his family in important meetings both within the Boss's own crime family and within other crime families. The consigliere is a close, trusted friend and confidant, the Mafia's version of an elder statesman, a 'right-hand man'. Jimmy Murphy was undoubtedly the equivalent of a Consigliere to Matt Busby who himself has been referred to as the Father of Manchester United.

A HAT-TRICK OF GOALKEEPERS

Herbert Birchenough played in goal for Manchester United on Christmas Day 1902 in the Second Division against Manchester City at United's Bank Street ground before 4,000 fans. The game ended 1-1, with Ernest Pegg scoring United's equaliser in the 68th minute after the visitors took the lead a quarter of an hour earlier when City's legendary winger, their talismanic Billy Meredith scored against Birchenough. It was only his 10th game for the club after signing for United from Glossop North End at the end of October 1902. However, Birchenough did not see out the full 90 minutes as he was injured during the game and half-back, Walter Cartwright, replaced him in goal, after the United custodian was carried off the pitch on a stretcher.

The following day, Boxing Day 1902, Herbert was not fit to play and James Whitehouse took over in goal when United drew 2-2 versus Blackpool at home in the league before a bumper crowd of 10,000 fans (scorers: Thomas Morrison and Alexander Downie). It was Whitehouse's 64th and last appearance for the club after signing for Newton Heath in September 1900, from Grimsby Town. In February 1903, he moved across the city and signed for Manchester City. Whitehouse was in goal for the club when they played their first ever game as Manchester United, a 1-0 away win versus Gainsborough Trinity on 6 September 1902 (scorer: Charles Richards). Meanwhile, a future Manchester United player appeared for Blackpool in the game – Harold Hardman was at Old Trafford in season 1908-09 when he played four games without scoring.

Amazingly, United played their third game in three days when they welcomed Barnsley to Bank Street on 27 December 1902, and quite unbelievably they had a third different goalkeeper for the game which was also a Second Division game. On this occasion John Saunders pulled on the No.1 jersey in a game the home side won 2-1 (scorers: Jack Peddie and Hubert Lappin). The former Newton Heath full-back, John McCartney, was the Barnsley manager. He made 20 appearances for The Heathens in season 1894-95, his only season with the club, and scored one goal, versus Crewe Alexandra in a 6-1 victory in his second game for the club in a Division Two game at Bank Street on 16 September 1894.

There is a famous saying: Unlucky Number 13. And, Whitehouse's appearance against Barnsley was his 13th game for the club, and his last. Apparently, the No.13 is unlucky for a number of reasons, one of which is religious, and is relevant to Whitehouse who joined Newton Heath Football Club in September 1900 from Grimsby Town and effectively became a 'Heathen'. During 'The Last Supper', Jesus Christ's Last Supper, there were 13 people around the table, Jesus Christ and his 12 apostles. Many Roman Catholics believe that the No.13 is unlucky because one of those 13 who attended The Last Supper was Judas Iscariot, the 13th person to sit at the table, and who later betrayed Jesus to the Romans for 30 pieces of silver.

On 10 January 1903, Birchenough returned and United lost 3-1 away to Burton United in a League fixture (scorer: Peddie). Birchenough left United at the end of the 1902-03 season having made 25 League appearances and five FA Cup games for the club.

Did You Know That?

THE GAME AGAINST Manchester City on 25 December 1902, was the first Derby played between Manchester United and Manchester City, after Newton Heath Football Club changed their name in April 1902 to Manchester United.

PART 8

MANCHESTER'S VICTORIAN BOO BOYS

DENIS LAW'S BACK HEEL GOAL

NEWTON HEATH BOOTED OUT OF FA CUP

UNITED'S FIRST GAME

FANS DOUBT FERGIE

THE PHOENIX RISES

MANCHESTER'S VICTORIAN BOO BOYS

On 18 March 1899, Newton Heath Football Club welcomed New Brighton Tower to their Bank Street ground for a Second Division encounter. The Heathens were enjoying their seventh season in the Football League, and their fifth consecutive season in the division. The club had high hopes of winning promotion to the top flight after finishing runners-up in season 1896-97 and fourth in season 1897-98 in the second tier of English football. But, the Merseyside club also held aspirations of winning promotion. Their previous encounter resulted in a 3-0 win for New Brighton Tower at their Tower Athletic home ground on 19 November 1898.

So, when 20,000 fans turned up at Bank Street, a joint record home attendance for the season matching the crowd for the game versus Manchester City on 10 September 1898 (a 3-0 win), they were expecting a victory which would help their push towards promotion. The visitors won 2-1 (scorer: Joe Cassidy) which put a serious dent in the fans' dreams of watching The Heathens play top flight clubs the following season. Teams such as Aston

Villa (First Division champions in season 1898-99), Sheffield United (FA Cup winners in 1899 and First Division champions in season 1897-98), Everton, Liverpool, Preston North End and Wolverhampton Wanderers.

When the referee brought the game against New Brighton Tower to an end after the regulation 90 minutes of play, a group of home fans ran on to the pitch and surrounded him. They booed and jeered him, they jostled him and hurled verbal abuse at him after he had, in the opinion of the fans of the home team, made several highly questionable decisions in favour of the visitors. Thankfully, two alert policemen who were on duty acted swiftly and ran to the aide of the startled official and escorted him safely to the comfort of his dressing-room.

The loss proved to be a costly one as Newton Heath then lost one, drew three and won four of their remaining games to finish fourth in the table and outside the promotion spots. New Brighton Tower finished fifth level with The Heathens on 43 points, but with an inferior goal difference (+19 to +24).

Did You Know That?

NEW BRIGHTON TOWER Football Club were founded in 1896 in New Brighton, Merseyside. Just like their neighbours, Liverpool (Anfield, 1892), Chelsea (Stamford Bridge, 1905), Sheffield United (Bramall Lane, 1889) and Thames (West Ham Stadium, 1928) they moved into a ground which did not already have a club using it as their home ground. New Brighton Tower FC were formed by the owners of New Brighton Tower, a steel lattice construction which was built to rival Blackpool Tower. It was envisaged that the steel tower, which was the tallest building in Britain when it opened around 1899, would attract visitors from May to September, whilst the football club would provide entertainment during the autumn and winter months. New Brighton Tower joined the Lancashire League at the start of the 1897-98 season and won it. They applied to join the Football League and although their application was initially rejected, they were admitted to the Second Division in season 1898-99 when the Football League decided to expand the second tier by admitting two more clubs. At the end of the 1900-01 season, the club was dissolved as poor home attendances (an average of 1,000) meant that their income was insufficient to support the running of a football club. Their place in the Second Division was taken by Doncaster Rovers, who had been formed in 1879.

LAW'S BACK-HEELED GOAL NEVER RELEGATED UNITED

Many Manchester City fans still claim that Denis Law's back-heeled goal in the Manchester Derby game at Old Trafford on 27 April 1974 sent the Red half of the city tumbling down into the Second Division. However, this is factually and historically incorrect. It is a complete myth.

On the final Saturday of the 1973-1974 First Division season, Manchester United faced their local neighbours in a game which could possibly decide whether or not United would be relegated. United had a really poor season and in their previous 40 games before they met City, they had won only 10, drawn 12 and were beaten 18 times. They were a struggling side in a season which did not have Bobby Charlton and Denis Law in the squad for the first time in 12 years, going back to season 1962-63. George Best broke into the United first team the season after Denis arrived, making his debut as a 17-year-old on 14 September 1963. Bobby had already decided he was retiring at the end of the 1972-73 season after loyally serving the club for 17 years.

Denis was expecting to start the 1973-74 season alongside the Belfast Boy and wanted to impress the new manager of the Scotland international team, Willie Ormond, as the 1974 FIFA World Cup finals were less than a year away. Denis was visiting family in his native Aberdeen in July 1973, enjoying his pre-season break, when he learned that his Manchester United career was over. He was in a pub close to where he was born in the Granite City when a news report came on the TV in a corner of the bar. Denis discovered that he had been placed on the transfer market by his manager, fellow Scot, Tommy Docherty. The King of Old Trafford was absolutely dumbstruck and slumped in his seat as the enormity of the fact that he would never play again for his beloved Manchester United began to slowly drip feed into his mind. *How could this be?* But it was not the first time that United's prolific striker (237 goals in 404 appearances, including a club record 46 goals in only 42 games in season 1963-64) suffered the indignity of being transfer listed.

In the spring of 1970, the man who succeeded Matt Busby as the manager of Manchester United, Wilf McGuinness, offered Denis' services to any suitor interested in signing the striker, but quite amazingly, no one approached United about The Lawman. In season 1969-70, Denis only managed to play in 16 matches for United, scoring three times, compared with his previous goals tally in a season of 29 in 44 games in his first year at Old Trafford (1962-63), his record haul the following campaign, 39 strikes in 52 outings in 1964-65, 24 in 49 games in 1965-66, 25 goals in season 1966-67 in 38 matches, 10 strikes in season 1967-68 in 28 games, and 30 goals in 45 appearances in the 1968-69 season. However, in season 1967-68, Denis injured his knee which he never really made a full recovery from.

But more importantly, Law's contribution of goals helped United win the FA Cup in season 1962-63 (he scored in the final), the First Division Championship in 1964-65, the First Division Championship in 1966-67 and the European Cup in 1968. In season 1963-64, Law's lethalness in front of goal earned him the Ballon d'Or, the first United player to be voted the best footballer in Europe. Denis missed the 1968 European Cup final victory over SL Benfica with a knee injury but his teammates recognised his contribution to Manchester United becoming the first English winners of European football's most coveted and prestigious trophy, and later brought the trophy to Denis's hospital bedside with a crate of beer to celebrate.

Dynasties rise and fall. Denis Law was a Manchester United dynasty in his own right, and is remembered today in front of Old Trafford in the form of the 'United Trinity' statue depicting Law, Best and Charlton. Egypt is synonymous with its Kings but their Pharaohs fade into the shadows of the great Pyramids which they built in their own honour. But, when United fans recall the exploits of the Three Kings of Manchester United. Law, Best and Charlton this famous Triumvirate may not have been Kings of an ancient world but in the football world, they were the Kings of European football. United's Three Kings did not have a Pyramid built to worship them, Old Trafford was their home where the United fans worshipped them. No other club in Europe had three Ballon d'Or winners playing together in the same team. Charlton was European football's No.1 player in season 1965-66 when he helped England win the World Cup and then two years later, a 22-year-old George Best won the Ballon d'Or in season 1967-68.

In season 1972-73, Denis's knee injury reappeared, restricting him to playing just 12 games, scoring two goals. His future at Old Trafford was on the precipice. Bobby was perhaps the first of the famous three to recognise that the dynasty he helped to build at Old Trafford since he joined the club as a Busby Babe, aged just 15 in January 1953, was gradually crumbling. At the start of the 1972-73 season, he told Docherty and the Manchester United Board of Directors that it would be his final year at the club. The season almost saw United relegated as they finished in 18th place in the table.

Goals were a priceless commodity for the team, which was reflected in the fact that Charlton finished the season as the club's top goalscorer in the league and in all competitions, with six in the league and one in the League Cup. He also netted twice in the Anglo-Italian Cup. Indeed, things became so bad that at one point that goalkeeper Alex Stepney even topped the goal scoring charts with two, both penalties. A fit Denis Law would always score goals: in season 1970-71 he scored 16 times from 34 outings, followed by 13 goals in 42 games in season 1971-72.

But, Denis, aged 33, did not feature in Docherty's plans of rebuilding a new Manchester United team as he focused on bringing young players to the club. Best was still only 27 but it would not be much longer before he too would become 'persona non grata' at Old Trafford as Docherty began to wield his authority in what would be his first full season as manager. And so, Tommy Docherty let Denis go but much to the shock and horror of the United fans. Denis signed for Manchester City, a club he played for in season 1960-61 when he was the Blues' top goalscorer with 23 from 43 appearances, before moving to Italy's AS Torino for a season in 1961-62 (27 league games, 10 goals).

Back to the Manchester Derby at Old Trafford on 27 April 1974. It was a beautiful sunny day and prior to kick-off the fans were enjoying the music being played as part of the pre-match entertainment. Two of these songs were *Seasons In The Sun* by Terry Jacks, which was the No.1 song in the UK charts at the time, and the 1974 Eurovision Sing Contest winner, *Waterloo*, by the Swedish group ABBA. Manchester United were facing their own Waterloo in order to be able to continue enjoying their own seasons in the sun, in the top flight of English football. Many popular jokes began with the line, '*Did you hear the one about the Irishman, the Englishman and the Scotsman?*' But, on 27 April 1974, the United fans were in no joking mood as their talismanic genius of an Irishman fell out of love with football and played his last ever game for the club on New Year's Day 1974; their English Busby Babe went from playing to managing when he was appointed the manager of Preston North End the previous summer; and their very own King of Scotland had, reluctantly, swapped his red United shirt for the blue of City.

April 1974, hadn't been a bad month for United, drawing 3-3 away to Burnley followed by two wins against clubs who were also scrapping it out in the relegation dog fight, 2-0 away to Norwich City and a 1-0 home victory over Newcastle United. United then secured a third successive win, 3-0 against Everton at Old Trafford. However, a 1-1 draw away to Southampton was followed by a 1-0 defeat against Everton at Goodison Park. A win over their neighbours would be a huge step towards avoiding the dreaded drop but United's destiny was not in their own hands because even a victory could still see them relegated. Norwich City were sitting rock bottom of the league table but United need a huge favour from The Canaries, who were already relegated and needed them to beat Birmingham City at St Andrew's, Birmingham.

When Law took to the Old Trafford pitch wearing the blue of Manchester City the United faithful stood and applauded him whilst the fans in the Stretford End who had dubbed him 'The King of the Stretford End' (there is a bronze statue of Denis in the Stretford End) during his United career cried out 'Law, Law, Law, Law, Law' as if they were one massive voice. It was like a gladiator who had returned to the Colosseum to entertain the audience one last time although Law was not to know that the game would be his last before the Old Trafford crowd. He was still idolised by the Red Army regardless of his move across the city none months earlier. Manchester City made Denis their captain for the game.

The first Manchester Derby of the season was a cagey affair, best remembered for the spat involving the City captain, Mike Doyle and United's diminutive, but firecracker of a striker, Lou Macari, which saw both players sent off in a 0-0 draw at Maine Road on 13 March 1974. Their second meeting was heading for a 0-0 draw until Law, with his back to the goal, casually back-heeled the ball in the 82nd minute of play and then watched in horror as it eluded Alex Stepney in the United goal. Law quickly realised what he had just done, and what affect it could possibly have on his former employer, and showed no elation whatsoever in scoring; there was no raising of his right arm in the air with his fist clenched holding the cuff of his shirt. As his teammates surrounded him to celebrate, the United fans poured out of the stands and made their way on to the pitch. Law's goal turned out to be his last kick in league football because when the game re-started three minutes later, Phil Henson had come on as a substitute for Law who was too distraught to play on.

He looked heartbroken as he sat in the away dressing-room, tears in his eyes at the thought that his goal could be the goal that would send United down into Division Two. It was Henson's league debut for the Blues. Shortly after the restart, the United fans invaded the pitch again and with a fire starting in the Stretford End, the referee, David Smith, took the decision to abandon the game. The Football League ordered the result to stand with City winning 1-0 and United were relegated to the Second Division for the first time since the end of season 1936-37 (finished in 21st place). However, it wasn't Denis' most nonchalant of flicks which relegated United; indeed, even if United had won the game, they would still have been relegated as Birmingham City beat Norwich City 2-1, a result which condemned United to the drop. Eric Todd reported on the United versus City game for *The Guardian* and wrote: *After a lapse of 37 mostly glorious years Manchester United face at least one season in the outer darkness, a fate which like that of the Roman Empire once was deemed to be impossible.*

Two days after United lost their Waterloo, when their relegation was confirmed, the Reds lost 1-0 away to Stoke City and would be playing their football in the second tier in season 1974-75 along with Norwich City (finished bottom) and Southampton (finished second from bottom) who went down with them. A team which had been crowned champions of Europe just six years earlier were now only the 21st best team in England.

In actual fact it was Everton's Mick Lyons who sent Manchester United nosediving into the Second Division when he scored the only goal of the game between the two clubs just four days earlier, 23 April 1974. St George's Day is celebrated in England on 23 April each year and celebrates the legend that St George slayed a dragon.

And so, the myth that the legendary Denis Law's back-heeled goal which he scored against Manchester United when he was playing for Manchester City relegated his former club is well and truly debunked.

Many years after the event, Denis was asked what he remembered about the goal and said, 'After 19 years of trying my hardest to score goals, here was one that I almost wished hadn't actually gone in. I was inconsolable. I didn't want it to happen.

'How long did the feeling last?

'How long ago was the game?

'There is your answer.'

Did You Know That?

LAW WENT ON to make one appearance for Scotland at the 1974 FIFA World Cup finals hosted by West Germany. On 14 June 1974, he helped the Scots beat Zaire 2-0 at the Westfalenstadion, Dortmund. It was his 55th and final appearance for his country, scoring 30 international goals, and after playing 602 career games, 303 goals, he took the decision to hang-up his football boots and retired from the game.

NEWTON HEATH BOOTED OUT OF THE FA CUP

In season 1886-87, Newton Heath Football Club entered the FA Cup for the first time since the club's formation in 1878. However, their participation in the competition, which was first contested in season 1871-72 and was won by Wanderers Football Club, who defeated Royal Engineers 1-0 in the inaugural final played at the Kennington Oval, London, ended in ignominious circumstances.

On 30 October 1886, The Heathens were drawn to play Fleetwood Rangers away in the First Round at Fleetwood Park, Fleetwood, Lancashire which was just a short distance away from Newton Heath's North Road, Monsall home ground. John 'Jack' Doughty put the visitors 1-0 up in the 10th minute but William Wright brought the home side level five minutes later. Harry Fisher put Fleetwood Rangers 2-1 in front 11 minutes into the second-half but within 60 seconds of the restart, Doughty scored again. The game ended 2-2 and the referee called the two captains into the centre circle to inform them that extra-time would be played to settle the outcome of the tie. John 'Jack' Powell, the captain of The Heathens, then informed his teammates of the referee's decision.

However, this historic game in the history of the club was prematurely truncated when the Newton Heath players informed their captain that they were not going to play extra-time and instead wanted a replay and another pay day. Powell, a Welsh international right-back (15 caps, 0 goals, 1878-88) was made captain for the game by secretary/manager A. H. Albut as the club captain, Sam Black, was injured. Despite his leadership abilities, Powell was unable to persuade his teammates to play extra-time and they walked off the pitch to enjoy a much needed shower, leaving their captain to explain their actions to the referee. Even Powell's fellow Welshman, Doughty (eight caps, six goals, 1896-90), refused to play extra-time thereby denying himself the opportunity of potentially scoring a hat-trick.

Powell approached the match referee and informed him that his players were unwilling to play extra-time. The referee informed Powell that he was abandoning the game and awarded the home side a win which effectively eliminated Newton Heath from what is now the world's most famous Cup competition. So, in their first ever entry into the history of the FA Cup, Newton Heath were effectively kicked out of the competition. The Newton Heath Board of Directors were so incensed at the decision that they refused to enter the FA Cup in the following three seasons, a self-imposed three-year exile.

Powell, born in Ffrwd, Wales on 25 March 1860, began his playing career with Druids Football Club in Wrexham in 1879 and moved to England in October 1883 to play for Bolton Wanderers. He became the first Welsh player to move to England in pursuit of a professional football career. However, professionalism in English football was not made legal until July

1885, and so, after spending 21 months with The Trotters he took the decision to leave Pike's Lane, Bolton after 21 months with the Lancashire club and in July 1885, he joined Newton Heath.

When he made the switch from Bolton to Manchester, he was given the job as a 'fitter' at the Lancashire and Yorkshire Railway in their Carriage and Wagon Works in Newton Heath. He not only joined a new club but he became a member of a division of the railway which seven years earlier formed Newton Heath Lancashire and Yorkshire Railway Cricket and Football Club.

Although E. Thomas is believed to be the first ever captain of Newton Heath, Sam Black is widely considered to be the first true star of the club after joining them from Burton Wanderers in 1882. A full-back with the build and strength of Wayne Rooney, he was made the club's captain upon his arrival and with many outstanding performances under his belt he soon drew the attention of bigger clubs. Shortly after winning the FA Cup in 1883, Blackburn Olympic (today known as Blackburn Rovers) attempted to lure him to Ewood Park but he declined their advances and captained The Heathens until 1887, helping the club to their first ever trophy success, the Manchester Senior Cup in 1886. When he left Newton Heath in 1887, he returned to his former club, Burton Wanderers. Sam was an amateur throughout his career.

On 22 March 1884, Sam Black, along with his teammates, J Blears, C Fulton and E Moran, became the first Newton Heath players to win representative honours when the four were chosen to represent the Manchester and District Football Association against a Liverpool and District XI.

Did You Know That?

IN SEASON 1886-87, The Heathens were not playing in any league as the inaugural English First Division season did not take place until season 1888-89. However, apart from friendlies, they participated in the Manchester Senior Cup and reached the final in 1887, losing 2-1 to West Manchester at Whalley Range, Manchester on 23 April 1887 (scorer: James Gotheridge).

MANCHESTER UNITED'S FIRST EVER GAME

On 6 September 1902, Manchester United travelled to Lincolnshire to play Gainsborough Trinity in the opening game of their 1902-03 Second Division season. The home side's ground, The Northolme, was opened in the 1850s, and was originally used as a cricket ground. Gainsborough Trinity moved to The Northolme in 1884 and at the time the only spectator facility was a small covered stand in the south-west corner of the ground. Players used the nearby pub, The Sun Inn, for changing rooms, and the landlord of the pub built an extension to the building for use by the football club. A 200-seat grandstand was later added to The Northolme, along the southern touchline and a covered terrace on the northern side of the pitch.

This was the first ever match played by Manchester United after Newton Heath Football Club went bankrupt in late April 1902 and out of its ashes a new club was formed. That club was

Manchester United.

In season 1900–01, Newton Heath Football Club was on the verge of bankruptcy. Things were that bad at the club that the fans conducted whip-rounds to pay for the team's railway fares to play away fixtures. The club organised a Grand Bazaar at St James's Hall, Oxford Street, Manchester late in the season in an effort to boost finances and raise the £1,000 which was needed to prevent the club from becoming bankrupt. At the bazaar the club captain's dog, Harry Stafford's St Bernard named Major, walked around the stalls in the hall with a collection box fastened around his collar so children could drop some pennies in his box. One day, Major walked out of the hall and wandered off. He eventually turned up at the home of John H. Davies, a very wealthy local brewery owner. Stafford is believed to have tracked down the dog after placing a notice in a local newspaper and Davies contacted him to tell him he had Major.

When Stafford called to the home of Davies to collect Major, Davies offered to purchase the pet as his daughter had fallen in love with the animal. Stafford told Davies that Major was not for sale but during their meeting Stafford told Davies about the Heathens' precarious financial position. As a direct result of their chance meeting, Davies saw a new business opportunity and, as a benefactor of other sports, he decided that he would get involved to financially support The Heathens when they needed his investment.

It proved to be one of the most decisive moments in the club's history.

But despite the financial success of the Grand Bazaar, the club was still in need of a major cash injection. In January 1902, the club's crippling debts amounted to £2,670 and a number of creditors pressed for payment. The club simply did not have the money to discharge their liabilities and so Newton Heath Football Club was adjudicated bankrupt. When the gates to their Bank Street ground were locked by their landlord, Stafford decided to call in Davies' promise to help. A meeting of the club's shareholders was held at Islington Town Hall, Ancoats, Manchester on 18 March 1902. Stafford, realising the quite perilous financial state the club were in, contacted Davies and offered to let him have Major if he helped out the club. Davies agreed and on 18 March 1902, Stafford took to the stage at the New Islington Hall to announce that he and four other gentlemen were willing to stake £200.00 each to save the club. The four were Davies and three of Davies' business acquaintants, Mr Jabez James Bown (Davies' right-hand man at his brewery), Mr Charles Jones (a cashier employed by Davies) and Mr James Taylor (a major shareholder in the Eagle Brewery). In return for their investment, they would take full control of the club. Newton Heath Football Club's existing Board of Directors were left with no other choice but to agree to the takeover. However, the Football Association declared that the reformed club would need to have a new name.

On 23 April 1902, Newton Heath Football Club beat Chesterfield 2–0 (scorers: Jimmy Coupar and Stephen Preston) at their Bank Street home in Division Two and finished 15th in the table, their last league game under that name. Three days later, 26 April 1902, Harry Stafford captained Newton Heath Football Club in their last ever game, a 2-1 win in the Manchester Senior Cup final against Manchester City at their rival's Hyde Road ground. It proved to be his only winners' medal in his time at Bank Street.

On 24 April 1902, a key meeting was arranged to form a new club. Those present were fans, directors and interested parties, and they were invited to suggest a new name. Manchester Celtic and Manchester Central were both suggested, the former perhaps reflecting links with the Irish community in the city. The latter was rejected as there was a train station named Manchester Central. Louis Rocca, who had served the club as a tea boy in the 1890s and played for the Reserve team a few times, was in attendance. Rocca, who lived in Oldham Road, Manchester was managing the family's ice-cream business at the time and he always maintained that he was the person who suggested the name Manchester United, which was unanimously agreed at the meeting to be the club's new name. Rocca went on to become a chief scout at United and assistant manager to Walter Crickmer. The team's new colours would be red jerseys and white shorts, although the team had played in red and white as early as 1892. The away kit was a green and white striped shirt with black shorts.

Harry Stafford and the club's Secretary, James West, were placed in charge of all football related matters which effectively made Stafford the club captain, joint manager and a director. However, now that he had a position on the Board of Directors of Manchester United, Stafford had to give up his professional status as a player and revert to amateur status. Harry Stafford was the last ever captain of Newton Heath Football Club and the first ever captain of Manchester United.

The new look United side took to the pitch to play Gainsborough Trinity wearing their brand new red shirts replacing the famous green and gold halves worn by Newton Heath Lancashire and Yorkshire Railway Football Club from their formation in 1878 at the local Wagon Works at the railway yard in Newton Heath, as follows James Whitehouse, Harry Stafford (capt), Thomas Read, William Morgan, William Griffiths, Walter Cartwright, Charles Richards, Ernest Pegg, Jack Peddie, Frederick Williams, Daniel Hurst. With the exception of Peddie, who was born in Hutchesontown, Glasgow, it was an all-English born side.

The game was played before 4,000 fans and ended 1-0 with the visitors, Manchester United, getting their season off to the perfect start thanks to a goal from Charles 'Chas' Richards who holds the distinction of being the first player to score a goal for Manchester United.

Richards was a one-season wonder for United after joining the newly formed Manchester United in August 1902 from Leicester Fosse. He was what you would call a journeyman of a player having had spells with Gresley Rovers, Newstead Byron, Notts County, Nottingham Forest and Grimsby Town. Richards left United for Doncaster Rovers in March 1903 having played 11 times and scoring two goals. He also scored in United's 7-0 victory over Accrington Stanley on 1 November 1902 in the Third Qualifying Round of the FA Cup.

Gainsborough Trinity Football Club was formed in 1873 as Trinity Recreationists, set up by the vicar of the Holy Trinity Church for young parishioners. In 1889, they became members of the Midland Counties League, losing their first match 2-1 to Lincoln City and going on to finish 7th out of 11 clubs. The club quickly became well known, and won their first Midland

League championship in 1890-91 and, after finishing runners-up in the Midland League in season 1895-96, were elected to the Football League Second Division.

Ironically Gainsborough Trinity's first ever Football League match was against Newton Heath Football Cub. The Second Division game was played on 1 September 1896 at The Heathens' Bank Street ground with the home side running out 2-0 winners (scorer: James McNaught two). Gainsborough Trinity held on to their place in Division Two but, based in an area with a small population, it was always a struggle and the club returned to the Midland League in 1912. Here they were to settle and earn more success, winning the Midland Championship in 1927-28, 1948-49 and 1966-67, also finishing runners-up twice.

Did You Know That?

IN 1902, THE novel *A True Story* by Lucian was published. The story of Newton Heath becoming Manchester United is not only a true story, it is history.

ALEX FERGUSON'S FUTURE AS UNITED BOSS WAS NEVER IN DOUBT

On 6 November 1986, the Manchester United Board of Directors appointed Alex Ferguson as the new manager of the club following the sacking of Ron Atkinson. Alexander Chapman Ferguson left the comfortable throne he had made for himself at Aberdeen

Football Club to become the sixth man since the retirement of Sir Matt Busby to restore the glory days at Old Trafford. United had not won the English First Division Championship crown since season 1966-67 and had not lifted a European trophy since they beat SL Benfica 4-1 after extra-time in the 1968 European Cup final at Wembley Stadium. Ferguson's first three seasons in the United hot seat were uneventful, with a highest league placing of runners-up spot in season 1987-88, reaching Round 6 of the FA Cup in 1988-89 and Round 5 of the League Cup in 1987-88. When United only won two of their opening eight league games in season 1989-90, drew two and lost four, scoring 13 and conceding 15, his tenure at the club looked to be hanging in the balance. At one game a United fan unveiled a homemade banner which read, *Ta Ra Fergie*.

Manchester City's 5-1 mauling of United at Maine Road on 23 September 1989, was all the ammunition the press needed to call for Ferguson's head. After the opening eight games of season 1988-89, United were 17th in the table (22 teams) and the players were collectively struggling to find a decent run of form. The fans felt humiliated, let down by the players after the Manchester Derby defeat. Bragging rights in the city were all so important to both halves of the Blue and Red divide. It meant a fan of either colour walking into work the day after the game with their head held imperiously high, chest puffed out like a peacock in pre-mating mood, and hoping to catch an envious glance from a co-worker who was feeling down in the dumps following his side's defeat in the most important game of the season.

But, despite United's lacklustre start to the 1989-90 season, there was no doubting Ferguson's pedigree as a manager who could land trophies. He was a very strict disciplinarian with his Dons (Aberdeen players) who nicknamed him 'Furious Fergie'. He actually fined his star striker John Hewitt, who scored the winning goal (112 minutes) in Aberdeen's historic 2-1 win over Real Madrid after extra-time in the 1983 European Cup Winners' Cup final, £20.00 after his star striker overtook him in his car on the road after a training session. But he was unquestionably, The Don at Aberdeen. When he arrived at Old Trafford, he made no secret of the fact that he thought there was an unhealthy drinking culture prevalent among some of the star players, with Paul McGrath, Norman Whiteside and the club captain, Bryan Robson, on his radar. The two Irish internationals were not part of Fergie's plans and he sold both; McGrath went to Aston Villa, and Big Norman moved to Everton.

Although he was the Old Trafford Board of Directors' first choice to replace Atkinson, Ferguson almost did not become the manager of Manchester United. When the club enquired about his availability, he was not only the manager of Aberdeen, he was also Scotland's manager who was in charge of the national squad at the 1986 FIFA World Cup finals, following the death of the legendary Jock Stein on 10 September 1985, after guiding Scotland to a place at the finals in Mexico. The media were reporting that the 44-year-old Ferguson would be offered the job as Scotland manager on a permanent basis and succeed Jock Stein. In March 1986, Ferguson was offered the job as manager of Tottenham Hotspur after Peter Shreeves was sacked but politely declined the London club's advances and the job went to David Pleat instead. That same month Don Howe resigned as Arsenal manager but Ferguson also rejected the advances of

The Gunners, which saw ex- Manchester United player George Graham (1972-75, 46 games, two goals), become the new boss of the London club. Who knows? Perhaps Ferguson was waiting on a call from Martin Edwards, the Chairman of Manchester United, as the United board was reportedly still extremely unhappy with Atkinson following United's 10 game unbeaten run at the start of the 1985-86 season only for the club to end the campaign in 4th place.

Not many football pundits thought that Ferguson could revitalise a club that was back-peddling and when they visited the City Ground, Nottingham on 7 January 1990 for an FA Cup Third Round tie, United had not won a game in their previous eight (four draws and four defeats). The wise money was on Ferguson to be sacked if Brian Clough's side knocked United out of the FA Cup just as they had done the previous season, a 1-0 loss at Old Trafford in Round 6. There was no doubt that Ferguson was on the brink of his United career. He was standing on the cliff edge staring down the precipice, perhaps thinking why he vacated his throne as the King of Scottish football. If United failed to beat Forest, and thereby save the club's season by winning the FA Cup, many football commentators, and a large number of United fans, considered his position as manager of the club would no longer be tenable. And the curse of trying to follow in the footsteps of the Father of Manchester United, Sir Matt Busby, would be passed on to a seventh would be successor.

However. United got their revenge over Nottingham Forest with a 1-0 win thanks to a goal from their diminutive striker, Mark Robins. Over the following years many articles were written about the game with the vast majority of them asserting that Ferguson would have been sacked had United lost. However, Sir Bobby Charlton always maintained that this would not have happened as the Board of Directors had faith in what Ferguson was trying to do at Old Trafford. They recognised his approach to developing Youth team players instead of asking the board to release money from the club's coffers to buy players who might only serve as a short-term fix. Ferguson may not have been a gypsy palm reader, but he knew a potential star when he saw one; Ryan Giggs is perhaps the greatest ever testimony to this particular attribute which he possessed in abundance. He was football's first wizard, many centuries after Merlin the Wizard advised King Arthur of England, and 15 years before J. K. Rowling entertained cinema goers with *Harry Potter and the Philospher's Stone* in 2001.

Round 4 gave United another away tie when they visited Hereford United on 28 January 1990. In season 1971-72, Hereford United achieved national prominence when, as a Southern League club, they beat First Division Newcastle United 2-1 in a Third Round replay at their Edgar Street home after drawing 2-2 at St James' Park in the first game. A goal from Clayton Blackmore with only four minutes to go gave United a 1-0 victory. And quite spookily, next up for United was Newcastle United at St James' Park on 18 February 1990. It was a pulsating Fifth Round tie which saw United take the lead after 16 minutes when Robins scored. Mark McGhee, who played under Ferguson at Aberdeen from 1979-84, levelled for The Geordies five minutes into the second-half scoring a penalty, but Danny Wallace put United back into the lead on the hour mark. Kevin Scott made it 2-2 in the 65th minute but Brian McClair's goal in the 77th minute sent United into the quarter-finals and kept alive the fans' hopes of the club winning some silverware.

For the fourth time in-a-row, United were drawn away in the competition, this time versus Sheffield United, a game United won 1-0 (scorer: McClair). Four teams went into the hat for the semi-final draw: Crystal Palace, Liverpool, Oldham Athletic and United. On 8 April 1990, Oldham Athletic and United drew an entertaining game 3-3 after extra-time at Maine Road (scorers: Bryan Robson, Neil Webb and Wallace). The replay took place three nights later at the same venue with United winning 2-1 after extra-time with goals from Robins and the United captain, Robson. Ex-United striker Andy Ritchie (1977-80) scored for Oldham Athletic in the game. Meanwhile, Denis Irwin who played in both games for Oldham Athletic would later join United. Crystal Palace caused a major upset defeating Liverpool 4-3 after extra-time just seven months after Liverpool beat them 9-0 at Anfield in the First Division.

On 12 May 1990, Crystal Palace and United were led out of the Wembley tunnel by their respective managers, with a former United hero in charge of Crystal Palace, Steve Coppell (1975-83). The match was a goal feast, ending 3-3 after extra-time with Mark Hughes scoring twice for United and Robson also scoring. When the two sides met for the replay on the evening of 17 May 1990, Ferguson made a dramatic change to his team when he dropped goalkeeper Jim Leighton and replaced him with Les Sealey. Leighton was an Aberdeen player from 1977-88 before Ferguson persuade him to join him at Old Trafford.

Manchester United: Les Sealey, Paul Ince, Lee Martin, Steve Bruce, Gary Pallister, Mike Phelan, Bryan Robson (capt), Neil

Webb, Danny Wallace, Brian McClair, Mark Hughes
Substitutes: Clayton Blackmore, Mark Robins.

Both sets of fans were treated to hearing their team's FA Cup final song prior to kick-off: Manchester United's squad recorded *We Will Stand Together* for the final, whilst the Crystal Palace players recorded a version of the club's anthem *Glad All Over*.

But it was the United players who were glad all over when the final whistle went after Lee Martin scored the only goal of the match in the 59th minute to give United a 1-0 win and their seventh FA Cup final win (1909, 1948, 1963, 1977, 1983 and 1985). It was Crystal Palace's first FA Cup final and Martin's second and last goal for the club in 109 games (1987-94).

Ferguson became the first manager to lead a team to victory in both the English and Scottish Cup finals (Aberdeen 1982, 1983, 1984 and 1986), an achievement matched by Brendan Rodgers in 2021 when he led Leicester City to FA Cup glory (Glasgow Celtic 2017 and 2018).

Did You Know That?

IN FEBRUARY 1982, Alex Ferguson was approached by Wolverhampton Wanderers with a view to him succeeding John Barnwell as the manager of the club. Wolves were on a downward spiral at the time and were the bookmakers' favourites to be relegated from the First Division. Ferguson rejected the West Midlands' club advances, perhaps concerned that the famous club, three times First Division champions, four times FA Cup winners and two times winners of the League Cup, were more than £2 million in debt. Wolves finished the 1981-82 season rock bottom of the table. And, at the end of the 1984–85 season, it was reported that Ferguson was seriously being considered for the position as the new manager of Liverpool after Joe Fagan announced his retirement. However, Kenny Dalglish accepted an offer to become their player/manager.

A PHOENIX RISES FROM THE ASHES

As John Steinbeck, the great American writer and winner of the 1962 Nobel Prize for Literature for his realistic and imaginative writings, combining as they do sympathetic humour and keen social perception, once said, 'It's so much darker when a light goes out than it would have been if it had never shone'.

In the history of English football, the Busby Babes shone brighter than any other team before them or since. Steinbeck's quote encapsulated the feelings of all Manchester United fans on 6 February 1958, when the Munich Air Disaster claimed the lives of 8 young Manchester United players, the nucleus of a side affectionately known by all football fans as 'The Busby Babes'.

The entire football world mourned their loss but only Manchester United fans could celebrate them. This was a time when there was intense rivalry between clubs, as opposed to the intense hatred towards other clubs which has seeped into the veins of football fans today. It was a time when fans regardless of their club affiliation appreciated the fact that a young player had made it through the junior ranks at a club and burst on to the big scene to begin a career as a professional footballer. There wasn't the vitriol which permeates the game today because players used the football pitch as their platform to express their talent, not a social media post to help inflate their own bursting ego.

If Matt Busby had witnessed any of his players openly seek public attention, he would have put them firmly in their box, and that box would be the 18-yard area of an opposing team in a Reserve team game. And like a Jack-in-the-Box, the offending player would not be allowed out of it until he had taken full responsibility for his mistake, apologised to his teammates, to his coaching staff, and to his manager for thinking he was a legend in his own mind. Perhaps the one exception under Busby's reign as Manchester United manager was The Belfast Boy, George Best, but then again George did not have to approach the media to promote his ego or standing in world football. George expressed his artistry on the field of play, his actions with a football at his feet spoke more than any words or photos in the tabloid press could ever describe, and as for the media, well they were never that far away from him, with many British newspapers employing their own in-house paparazzi whose sole responsibility was to photograph the world's most famous footballer wherever he went. And, on many occasions, especially when the young handsome Irishman was dating a Miss World, George's off the field activities were enough to produce his own 'Encyclopaedia Bestanica'.

But to the credit of every Busby Babe, seeking adulation from outside the confines of their second home, for many of them their first home was Old Trafford, by contacting the media to promote their career was simply an anathema to their upbringing under the shrewd guidance of their mentor, Jimmy Murphy. They were a Busby Babe, a description thousands of teenagers up and down the country would have loved to be associated with them. They were signed by Manchester United when they left school for one reason and one reason only, and that was because Messrs Busby and Murphy had the utmost confidence in the young boy's ability.

In season 1956-57, United narrowly missed out on becoming the first English side in the 20th century to win the coveted, and highly prized Double of First Division Championship and FA Cup. Their coronation as league champions was achieved at a canter, winning the title by eight points over Tottenham Hotspur, scoring 103 goals and conceding 54 (Spurs scored 104 and let in 56). But they fell at the last hurdle, losing the 1957 FA Cup final 2-1 to Aston Villa at Wembley Stadium (scorer: Tommy Taylor). It would have been a mammoth achievement had United lifted both trophies given the fact that they went into the FA Cup final having played eight games more than their opponents. Villa's longest away trip of the season was their 241 miles journey to play Newcastle United and the only time they left English soil was to play Cardiff City away in Wales, a mere 123 miles from Birmingham.

When Chelsea won the 1955-56 First Division Championship they were invited by *L'Equipe* magazine, the tournament's organisers, to participate in the inaugural European Cup competition the following season. But following pressure levied on them by the Football League, including the threat of penalties in the shape of a points deductions if they did not adhere strictly to their 42 game league campaign, the London club buckled and declined the offer to test themselves against the champions of other European Leagues. When Manchester United were sent a similar offer in the summer of 1956 after being crowned champions of England, their forward thinking manager, Matt

Busby, told his Chairman, Harold Hardman, to accept the invitation, which he did, much to the annoyance of the hierarchy of English football. So, in season 1956-57, in addition to their 42 league games and six FA Cup games, United also played eight games in the European Cup, all midweek.

Villa's road trip to the North East of England on 20 April 1957, when they beat Newcastle United 2-1 at St James' Park, seemed like a jaunt compared to United's travels which included a 241 miles journey to play Portsmouth at Fratton Park, a 437 miles flight to Belgium to face RSC Anderlecht, a 586 miles journey to play Borussia Dortmund in West Germany, a 1,047 miles journey to Bilbao, Spain where they played Athletic Bilbao in the European Cup quarter-finals and rounded off with a 2,526 miles roundtrip to the Spanish capital, Madrid, to pit themselves against the reigning European Cup holders, Real Madrid, in the semi-finals of the newly established competition. Perhaps all of the travelling finally caught up on the United players, or perhaps the expectations placed on their shoulders to win the Double was just too heavy a weight to carry, and they succumbed to Aston Villa on the day. A case of so near, yet so far.

Matt Busby enjoyed his team's European Odyssey and when United claimed back-to-back First Division Championship titles in season 1956-57, he told his secretary that if a letter arrived with the crest and address of the Football League on it, to put it in the bin as it would be another demand from the Football League informing Manchester United Football Club in no uncertain terms that it wholly disapproved of them flying the flag for English clubs in Europe. Fast forward 43 years and the hierarchy of English football, who were so hell bent on trying to stop United in their tracks in the mid-1950's, were practically begging United to fly the flag for England in the inaugural FIFA World Club Championship in season 1999-2000. At stake was England's bid to host the FIFA World Cup finals in 2006 for the first time since they were crowned the World Champions 40 years previously at Wembley Stadium on 30 July 1966 with three United players in their squad (Bobby Charlton, John Connelly and Nobby Stiles). England played host to the 1996 European Championship finals but in comparison to the World Cup it was like the Football League Cup being compared to the UEFA Champions League.

United were hesitant at first about accepting FIFA's offer to play in the tournament which was being hosted by Brazil from 5-14 January 2000. It would mean being away from Manchester for three weeks, which included a 12 hours flight covering 5,823 miles plus time to acclimatise to the heat of Rio de Janeiro and Sao Paulo, the two venues for matches. Fixture congestion was a major issue for United meaning they would miss three Premier League games and at least one FA Cup game. However, when the Football Association told United they would be allowed to opt out of the FA Cup and that they would accommodate United when it came to re-arranging missed Premier League games, United did what no other reigning FA Cup holders had ever done before in the 118 year history of the FA Cup and opted out of defending the trophy and withdrew their participation in it. The Government were also involved in the decision making process as it wanted England's bid to succeed. So, at the request from the upper echelons of the English game, the Football Association, an organisation Sir Matt Busby treated with disdain, Sir Alex

Ferguson and Manchester United traded world football's oldest domestic competition – it was first played for in 1871-72 – for FIFA's new baby, the FIFA World Club Championship. The tournament was a disaster for United who failed to qualify from their group which was won by Brazil's Vasco da Gama who went on to lose the final to their bitter rivals in the Campeonato Brasileiro Serie A (the Brazilian Premier League), Corinthians. The only thing United players came home with was a suntan, a bag of duty free goodies and the thought of a few midweek games to play catch-up on their rivals for the race for the Premier League title.

Needless to say, in season 1957-58 Busby could not wait to see how his 'Babes' would fare once more against Europe's elite clubs. The previous season's European adventures had merely whet his appetite and all-consuming desire to make his club, Manchester United, the best team in Europe. But Busby knew fixture congestion could once again hinder United's chances of completing the unprecedented clean sweep of First Division, FA Cup and European Cup. Even the mighty Real Madrid were unable to bag all three equivalent trophies in the same season. In the inaugural European Cup campaign, season 1955-56, Real Madrid were crowned the first ever champions of Europe, or as etched on the famous trophy, 'Coupe des Clubs Champions Européens'. But their exploits in Europe took their toll on their domestic campaign when they could only finish third in La Liga (Athletic Bilbao won their sixth title) and they also lost 5-4 on aggregate over two legs in the semi-finals of the Copa del Rey (Spanish FA Cup). The following season, 1956-57, after beating United 5-3 over two legs in the semi-finals of the European Cup they defeated Italy's ASF Fiorentina 2-0 in the 1957 European Cup final at their home ground, Estadio Santiago Bernabeu. That season they reclaimed the La Liga title but in the Copa del Rey they were completely embarrassed after being thrashed 8-3 over two legs by the eventual winners, FC Barcelona.

However, the United Boss was confident that his squad of three goalkeepers, six full-backs, seven half-backs, four wingers and four strikers could meet the challenges that lay ahead. And, Busby also had at his disposal something that no other manager had, the best Youth team in England. In season 1956-57, the Manchester United Junior Athletic Club, their Youth team, won their fifth consecutive FA Youth Cup final since the inception of the competition in season 1952-53 with a team captained by Duncan Edwards, along with Gordon Clayton, Bruce Fulton, Paddy Kennedy, Ronald Cope, Eddie Colman, Noel McFarlane, Liam Whelan, Albert Scanlon, Eddie Lewis and David Pegg. Edwards, Colman, Whelan and Pegg all collected First Division winners' medals and FA Cup runners-up medals with United in season 1956-57.

Things did not go United's way in the league in season 1957-58 but in the FA Cup and European Cup they were flying high. By the time the FA Cup Third Round came along, 4 January 1958, United had already qualified for the quarter-finals of the European Cup with the first leg versus Red Star Belgrade to be played at Old Trafford on 14 January 1958, followed by a 2,364 miles round flight to the Yugoslav capital three weeks later, 5 February 1958, for the second leg. United beat Workington 3-1 at Borough Park, Workington in the FA Cup Third Round with a hat-trick from Dennis Viollet. On 25 January 1958, United beat Ipswich Town 2-0 in Round 4 with Bobby Charlton scoring twice. Busby played the same side in both games: Harry Gregg, Bill Foulkes, Roger Byrne, Mark Jones, Duncan Edwards, Eddie Colman, Kenny Morgans, Bobby Charlton, Albert Scanlon, Tommy Taylor and Dennis Viollet. Busby was not a manager for tinkering with his team.

United beat the Yugoslavian Champions 2-1 in the first leg with goals from Charlton and Colman. A 3-3 draw in Belgrade was good enough to send United into the semi-finals of the European Cup for the second successive season (scorers: Charlton 2 and Viollet). However, the next day, 6 February 1958, the plane carrying the United team, officials, press, some other passengers and six crew members crashed at Munich-Riem Airport, West Germany where it had stopped off to refuel en route from Belgrade to Manchester. The crash claimed the lives of 21 of the 44 people onboard, eight of them Manchester United players, with 21 survivors of which 19 were injured, some quite severely. United were due to play Wolverhampton Wanderers, the league leaders, two days later, 8 February 1958, but the game was postponed as a mark of respect for those who perished in Munich. The following Saturday, 15 February 1958, was FA Cup Round 5 day but again the match against Sheffield Wednesday was postponed. The club had the pressing matter of attending funerals and caring for the injured players and officials to worry about more than fulfilling a fixture commitment.

Thirteen days after the Munich Air Disaster, United steadied themselves to recommence their season and played Sheffield Wednesday on 19 February 1958 at Old Trafford in Round 5 of the FA Cup. Matt Busby was still lying in his hospital bed in the

Rechts der Isar Hospital in the Haidhausen district of Munich, West Germany recovering from his horrific injuries. Duncan Edwards was also a patient at the hospital and would have been the first name Busby put on his team sheet to play. Busby's right-hand man, Jimmy Murphy, who was not on the flight, was given the arduous task of running the club and consoling the families of the seven United players who died instantly in the Munich Air Disaster: Geoff Bent, Roger Byrne, Eddie Colman, Mark Jones, David Pegg, Tommy Taylor and Liam Whelan. It was all the harder for Murphy to cope with because in addition to his role as the Manchester United Assistant Manager, he was also the manager of United's Youth Team and six of the seven players who died instantly in the crash were developed by him in the club's nursery. The one exception was Tommy Taylor who United bought from Barnsley for £29,999 in March 1951.

On the morning of 19 February 1958, Murphy had to somehow set his grief temporarily to one side having lost 'his boys' and look around the club to see if he could put a team together to play Sheffield Wednesday. Just 18 days earlier, 1 February 1958, he sat beside Busby in the dugout at Arsenal Stadium and purred with delight when he watched many of the players he developed as trainees at the club beat Arsenal 5-4 in the First Division, The Busby Babes' last ever game on English soil (scorers: Taylor 2, Charlton, Edwards and Viollet).

The next time Murphy saw his Boys together was when the seven coffins containing their bodies were placed side-by-side in a dimly lit gymnasium at Old Trafford which served as a temporary morgue. In the darkness Murphy could take a walk among his Boys, his very own shining stars, one last time, whispering his thoughts to each one of them as he stood over their coffins. The Munich Air Disaster was one of football's darkest days but it brought the people of Manchester together as one. United and City fans bonded, their local rivalry put to one side, in memory of lost loved ones which also included a former Manchester City player, Frank Swift. Swift played for City for his entire football career, 1933-39, and when he retired from the game he began a new career becoming a sports journalist for the News of the World newspaper. He died aged 44 in Munich having travelled to Belgrade to report on United's match against Red Star Belgrade.

The Italian club, Torino, knew what it felt like to lose a team full of so much promise. On 4 May 1949, the 'Superga Air Disaster' occurred when an Avio Linee Italiane (Italian Airlines) Fiat G.212 airplane carrying the entire AS Torino football team crashed into the retaining wall at the back of the Basilica of Superaga, which is situated on a hill on the outskirts of Turin. All 31 onboard lost their lives. The team was flying home from a friendly versus SL Benfica in Lisbon, with the crash attributed to dense fog and spatial disorientation as a result of a faulty altimeter in the cockpit of the aircraft. The team were dubbed 'Grande Torino' and were Italy's best team during the decade having won Serie A (Italian First Division Championship) five times (1942-43, 1945-46, 1946-47, 1947-48 and 1948-49) and the Coppa Italia (Italian FA Cup) in their 1942-43 Double winning season.

For Murphy to select a team to field for the game was like trying to complete a jigsaw but knowing that you did not have all of the pieces you needed. Two of the survivors from the Munich Air Disaster, Bill Foulkes and Harry Gregg, knocked on the door of the manager's office at Old Trafford, Murphy's new home for the next three months, and told their new Boss that they wanted to play. It was the least they thought they could do to honour the memory of their fallen teammates whose funerals they attended and perhaps help to wipe away their tears, even it was for only 90 minutes of football.

Murphy did not have a team sheet, more a scrap of paper on which he scrambled down the names of the 11 players which he gave to the referee, Mr A. Bond (London), within minutes of the kick-off. Indeed, in the *United Review* (the match programme) that evening where once you would find the names of the players of the two teams playing, the top of the middle spread where the United team would normally be listed, was left blank. Quite poignantly the title of this particular *United Review* read: UNITED WILL GO ON..."

The team Murphy selected for the game was: Harry Gregg, Bill Foulkes (capt), Ian Greaves, Ronald Cope, Stan Crowther, Frederick Goodwin, Colin Webster, Ernie Taylor, Shay Brennan, Alex Dawson, Mark Pearson. Needless to say, they had never played together before and four of them were actually making their debut for the club: Brennan (age 20), Crowther (age 22), Pearson (age 18) and Ernie Taylor (age 32) who joined United from Blackpool in an £8,000 transfer deal a week before the game.

Imagine playing an important game like an FA Cup Fifth Round tie with a relatively inexperienced side, with almost half of them pulling on the United shirt for the very first time. Well, that was the predicament Murphy found himself in. Aside from Foulkes, Gregg and the four debutants, the other five players had only made a combined total of exactly 100 appearances for United: Greaves 19, Goodwin 25, Cope 2 two, Dawson four and Webster 50. In stark contrast, Albert Quixall, the Sheffield Wednesday captain, had played more than 200 times for The Owls. Aston Villa's Stan Crowther and his manager, Eric Houghton, drove to Manchester to watch the game, or so Crowther thought. But Houghton thought his tough wing half could help United out in their hour of need. Despite being cup-tied having already played for Villa in the two previous rounds, the Football Association granted United a special dispensation to sign Crowther for £18,000 just one hour before the game started. The canny Houghton had even visited the Aston Villa boot room before making the journey to Manchester and put Crowther's football boots in the back of his car. Crowther had starred for Aston Villa in the 1957 FA Cup final when he and his teammates stopped United from clinching the Double.

A crowd of 59,848 went to Old Trafford to see how their club and the players that were still left at it would deal with the aftermath of what happened less than two weeks earlier on a slush covered runway in Munich. It was an emotionally charged night for all involved, on and off the pitch. The players from both clubs wore black armbands as a mark of respect to those who were no longer with them and a minute's silence was impeccably observed before the kick-off just as it had been at many grounds up and down the length of the country post the disaster. The Busby Babes weren't just Manchester's team, they were England's team, their champions, the best team in the land who were seeking to conquer Europe and a team every kid growing up wanted to be part of.

The wave of emotion and outpouring of sympathy which rained

down on the United players from all four stands swept them to a 3-0 victory with one of the new kids, Brennan, scoring twice and a goal from Dawson, his fourth in his first five games for United. Brennan was actually a right-back but with limited options in his attack, Murphy played him as an inside right against The Owls. Two days after the game, Duncan Edwards succumbed to his serious injuries.

United made it all the way to Wembley Stadium to contest the 1958 FA Cup final but lost 2-0 to Bolton Wanderers. Murphy led the team out of the tunnel whilst Matt Busby took a seat on the bench as he was still recuperating. This was the beginning of a new era, a new chapter in the illustrious history of Manchester United. A Phoenix had risen from the ashes.

Did You Know That?

IN SEPTEMBER 1958, Matt Busby brought Albert Quixall to Old Trafford from Sheffield Wednesday for what was a new British record transfer fee at the time of £45,000. Busby, who had recovered from his own injuries, set about building his third great Manchester United side. His dream of making United the best club in Europe still burnt deep inside of him. Thirteen years after the Sheffield Wednesday game in which the players wore black armbands, Manchester United introduced black into their first team kit, black socks, on a permanent basis and it has remained there ever since. Between October 1960 and April 1963, the socks were white with the traditional red shirt and white shorts. In May 1963, red socks were introduced and remained part of the first team home strip until the end of the 1970-71 season. Season 1971-72 heralded in the iconic black socks with two red bars at the top of them sandwiched by white in the middle.

PART 9

CLUB SUED BY THE PRESIDENT

BABES IN THE WOOD

FERGIE RIDES THE SINGLES CHARTS

PUB FOOTBALL

A FIRST PENALTY SHOOT-OUT

VIV AND GARRY

BABES IN THE WOOD

On 12 October 1957, Nottingham Forest opened their new East Stand at their City Ground home in Nottingham. The newly constructed stand cost £40,000 to build and seated 2,500 fans. Billy Walker, the Forest manager, and his Board of Directors could not have wished for a better opponent to christen the new stand when Manchester United visited Nottingham for First Division match. Matt Busby's young Manchester United side were the pride of English football, the reigning First Division champions and were playing in their second consecutive season in the European Cup.

One of the top movies in 1957, was *Gunfight at the O.K. Corral*, but despite the appeal of Kirk Douglas and Burt Lancaster in this Hollywood blockbuster, their appeal to movie goers paled into significance to the appeal of the famous Busby Babes. They did not entertain fans for a single show of 90 minutes, they wooed fans every time they appeared on a pitch with their swashbuckling style of play which even Nottingham's most famous son, Robin Hood, a highly skilled archer and swordsman, could not match. And when Manchester United visited your city or town, a gunfight was ensured.

Indeed, such was the appeal of the Busby Babes, United's visit to the City Ground set Nottingham Forest's record home attendance at the time of 47,804 fans.

Prior to their visit to football's equivalent of Sherwood Forest, United had played 11 league games, winning seven, including a 4-1 thumping of Manchester City at Old Trafford and a similar home result against Aston Villa. Busby's team had accumulated 28 goals and had conceded 17. The Busby Babes would never become a team that would be given the prestige of being referred to as 'Invincibles,' like the legendary Preston North End side who won the inaugural First Division Championship in 1888-89 and the FA Cup the same season without losing a single game. Preston North End won 18 and drew four of their league games to win the title with 40 points, Aston Villa were runners-up on 29 points.

Busby's mantra, indeed his football philosophy, was the same for every game regardless of the opposition. He simply told his players before a game and during the half-time break, that no matter what the score was, or how many goals their opponents had scored, and may yet score, he had the utmost faith in them to score at least one more goal than the opposition by the time the referee blew for time. Busby very rarely sent a team out to play it tight at the back for the first 15 minutes or so and then gradually ease their way into a game. Although, admittedly he did try and do this on 9 March 1966 in Lisbon, Portugal. United were in the Portuguese capital to play SL Benfica in the second leg of their European Cup quarter-final tie holding a quite slender 3-2 lead from the first leg at Old Trafford. The reigning Champions of Portugal, winners of the European Cup in 1961 and 1962, were among the most feared sides in European club football during the 1960s and had never lost a game in European competition at their Stadium of Light home. Added to this, when United met them, they had the 1965 Ballon d'Or winner in their team, Eusebio. Thankfully, one of Busby's greatest ever Babes paid no attention to his manager's pre-game talk on a balmy night in Lisbon and ignored his express instructions to be defensive from the kick-off by scoring twice inside the first 15 minutes to give United the advantage in the tie. His name was George Best and he helped United to a famous 5-1 victory, and Busby would not be the only United manager the young boy from Belfast would not obey.

Busby always wanted his side to entertain the fans but was fiercely opposed to any of his players showboating, although there was very little he could do about Best who looked like he was showing off every time the ball touched his feet, such was the young Northern Ireland international's artistry and genius. At his peak, George was the ultimate Showman and the fans loved him for it. Sir Winston Churchill once famously said, 'Russia is a riddle wrapped in a mystery inside an enigma'. Best was all of this and more. In Greek mythology a Pandora's Box released physical and emotional curses upon mankind. To United fans, George Best was a real-life God, who physically tortured opponents who were left cursing him as he left them in his wake and if any player was trying to get too rough with him, George went back for more and humiliated the player who dared to cause him injury. As his great friend and teammate

Paddy Crerand once said, 'George had twisted blood.'

Busby openly encouraged his teams to attack from the back by going through the midfield and up to the attack. And, on the odd occasion when the opposition had the ball, it was the role of his frontmen to be the first line of defence. Football fans everywhere loved the Babes' style of play and only wished their team could be a mirror image of the young men from Manchester.

In fact, Matt Busby's side were so good a song was released about them in 1957 by Edric Connor entitled *United Calypso*. The lyrics to the famous song are:

> *Oh Manchester, Manchester United,*
> *A bunch of bouncing Busby Babes,*
> *They deserved to be knighted,*
> *Whenever they're playing in your town,*
> *Be sure to get to that football ground,*
> *Take a lesson, come and see,*
> *Football taught by Matt Busby,*
> *Oh Manchester, Manchester United,*
> *A bunch of bouncing Busby Babes,*
> *They deserved to be knighted,*
> *Whenever they're playing in your town,*
> *Be sure to get to that football ground,*
> *Take a lesson, come and see*
> *Football taught by Matt Busby*

Connor's song title was so apt to describe Manchester United because the name 'Calypso' derives from the Ancient Greek meaning 'to cover,' 'to conceal' or 'to hide'. In Greek mythology

Calypso means 'she who conceals'. There was no mythology about Manchester United when they visited the City Ground to play Nottingham Forest, they were the real deal, 27 years before boxer Evander Holyfield, nicknamed 'The Real Deal', won the gold medal in the Light Heavyweight division in boxing at the 1984 Olympic Games hosted by Los Angeles.

And so, back to the Nottingham Forest match. Ironically, the Busby Babes were being protected by a wood at the time, as Ray Wood was their goalkeeper. The home side were no match for United's young, but experienced side captained by the 28-year-old English international right-back, Roger Byrne. Roger was only a few years older than many of his teammates but he was their undisputed leader, moving United up-field like an Army General homing in on their opponents in battle. Liam Whelan, aged 22, a Republic of Ireland international winger put United 1-0 up before all of the spectators in the new stand had taken their seats, scoring in the third minute of play. Stuart Imlach brought the home side level two minutes after the interval but United just moved up another notch with Dennis Viollet scoring the winning goal of a 2-1 victory in the 53rd minute.

Only three of United's team were not Busby Babes, having commenced their careers with other clubs: Ray Wood was purchased from Darlington, Johnny Berry was signed from Birmingham City and Tommy Taylor was brought in from Barnsley. The remaining eight, an unlucky figure as it later turned out to be when eight Busby Babes lost their young lives in the Munich Air Disaster less than four months later. Roger Byrne, Bill Foulkes, Jackie Blanchflower, Duncan Edwards, Eddie Colman, Liam Whelan, David Pegg and Dennis Viollet all starred in the win at the City Ground. Sadly, Taylor, Byrne, Edwards, Colman, Whelan and Pegg all perished in the crash whilst Berry and Blanchflower never kicked a ball again such was the severity of the injuries they had sustained. Geoff Bent and Mark Jones also lost their lives on that fateful day in Munich.

In 1932, Walt Disney released an animated version of the *Babes in the Wood* traditional English children's tale. On 12 October 1957, the real Babes in the Wood visited the City Ground, Nottingham and unlike the babes in the story, the United players came away unscathed.

Did You Know That?

NOTTINGHAM FOREST IS the only club to have won the European Cup/UEFA Champions League more times than they have been champions of their own country. Brian Clough's superb Forest side won their only First Division Championship (now called the Premier League) title in season 1977-78. As champions of England, they participated in the European Cup in season 1978-79 and beat Liverpool, the holders, 2-0 over two legs in their Round of 32 tie, en route to defeating Sweden's Malmö FF 1-0 in the final in Munich. Forest finished runner-up to Liverpool in the 1978-79 First Division Championship race but automatically qualified for the European Cup the following season as holders of the trophy. On 28 May 1980, Forest and Clough retained the European Cup after beating the West German side, Hamburg, 1-0 in the final played in Rome. As for the scousers, they got hammered 4-2 over two legs in the First Round by Dinamo Tblisi. Two future United players were in both of Nottingham Forest's European Cup winning teams, Viv Anderson and Garry Birtles.

PUB FOOTBALL

On 5 August 1970, Manchester United made history by taking part in the first ever penalty shootout in a professional game in English football.

In the summer of 1970, The Watney Cup became the first sponsored competition in English football. Officially known as the Watney Mann Invitation Cup, though it was known simply as the Watney Cup, was the first domestic cup competition to bear the name of a sponsor, Watney Mann being a brewer of popular beer (the brewery's Red Barrel beer). The tournament was contested by two teams from each of the top four divisions in English football, with qualification based on the most number of goals scored by a club in the previous league season, provided that the club did not qualify for one of Europe's three club competitions (European Cup, European Cup Winners' Cup and UEFA Cup) or had been promoted from the Second, Third or Fourth Division. Unlike the FA Cup, the tournament's organisers decided that replays would not be played but extra-time would be enforced if required and if the score was still level after 120 minutes, then the tie would be decided by a penalty shootout. The final was a one leg tie which was played at the home ground of one of the two finalists.

Such was the interest in the tournament, it was televised live. Each club received an equal share of the gate receipts and TV revenue, as well as £4,000 for entering the competition. Another £500 went to each First Round winners, £500 more for a victory in the semi-finals and £1,000 for the winners. The Football League and the Football Association shared £50,000 from the sponsors.

The 1970 Watney Cup tournament was contested by Derby County and Manchester United from the top flight who had finished the 1969-70 season – Everton were crowned champions – in fourth and eighth place respectively. Wilf McGuinness had just spent his first season in charge of Manchester United, the club he signed for as a trainee in January 1953 aged 15, signed professional for on 25 October 1954, the day of his 17th birthday, and who he played 85 times for, scoring two goals from 1955-60.

The Division Two representatives were Sheffield United and Hull City, finishing their league campaigns in sixth and thirteenth position, with Huddersfield Town crowned champions. Leyton Orient won Division Three but their representatives were fourth placed Fulham and eighth placed Reading. The last two places were filled by Aldershot (sixth place in the table) and Peterborough United who ended the 1969-70 season two places behind them in Division Four which was won by Chesterfield.

In Round 1 of the inaugural Watney Cup, which was effectively the quarter-finals as there was only eight participants, Aldershot lost 6-0 at home to Sheffield United, Derby County beat Fulham 5-3 away after extra-time, Peterborough United lost 4-0 at home to Hull City and United beat Reading 3-2 away (scorers: Bobby Charlton 2 and Paul Edwards). The draw for the semi-finals saw Derby County handed a home tie versus Sheffield United, whilst United were given a 100-mile road trip to East Riding of Yorkshire to play Hull City at their Boothferry Park home.

The Rams (Derby County) beat The Blades (Sheffield United) 1-0 at the Baseball Ground, Derby. However, United looked toothless against Hull City, nicknamed The Tigers, and drew 1-1 after extra-time (scorer: Denis Law). Manchester United won the sudden death penalty shootout 4-3 to progress to the final. George Best became the first player to take a penalty in the inaugural shootout of a domestic English cup competition and scored against Ian McKechnie. Amazingly, Denis Law, the man who scored for United in the game, a player who rarely missed an opportunity presented to him in the opposition's box, missed his spot kick which was saved by McKechnie. The Lawman became the first player to miss a penalty in a domestic English cup competition. However, McKechnie later blotted his copybook by missing the vital spot kick that saw Manchester United progress to the final.

On 8 August 1970, Derby County beat Manchester United 4-1 in the inaugural Watney Cup final at their Baseball Ground home. George Best scored United's goal. Derby County's win over United in the 1970 Watney Cup final was the first trophy won by the legendary Brian Clough as a manager. United took the competition seriously and fielded the following side versus The Rams: Alex Stepney, Paul Edwards, Tony Dunne, Pat Crerand, Ian Ure, David Sadler, Willie Morgan (sub: Nobby Stiles), Denis Law (sub: John Fitzpatrick), Bobby Charlton, Brian Kidd and George Best. Six of the players who played in the 1970 final had won the 1968 European Cup with the club, the exceptions being Edwards, Ure, Morgan, Fitzpatrick and Denis Law who missed the 1968 European Cup final triumph through injury. Derby County made a profit of £13,910 from the tournament before deduction of players' bonuses.

Did You Know That?

MANCHESTER UNITED ENTERED the tournament again the following season, 1971-72, after finishing eighth in Division One but suffered a major embarrassment when they lost 3-1 away to Halifax Town (scorer: Best) in the First Round. It was Frank O'Farrell's first game in charge of Manchester United. In season 1972-73, United finished in 18th place in the First Division, just three places away from suffering the indignity of being relegated, a fate endured by West Bromwich Albion, who finished bottom, and Crystal Palace. However, perhaps chastened by the previous year's humiliation, United became the first, and only, club to refuse an invitation to participate in the tournament. Their place was taken by Sheffield United who had finished the season in 14th position along with fifth placed Wolverhampton Wanderers.

The tournament only lasted four seasons and was won by Colchester United in 1971, Bristol Rovers in 1972 and Stoke City in 1973.

FERGIE AND THE UK SINGLES CHARTS
HIS FIRST SEASON 1986-87

Div 1: 11th.
FA Cup: 4th Round (lost 2–1 at home to Coventry City).
League Cup: 3rd Round replay (lost 4–1 away to Southampton).
Leading goal scorer: Peter Davenport, 16 goals.
DID YOU KNOW THAT? When Alex Ferguson was appointed the manager of Manchester United on 6 November 1986, Nick Berry was enjoying his only No.1 in the UK chart with *Every Loser Wins*.

HIS SECOND SEASON 1987-88

Div 1: Runners-up to Liverpool.
FA Cup: 5th Round (lost 2–1 away to Arsenal).
League Cup: 5th Round (lost 2–0 away to Oxford United).
Leading goal scorer: Brian McClair, 31 goals.

United finish in the top two of the First Division for the first time in seven years.

DID YOU KNOW THAT? On 14 November 1987, T'Pau claimed the 600th UK No.1 single of all time with *China In Your Hand*, the band's first and only No.1 hit which spent five weeks in the top spot.

HIS THIRD SEASON 1988-89

Div 1: 11th.
FA Cup: 6th Round (lost 1–0 at home to Nottingham Forest).
League Cup: 3rd Round (lost 2–1 away to Wimbledon).
Leading goal scorers: Mark Hughes and Brian McClair, 16 goals.

DID YOU KNOW THAT? Cliff Richard had the 1988 Christmas UK No.1 single with *Mistletoe & Wine*, his 12th No.1 hit and his first solo No.1 for nine years.

HIS FOURTH SEASON 1989-90
(HIS FIRST TROPHY)

Div 1: 13th.
FA Cup: Winners (defeated Crystal Palace 1–0 in a replay at Wembley).
League Cup: 3rd Round (lost 3–0 at home to Tottenham Hotspur).
Leading goal scorer: Mark Hughes, 15 goals.

DID YOU KNOW THAT? When United won the FA Cup on 17 May 1990, Adamski was enjoying his only UK No.1 single with the song *Killer*.

HIS FIFTH SEASON 1990-91 (EUROPEAN WINNERS)

Div 1: 4th.

FA Cup: 5th Round (lost 2–1 away to Norwich City).

League Cup: Finalists (lost 1–0 to Sheffield Wednesday at Wembley).

European Cup Winners' Cup: Winners (defeated Barcelona 2–1 in Rotterdam).

Leading goal scorers: Mark Hughes and Brian McClair, 21 goals.

DID YOU KNOW THAT? When United won the European Cup Winners' Cup on 15 May 1991, Cher was enjoying her second UK No.1 single with the *Shoop Shoop Song*.

HIS SIXTH SEASON 1991-92

Div 1: Runners-up to Leeds United.

FA Cup: 4th Round (drew 2–2 with Southampton at home in a replay before losing on 4–2 penalties).

League Cup: Winners (defeated Nottingham Forest 1–0 at Wembley).

European Cup Winners' Cup: 2nd Round (lost 4–1 on aggregate to Atletico Madrid).

UEFA Super Cup: Winners (defeated Red Star Belgrade 1–0 at Old Trafford).

Leading goal scorer: Brian McClair, 25 goals.

DID YOU KNOW THAT? When United won the League Cup on 12 April 1992, Shakespears Sister were enjoying their only UK No.1 single with the song *Stay*.

HIS SEVENTH SEASON 1992-93
(CHAMPIONS)

Premier League: Champions.
FA Cup: 5th Round (lost 3–1 away to Sheffield United).
League Cup: 3rd Round (lost 1–0 away to Aston Villa).
UEFA Cup: 1st Round (lost 4–3 on penalties after 0–0 aggregate draw with Torpedo Moscow).
Leading goal scorer: Mark Hughes, 16 goals.

In season 1992–93, United lifted the FA Premier League, their first championship in 26 years, thereby removing at least one albatross from around the neck of Alex Ferguson. United won 24 of their 42 league games to edge past Aston Villa and Norwich City in a hard-fought inaugural campaign.

DID YOU KNOW THAT? When United were presented with the inaugural Premier League Championship trophy at Old Trafford on 3 May 1993, George Michael with Queen and Lisa Stansfield occupied the No.1 spot in the UK chart with their Five Vive EP, the main track of which was the Queen single *Somebody To Love*. However, it was another Queen favourite which was belted out of Old Trafford's PA system that evening and summed up the season – *We Are The Champions*."

HIS EIGHTH SEASON 1993-94
(DOUBLE WINNERS)

Premiership: Champions (two).

FA Cup: Winners (defeated Chelsea 4–0 at Wembley).
League Cup: Finalists (lost 3–1 against Aston Villa at Wembley).
UEFA Champions League: Second Round.
Leading goal scorer: Eric Cantona, 25 goals.

The 1993–94 campaign began with success in the season's curtain-raiser, victory in the FA Charity Shield, and ended with United becoming only the sixth team in history to lift the domestic Double of League and FA Cup. United narrowly missed out on a domestic clean sweep of the trophies when Aston Villa beat them 3–1 at Wembley in the League Cup final.

DID YOU KNOW THAT? When United lifted the Premier League title at Old Trafford for the second successive season on 8 May 1994, Tony di Bart was enjoying his only UK No.1 single with the song *The Real Thing*. Six days later when they beat Chelsea 4-0 in the FA Cup final, the Scottish band Stiltskin were enjoying their only UK No.1 single with the song *Inside*. On 21 May 1994, the Manchester United squad rocketed to the top of the music charts with *Come On You Reds* which remains the club's solo No.1 single.

HIS NINTH SEASON 1994-95
(SO NEAR, YET SO FAR)

Premiership: Runners-up to Blackburn Rovers.
FA Cup: Finalists (lost 1–0 to Everton at Wembley).
League Cup: 3rd Round (lost 2–0 away to Newcastle United).
UEFA Champions League: Group Stages.
Leading goal scorer: Andrei Kanchelskis, 15 goals.

DID YOU KNOW THAT? On 28 October 1995, Coolio featuring LV enjoyed being at No.1 in the UK Singles Charts with *Gangsta's Paradise*, which was also No.1 in the US Billboard Chart.

HIS TENTH SEASON 1995-96
(THE DOUBLE, DOUBLE)

Premiership: Champions (three).
FA Cup: Winners (defeated Liverpool 1–0 at Wembley).
League Cup: 2nd Round (lost 4–3 on aggregate to York City).
UEFA Cup: 1st Round (lost on away goals rule to Rotor Volgograd).
Leading goal scorer: Eric Cantona, 19 goals.

DID YOU KNOW THAT? When United won the Double after beating Liverpool in the FA Cup final on 11 May 1996, George Michael was enjoying his seventh and last UK No.1 single with *Fastlove*.

HIS ELEVENTH SEASON 1996-97
(CHAMPIONS AGAIN AS ERIC LEAVES)

Premiership: Champions (four).
FA Cup: 4th Round (lost 1–0 away to Wimbledon in a replay).
League Cup: 4th Round (lost 2–0 away to Leicester City).
UEFA Champions League: Semi-Finals (lost to Borussia Dortmund).
Leading goal scorer: Ole Gunnar Solskjaer, 19 goals.

DID YOU KNOW THAT? When United lifted the Premier League trophy following a 2-0 win over West Ham United at Old Trafford on 11 May 1997, Gary Barlow was enjoying his second and last UK No.1 single with *Love Won't Wait*.

HIS TWELFTH SEASON 1997-98

Premiership: Runners-up to Arsenal.
FA Cup: 5th Round (lost 3–2 away to Barnsley in a replay).

League Cup: 3rd Round (lost 2–0 away to Ipswich Town).
UEFA Champions League: Quarter-Finals (lost to AS Monaco).
Leading goal scorer: Andy Cole, 25 goals.

DID YOU KNOW THAT? On 21 February 1998, Celine Dion had the UK No.1 single, *My Heart Will Go On*, the theme song to the blockbuster movie *Titanic*.

HIS THIRTEENTH SEASON 1998-99 (TREBLE WINNERS)

Premiership: Champions (five).
FA Cup: Winners (defeated Newcastle United 2–0 at Wembley),
League Cup: 5th Round (lost 3–1 away to Tottenham Hotspur),
UEFA Champions League: Champions (defeated Bayern Munch 2–1 at Barcelona).

In the last ten days of the 1998–99 season, United beat Tottenham Hotspur in the final league game of the season to regain their crown as champions of England; they then beat Newcastle United 2–0 in the FA Cup final; and in the following week, on that unbelievable night of 26 May in Barcelona's Camp Nou stadium, United fought back from the brink of defeat to beat Bayern Munich 2–1 in the UEFA Champions League final thanks to two dramatic late goals scored from corners by Teddy Sheringham and Ole Gunnar Solskjaer. United had achieved what many considered to be impossible: they had won the Treble and this unique achievement led the Boss to utter perhaps his most famous quote of all, 'Football, bloody hell.' It proved to be lucky No.13 season for Fergie.

Leading goal scorer: Dwight Yorke, 29 goals.

DID YOU KNOW THAT? When United beat Bayern Munich 2-1 at Camp Nou, Barcelona on 26 May 1999 to win the Treble, Boyzone were enjoying their sixth and last UK No.1 single with *You Needed Me*.

HIS FOURTEENTH SEASON 1999-2000 (CHAMPIONS)

Premiership: Champions (six).
FA Cup: Did not participate.
League Cup: 3rd Round (lost 3–0 away to Aston Villa).
UEFA Champions League: Quarter-Finals (lost to Real Madrid).
Leading goal scorer: Dwight Yorke, 24 goals.

DID YOU KNOW THAT? When United lifted the Premier League trophy following a 3-1 win over Tottenham Hotspur at Old Trafford on 6 May 2000, Oxide and Nutrino, two 17-year-olds, were enjoying their only UK No.1 single with *Bound 4 Da Reload*, a garage dance track based on the theme from the BBC TV show *Casualty*.

HIS FIFTEENTH SEASON 2000-01 (CHAMPIONS)

Premiership: Champions (seven).
FA Cup: 4th Round (lost 1–0 at home to West Ham United).
League Cup: 4th Round (lost 2–1 away to Sunderland).
UEFA Champions League: Quarter-Finals (lost to Bayern Munich).
Leading goal scorer: Teddy Sheringham, 21 goals.

DID YOU KNOW THAT? When United lifted the Premier League trophy following a 1-0 loss to Derby County at Old Trafford on 5 May 2001, S Club 7 were enjoying their third UK No.1 single with *Don't Stop Movin*.

HIS SIXTEENTH SEASON 2001-02

Premiership: Runners-up to Arsenal.
FA Cup: 4th Round (lost 1–0 away to Middlesbrough).
League Cup: 3rd Round (lost 4–0 away to Arsenal).
UEFA Champions League: Semi-Finals (lost to Bayer Leverkusen).
Leading goal scorer: Ruud van Nistelrooy, 36 goals.

DID YOU KNOW THAT? On 15 September 2001, Bob the Builder claimed the UK No.1 single with *Mambo No.5*, the TV animated character's second No.1 hit.

HIS SEVENTEENTH SEASON 2002-03 (WE GOT OUR TROPHY BACK!)

Premiership: Champions (eight).
FA Cup: 5th Round (lost 2–0 at home to Arsenal).
League Cup: Finalists (lost 2–0 against Liverpool at Millennium Stadium, Cardiff).
UEFA Champions League: Quarter-Finals (lost to Real Madrid).
Leading goal scorer: Ruud van Nistelrooy, 44 goals.

DID YOU KNOW THAT? When United lifted the Premier League trophy following a 3-1 win over Charlton Athletic at Old Trafford on 3 May 2003, Busted were enjoying their first UK No.1 single with *You Said No*.

HIS EIGHTEENTH SEASON 2003-04

Premiership: 3rd.

FA Cup: Winners (defeated Millwall 3–0 at the Millennium Stadium, Cardiff).
League Cup: 4th Round (lost 2–0 away to West Bromwich Albion).
UEFA Champions League: Second Round (lost to FC Porto).
Leading goal scorer: Ruud van Nistelrooy, 30 goals.

DID YOU KNOW THAT? Michael Andrews featuring Gary Jules had the 2003 Christmas UK No.1 single with *Mad World*.

HIS NINETEENTH SEASON 2004-05
Premiership: 3rd.
FA Cup: Finalists (drew 0–0 with Arsenal after extra time at the Millennium Stadium, Cardiff, before losing on penalties).
League Cup: Semi-Final (lost 2–1 on aggregate to Chelsea).
UEFA Champions League: 2nd Round (lost to AC Milan).
Leading goal scorer: Wayne Rooney, 17 goals.

DID YOU KNOW THAT? At the start of the season Buster were No.1 with *Thunderbirds*, a song from the soundtrack of the movie of the same name.

HIS TWENTIETH SEASON 2005-06
Premiership: Runners-up to Chelsea.
FA Cup: 5th Round (lost 1–0 away to Liverpool).
League Cup: Winners (defeated Wigan Athletic 4–0 at Millennium Stadium, Cardiff).
UEFA Champions League: Group Stage.
Leading goal scorer: Ruud van Nistelrooy, 24 goals.

DID YOU KNOW THAT? On 5 November 2005, Westlife were top of the UK Singles Charts with *You Raise Me Up*, the Irish boy band's 13th No.1 hit.

HIS TWENTY-FIRST SEASON 2006-07 (CHAMPIONS)

Premiership: Champions (nine).
FA Cup: Runners-up (lost 1–0 to Chelsea in the first FA Cup final at the new Wembley Stadium).
League Cup: 4th Round (lost 1–0 away to Southend).
UEFA Champions League: Semi-Finals (lost to AC Milan).
Leading goal scorers: Cristiano Ronaldo & Wayne Rooney, 23 goals.

DID YOU KNOW THAT? When United lifted the Premier League trophy following a 1-0 loss to West Ham United at Old Trafford on 13 May 2007, Beyoncé and Shakira were at No.1 in the UK Singles Chart with *Beautiful Liar*. It was Beyonce's third UK No.1 and Shakira's second.

HIS TWENTY-SECOND SEASON 2007-08 (CHAMPIONS)

Premiership: Champions (10).
FA Cup: 6th Round (lost 1–0 at home to Portsmouth).
League Cup: 3rd Round (lost 2–0 at home to Coventry City).
UEFA Champions League: Winners defeating Chelsea 6-5 on penalties after the game ended 1-1 at the Luzhniki Stadium, Moscow.
Leading goal scorer: Cristiano Ronaldo, 42 goals.

DID YOU KNOW THAT? When United lifted the Premier League trophy following a 2-0 win over Wigan Athletic at the JJB Stadium on 11 May 2008, Madonna featuring Justin Timberlake was at No.1 in the UK Singles Chart with 4 *Minutes*. It was Madonna's thirteenth UK No.1 and Justin Timberlake's third. It was still at No.1 when United lifted the Champions League trophy in Moscow.

HIS TWENTY-THIRD SEASON 2008-09 (CHAMPIONS)

Premiership: Champions (11) equaling Liverpool's record of 18 titles.

FA Cup: Semi-Finals (lost 4-2 on penalties to Everton after a 0-0 draw).

League Cup: Winners (defeated Tottenham Hotspur 4-1 on penalties after a 0–0 draw at Wembley).

UEFA Champions League: Runners-Up to FC Barcelona losing 2-0 at Stadio Olimpico, Rome.

Leading goal scorer: Cristiano Ronaldo, 26 goals.

DID YOU KNOW THAT? When United lifted the Premier League trophy following a 0-0 draw with Arsenal at Old Trafford on 16 May 2009, Tinchy Stryder featuring N-dubz were at No.1 in the UK Singles chart with *Number 1*. This was the first time ever that a single called Number 1 had made it to the top of the UK charts. This was the 4th hit for the British DJ and performer.

HIS TWENTY-FOURTH SEASON 2009-10

Premiership: Runners-Up to Chelsea.
FA Cup: 3rd Round (lost 1-0 at home to Leeds United).
League Cup: Winners (defeated Aston Villa 2-1 at Wembley).
UEFA Champions League: Quarter-Finals (lost 5-3 on

aggregate to Bayern Munich, 2-1 away and 3-2 at home).
Leading goal scorer: Wayne Rooney, 24 goals.

DID YOU KNOW THAT? Lady Gaga had the 2009 Christmas No.1 hit single with *Bad Romance*, her third No.1 of the year.

HIS TWENTY-FIFTH SEASON 2010-11 (CHAMPIONS)

Premiership: Champions (12).
FA Cup: Semi-Finals (lost 1-0 to Manchester City).
League Cup: 6th Round (lost 4-0 away to West Ham United).
UEFA Champions League: Runners-Up to FC Barcelona losing 3-1 at Wembley Stadium. Leading goal scorer: Dimitar Berbatov, 21 goals.

DID YOU KNOW THAT? When United lifted the Premier League trophy following a 4-2 win over Blackpool at Old Trafford on 22 May 2011, Pitbull/Ne-Yo/Afrojack/Nayer were at No.1 in the UK chart with *Give Me Everything*. It was Pitbull's second UK No.1, Ne-Yo's fourth and the first for Afrojack and Nayer.

HIS TWENTY-SIXTH SEASON 2011-12

Premiership: Runners-up on goal difference to Manchester City.
FA Cup: 4th Round (lost 2-1 away to Liverpool).
League Cup: 5th Round (lost 2-1 at home to Crystal Palace).
UEFA Champions League: Failed to qualify from Group.
Europa League: Round of 16 (lost 5-3 on aggregate to Atletico Bilbao, 3-2 at home and 2-1 away).
Leading goal scorer: Wayne Rooney, 34 goals.

DID YOU KNOW THAT? On 15 October 2011, Rihanna featuring Calvin Harris were top of the UK charts with *We Found Love*, Rihanna's sixth No.1 hit and Harris' third.

HIS TWENTY-SEVENTH & FINAL SEASON 2012-13 (CHAMPIONS 20!)

Premiership: Champions (13).

FA Cup 6th Round: (lost 1-0 away to Chelsea in a replay after a 2-2 draw).

League Cup: 4th Round (lost 5-4 after extra-time away to Chelsea).

UEFA Champions League: (lost 3-2 on aggregate to Real Madrid in Round of 16).

On 8 May 2013, the Boss announced his retirement. On 12 May 2013 he took charge of United for the last time at Old Trafford and one week later he led the team out for the last time, his 1,500th game as the manager of Manchester United.

Leading goal scorer: Robin van Persie, 30 goals.

DID YOU KNOW THAT? When United lifted the Premier League trophy following a 2-1 win over Swansea City at Old Trafford on 19 May 2013, Daft Punk featuring Pharrell Williams was at No.1 in the UK chart with *Get Lucky*. United fans were getting ready for the arrival of David Moyes as manager.

PART 10

TALE OF FIVE GOALKEEPERS

WARTIME FOOTBALL

BOYCOTT IGNORED BY THE REDS

THE CLUB'S FIRST GREAT CAPTAIN

BIRTH OF THE UNITED REVIEW

ON THE BRINK OF EXTINCTION

A TALE OF FIVE GOALKEEPERS

In 1951, the English author, Enid Blyton, had her 10th novel in the 'Famous Five' series published which was entitled *Five on a Hike Together*. A year later, Manchester United sent five goalkeepers on a hike together in the First Division Championship.

During the 1952-53 season, United used five different goalkeepers in their 42 First Division games. The defending champions opened the season with a 2-0 home win over Chelsea with Ray Wood in goal. Wood joined Manchester United from Darlington in late November 1949, and made his debut for the club on 3 December 1949, a 1-1 draw versus Newcastle United in the League at Old Trafford.

The Greatest Show on Earth, was the No.1 box office movie attraction in 1952, in which Brad Braden (played by Charlton Heston) is the no-nonsense general manager of the world's largest railroad circus. Manchester United were football's equivalent of a travelling circus in season 1952-53, English football's biggest attraction, and Matt Busby was the 'real life' Brad Baden.

Jack Crompton was in goal for United's next league game four days later, a 2-1 away defeat at Arsenal. The United veteran, he signed for the club as a trainee in June 1944 aged 22 and signed professional terms in January 1945, had played 166 times for the club kept his place in the side for the next four games.

When Bolton Wanderers visited Old Trafford on 13 September 1952, Reg Allen was in goal. He had signed for United from Queens Park Rangers in June 1950, becoming the first goalkeeper to command a five-figure fee. During the Second World War, Allen had served as a commando and in 1941, he was captured in North Africa while attempting to sabotage a German ship, and spent nearly four years as a prisoner of war. In his first season with the club, 1950-51, Allen played 44 times and in United's championship winning season in 1951-52, he made 34 appearances. Wood played in the following two matches before Allen made his second appearance of the season between the sticks versus Wolverhampton Wanderers at Molineux Stadium on 4 October 1952. United lost the match 6-2 and it proved to be Allen's last ever game for the club. It was reported that when Allen returned to the dressing-room at half-time with the score level at 2-2, he just flipped and walked out leaving the United captain, Johnny Carey, to take over in goal as there was no substitutes allowed. Following the passing of Jack Crompton on 4 July 2013, *The Independent's* obituary of him noted in passing that Reg Allen was *frequently brilliant but periodically unwell*, and in 1952 he lost his place in the first team after a dressing-room breakdown. Clearly, the nightmares of spending so much time in Stalag 344 in Nazi-controlled Poland haunted him. Wood then played again before Crompton had a run of 10 consecutive appearances, but Wood took control of the No.1 green jersey for the following seven league games.

However, when United visited Sunderland on 18 February 1953, Crompton was selected to play, Allen was not fit to play and Wood was on duty with the Royal Air Force. When the United squad arrived at Roker Park around lunchtime on the day of the game, Crompton took ill on the journey and the club doctor declared him too unwell to play. At the time, there was no train in time for the game. So, Matt Busby turned to the one player in his squad he could ask to play out of position in the game at Roker Park, Sunderland, his captain, Johnny Carey. Johnny was an extremely versatile player and welcomed the chance to show his prowess in goal again even though he had conceded four goals against Wolverhampton Wanderers. The Sunderland fans could not believe their luck and expected a goal fest. In the end, Carey played an exceptional game in the green jersey, only this time it was not the green of Northern Ireland or the Republic of Ireland he had proudly worn in international games. The game ended 2-2. Carey did what he was asked to do in his sticking plaster role.

Wood played in the next league outing before the ever-reliable Crompton returned for an eight-game run in goal. In United's fourth last league game of the campaign, they travelled to the North East and played Newcastle United at St James' Park. In September 1942, Robert Leslie 'Les' Olive joined Manchester United as a trainee aged just 14 when he left school near his home in Salford, Manchester. Because of the atrocities of the Second World War, Wood did not turn professional at Old Trafford until September 1952. United's aspirations of retaining the First Division Championship title were out of reach when they faced Newcastle United; they eventually ended the season in eighth place, and so, Busby decided to hand Olive his senior debut alongside another debutant, Dennis Viollet. The 24-year-old Olive played well and helped United to a 2-1 victory over The Magpies. Olive thereby became the fifth different custodian selected by Busby during the season. Olive retained his place in the side for the next game, a 2-2 home draw against West Bromwich Albion. Jack Crompton played in United's final two league encounters.

United reached the Fifth Round of the 1952-53 FA Cup competition with Wood playing in nets for all four matches. At the end of the 1952-53 season, Allen was sold to Altrincham having played 80 games for United.

In 1952, Isaac Asimov released his novel, *Foundation and Empire*. The book tells the incredible story of a new breed of man who create a new force for galactic government. Matt Busby's 1948-55 team were his first great side, FA Cup winners in 1948 and league champions in 1951-52, and were the foundation of the three magnificent teams he assembled.

Did You Know That?

BUSBY'S USE OF five different goalkeepers in season 1952-53 equalled the club record of using five different goalkeepers in a season which was set in season 1895-96, when the club were known as Newton Heath Football Club. Hugh Douglas, George Perrins, Joseph Ridgway, Robert Stephenson and Walter Whittaker all played in goal for The Heathens which saw them finish sixth in the Second Division.

WARTIME FOOTBALL

On 6 May 1939, Manchester United beat Liverpool 2-0 at Old Trafford in the First Division thanks to two goals from their leading goalscorer in the season, Jimmy Hanlon, 12 goals in all competitions. A certain Matt Busby played at right-half for Liverpool in the game, his 122nd and last ever game for the Merseyside club (he scored three goals). Indeed, it was his final competitive game. Only 12,000 fans turned up to watch the game as Salford were playing Halifax in the 1939 Rugby Challenge Cup final at Wembley Stadium that same day. Salford lost the game 20-3 before a crowd of 55,453 fans.

United ended the 1938-39 campaign in 14th place in the table which was won by Everton, their fifth English crown. United went into the 1939-40 season with hopes of winning their first league championship since 1910-11, and possibly a second FA Cup success following their 1909 victory. Walter Crickmer, the Manchester United club Secretary, was still in charge of first team affairs whilst his eventual successor, Busby, was making guest appearances for Hibernian Football Club during the war.

Prior to playing for Liverpool (1936-41), Busby joined Manchester City from Denny Hibernian on 11 February 1928 on a one-year contract which paid the 18-year-old boy from Bellshill, Scotland £5.00 per week.. Prior to moving to Manchester to embark on a career as a professional footballer, Busby was working full-time as a collier at his local coal mine and at the weekends he played amateur football for his hometown

Stirlingshire club, Denny Hibernian.

Although United had only achieved a placing of 14th in the 1938-39 First Division, there was more than an air of optimism at the club that season 1939-40 would be a successful one. A number of youngsters had progressed from the Manchester United Junior Athletic Club (MUJAC), the name given to Manchester United's Youth team many years before the term 'The Busby Babes' was first used, including Johnny Carey, Jack Rowley and Stan Pearson. All three had made their first team debuts in season 1937-38 helping United to runners-up spot in the Second Division and promotion to the top flight, and going into the 1939-40 season, all three were aged just 20. The future looked bright, bright red.

To confirm the optimism held by Crickmer and his coaching staff, in season 1937-38 Manchester United won the Central League Championship for the first time in 18 years, the club's 'A' team lifted the Manchester League title and the youngsters, MUJAC, won the Chorlton League. United also won the Manchester Senior Cup.

On the opening day of the 1939-40 season, Manchester United defeated Grimsby Town 4-0 at Old Trafford on 26 August 1939, and four days later they drew 1-1 with Chelsea at Stamford Bridge, London. United were back in the capital three days later when they lost 2-0 at The Valley to Charlton Athletic. It would be 49 days before United would play again, a 4-0 home loss to Manchester City at Old Trafford on 21 October 1939, but by this time, the world had changed immensely, and for the first time in 21 years, the world was once again at war. Nazi Germany invaded Poland on 1 September 1939, which resulted in France and the United Kingdom declaring war on Germany.

The 4-0 loss to their neighbours was the first of 25 games the club played in the War Regional League (Western Division) as the Football League had suspended English League football following Britain's declaration of war against Nazi Germany. The dreams of many young promising players up and down the country earning a living as a professional footballer were shattered as a result of League football being suspended until the hostilities ended. United finished fourth in the War Regional League (Western Division). Games 26-29 of the 1939-40 season, were classified as War League Cup games as the FA Cup was also suspended as a result of the ongoing atrocities in Europe. Portsmouth beat Wolverhampton Wanderers 4-1 in the 1939 FA Cup final.

In season 1940-41, United played 35 games. Games 1-19 were in the North Regional League First Competition. Games 20 and 21 were League War Cup matches, a 2-2 draw at Old Trafford with Everton on 15 February 1940 and a 2-1 defeat to the same opponents at Goodison Park the following Saturday. Games 22-35 were in the North Regional League Second Competition. A total of 36 teams played in the league with the final league positions decided on goal average. No points were awarded for a win or a draw. Manchester United finished 7th in the table. During the season, United were to play Blackburn Rovers at Old Trafford on 28 December 1940. However, on the nights of 22 and 23 December 1940, the German Luftwaffe carried out an aerial bombing of Manchester, Salford and Trafford Park which became known as 'The Manchester Blitz'. The British Prime Minister, Winston Churchill, said, 'Hitler did his worst, and

Mancunians did their best'. The game was played at a neutral venue, Stockport County's Edgley Park ground, which proved lucky for the Reds as they walloped Blackburn Rovers 9-0 with John 'Jack' Smith netting five goals.

Then on the nights of 11 and 12 March 1941, just a few days after United whacked Bury 7-3 at Old Trafford (Johnny Carey and Jack Rowley both scored a hat-trick), Hitler's bombers were back over the city and dropped tonnes of bombs on the Trafford area which demolished the stands at Old Trafford and destroyed the pitch. Carey later recalled, 'On the Tuesday I had just finished a 12-hour shift working overnight at Metrovicks in Trafford Park when I was riding home on my bike, and in the distance a huge ball of flame was hovering over the old ground. It not only did not look good, but would see the end of first team football for seven years'. United's Irish international was quite correct as the club was forced to play their remaining league games of the season (and for the following eight years) at the home of their neighbours, Manchester City's Maine Road ground. On 14 April 1941, United were 'away' to Manchester City and hammered them 7-1 on their own turf, with Jack Rowley scoring four times. It was City's heaviest home defeat since Maine Road was opened in 1923.

The 1941-42 season saw United play 37 matches with the season split into two league championships. Games 1-18 were played in the Football League Northern Section (First Championship) with United finishing in fourth position. Games 19-37 were for the Football League Northern Section (Second Championship) which United won. In the Second Championship points were calculated on 23 games and the results also included games played in the League War Cup Qualifying and Knockout Rounds plus

Regional Cup games, in United's case the Lancashire Cup.

The two leagues in one season continued for the next three seasons with mixed fortunes for United. In season 1942-43 they ended the campaign in fourth and sixth places respectively in the table. The following season, 1943-44, brought a runners-up place in the First Competition and a 9th place finish in the Second Competition. Season 1944-45 saw United finish the first half of the campaign in an embarrassing 30th place followed by a 9th place end to the second half of the season. However, the club did reach the 1945 North Cup final but lost 3-2 over two legs to Bolton Wanderers, which was played at home (Maine Road) and away (Burnden Park, Bolton). The final season of the War League was contested in 1945-46, with Manchester United finishing in a respectable fourth place in the Football League North under the leadership of their new manager, Matt Busby.

During the war, footballers would guest for clubs wherever they were stationed at that time. Whilst serving in the British Army, Johnny Carey guested for Middlesbrough, Cardiff City, Manchester City, Shamrock Rovers, Everton and Liverpool.

The 1946-47 season saw a return to the First and Second Division Championships.

Did You Know That?

DESPITE THE SECOND World War breaking out across Europe on 16 September 1939, Manchester United played Bolton Wanderers. This was the club's first ever friendly game. At the start of the war, part of the premises at Old Trafford and at the club's Cliff Training Ground at Lower Broughton, Manchester were taken over by the military and the Royal

Air Force respectively. Just as in the First World War, the fighting in Europe claimed the lives of Manchester United senior and reserve team players: Francis Carpenter was killed during the retreat to Dunkirk, being listed as missing; George Curliss was flying from RAF Kelstern in Lincolnshire when his aircraft disappeared on a bombing raid of the Kiel Canal in northern Germany. The squadron war diary recorded 'no contact' from his plane whilst it was his very first ever mission; Frederick Okoro was killed in action on 2 November 1942 and Hubert Redwood died of tuberculosis on 28 September 1943. George Gladwin was injured so badly in 1942 that his football career was prematurely ended and Allenby Chilton was wounded but not seriously. Walter Spratt represented Manchester United 12 times during the First World War having signed for the club from Brentford in early 1915 and played only one game after the conflict ended. During the Second World War he was living in London and working in Southwark as a dispatcher for Mosers and was among 35 people killed by a German V2 rocket attack on Southwark on 22 January 1945.

BOYCOTT OF WATCHING MANCHESTER UNITED PLAY IGNORED BY REDS

The 1930-31 season is one of the most humiliating in the history of Newton Heath Football Club and Manchester United Football Club. The previous season United finished 17th in the First Division on 38 points with 15 wins, eight draws and 19 defeats in their 42 league games. They scored 67 goals, Harry Rowley and Joe Spence each scored 12, and they conceded 88 with veteran Alf Steward playing in 38 league games. In the FA Cup, they limped out in Round 3 going down 2-0 at Old Trafford to Swindon Town who were playing in Division Three South.

The most important game of the season played at Old Trafford during the 1929-30 season (finished 17th) was played on 22 March 1930 and it did not even feature Manchester United. On 22 March 1930, the match programme for the game which was called 'RED & WHITE', many years before it became known as 'THE UNITED REVIEW', carried an advertisement stating: *PARK YOUR CAR at the COUNTY CRICKET CLUB GARAGE, OLD TRAFFORD.* Looking back now at this programme it is difficult to understand the marketing appeal of the advertisement as by the time most fans had purchased the souvenir programme, which cost 2d, they would already have parked-up and made their way to the stadium. The programme was Vol. XVII, No.33 and had a photograph of James 'Jimmy' Seed (the captain of Sheffield Wednesday) and Thomas 'Tom' Wilson (the captain of Huddersfield Town) on the front cover with the caption of *THE RIVAL CAPTAINS.* The game was the FA Cup semi-final which was played out by Huddersfield Town and Sheffield Wednesday. The Terriers (Huddersfield Town) beat The Owls (Sheffield Wednesday) 2-1 but Huddersfield Town lost the 1930 FA Cup final 2-0 to Arsenal at Wembley Stadium,.

Manchester United set four unwanted records in season 1930-31. Firstly, they lost all 12 of their opening league matches, which included a 6-0 and 7-4 tanking at home to Huddersfield Town and Newcastle United respectively. They also lost 4-1 to Manchester City, 5-1 to West Ham United and 4-1 against Portsmouth away from home. This was not only a club record but also a record for the First Division. Secondly, United won seven, drew eight and lost a club record 27 league games in a season giving them a meagre 22 points from 42 league outings. Their points tally was a club record low from 42 games whilst Newton Heath Football Club could only manage 14 points in season 1893-94 (United's lowest number of points – three points for a win came in season 1989-90 under Alex Ferguson when they could only register 48 points from 38 matches). Fourthly, United scored 53 times in their 42 league games, but conceded a club record 115 goals, with the hapless Steward partly responsible for them having played in 38 of the games. Bizarrely, Blackpool conceded 125 goals during the season but unlike Manchester United, who finished bottom of the First Division, along with Leeds United who were one place above them – both were relegated to the Second Division – Blackpool survived the drop after ending the season one point above Leeds United.

After Manchester United lost their opening 10 league games of the season, and were sitting bottom of the First Division with no points and a minus goal difference of 29, it was too much for one group of fans. Some 68 years before *Shareholders United Against Murdoch*, which subsequently became the 'Manchester United Supporters' Trust' (MUST) was formed in 1998 to stop a proposed takeover of Manchester United by the media tycoon, Rupert Murdoch, a large group of very disgruntled Reds formed a Supporters' Action Group. However, the United fans in 1930 could not call upon the social media monster that fans' pressure groups have at their fingertips today to advertise their dissatisfaction with their team's Board of Directors, whose resignations they were calling for.

The club's 11th league game of the 1930-31 season was against Arsenal on 18 October 1930, and the disgruntled Reds placed advertisements in the local press calling upon fans of the club to boycott the game. On the day of the game the same group of angry Reds paraded the concourses of Old Trafford with a placard in one hand and a leaflet in the other calling upon all Manchester United fans to boycott attending the match. However, the loyal Reds paid no heed to the call to boycott watching their team play and 23,406 fans attended the game which was the club's highest home attendance of the season at the time. United lost 2-1 with George McLachlan scoring United's only goal of the game.

United's record home attendance of the 1930-31 season was set on 7 February 1931, when they lost 3-1 at home to their rivals, Manchester City, before a crowd of 39,876. Joe Spence scored for United. At the end of the season Herbert Bamlett was replaced as manager with the club secretary, Walter Crickmer, taking charge of first team selection.

However, the 1930-31 season was not a complete disaster as Manchester United won the Manchester Senior Cup for the 14th time since the formation of Newton Heath Lancashire and Yorkshire Railway Cricket and Football Club in 1878.

Did You Know That?

UNITED'S DIFFICULTIES ON the pitch in season 1930-31 mirrored their financial position off it. The club, and not for the first time, were in deep financial trouble. Old Trafford was owned by a local brewery and the club's Board of Directors asked their landlord to suspend mortgage interest payments until the books were close to being in the black. The club also owed a significant sum to the Inland Revenue in respect of income tax arrears. However, in December 1930, the club faced bankruptcy for a second time (the first was in season 1901-02 as Newton Heath Football Club) when the bank refused to extend more credit which meant players' wages could not be paid. But, as time has shown, history has a habit of repeating itself and for Manchester United Football Club, history came about for the club for the second time in 28 years. In 1902, John Henry Davies rescued the club when Newton Heath Football Club became Manchester United Football Club. And in early December 1931, the club had a second benefactor to thank for their survival, their Guardian Angel, and his name is James W. Gibson who placed the princely sum of £2,000 at the club's disposal and paid all of the back wages owed to the players. He even ensured every player's family had a turkey to enjoy for their Christmas dinner. However, James W. Gibson expected nothing in return for his generosity, he just wanted the club to survive and entertain his fellow Mancunians.

MANCHESTER UNITED's FIRST GREAT CAPTAIN MARVEL

Harry Stafford was born on 29 November 1869 in Crewe, England. Stafford began his playing career with his hometown club's junior side, Crewe Alexandra Hornets. After impressing the club's first team selectors, a 20-year-old Stafford was given his first team debut for Crewe Alexandra (nicknamed The Railwaymen) on 22 September 1890, in a Football Alliance match at home versus Birmingham St. George's at the Alexandra Recreation Ground (also known as Nantwich Road). The home side lost 4-1 and that same season Stafford played league matches against Newton Heath Football Club

After Stafford played some 150 games for The Railwaymen, he became a railwayman and signed for Newton Heath Football Club in March 1896. He turned professional on 22 March 1897 after the ban on professional sportsmen being employed at the Crewe Works of the London & North Western Railway (LNWR) was lifted. Newton Heath severed their ties with the Lancashire and Yorkshire Railway in 1892 and were simply known as Newton Heath Football Club by the time Stafford signed for the club.

During his career at the Alexandra Recreation Ground, he won Cheshire Senior Cup winners medals in 1891-92 and 1892–93. In addition to his football career, Stafford was a capable athlete who ran various distances from 100 yards to the half-mile. He was also an exceptional hurdler and represented the Crewe Alexandra Athletic Club for several years until turning professional with Newton Heath disqualified him from competing in amateur athletics.

On 3 April 1896, Stafford made his debut for Newton Heath in a 4-0 home victory in the Second Division over Darwen at Bank Street, Clayton. William Kennedy scored a hat-trick with James McNaught also scoring in the game.

In February 1900, after 16 years of service, Stafford left his job as a boilermaker at the LNWR to became the landlord of the Bridge House Inn in Wrexham, Wales.

On 6 March 1901, Stafford's testimonial match (he shared the nett proceeds with his close friend and teammate, Walter Cartwright) took place versus New Brighton Tower at Bank

Street. The game was to be played with a gilded ball and the pitch illuminated by Wells Lights, contraptions that generated gas from tar oil. Unfortunately, the weather was extremely wet and windy and the lights kept going out, causing the match to be abandoned after 15 minutes. The following week the game was replayed when New Brighton lined-up against a Manchester Select XI billed as 'Manchester United', the first time the words had been used together in a footballing context.

Harry captained Newton Heath Football Club for the last time in a league game on 23 April 1902, in a 2-0 Second Division home win over Chesterfield at Bank Street. It was the second last ever game played by The Heathens with Stephen Preston scoring the club's last ever league goal. Three days later Harry captained the club for the last time when he lifted the Manchester Senior Cup after they beat Manchester City 2-1 at Hyde Road, Manchester (City's home), with Fred Erentz scoring the winner from the penalty spot.

On 24 April 1902, Newton Heath were adjudicated bankrupt and forced into liquidation, but thanks to Stafford raising the £1,000, the club was saved. Newton Heath Football Club were no more but in their place a new club was born, Manchester United Football Club, a new beginning for the officials and players.

On 6 September 1902, Manchester United Football Club played their first ever game defeating Gainsborough Trinity 1-0 away in a Division Two game. Inside-right, Chas Richards, had the honour of scoring the club's first ever goal but Stafford stole the headlines becoming the last ever captain of Newton Heath Football Club and the first ever captain of Manchester United Football Club. United ended their inaugural season (1902-03) in 5th place in the league but had to watch their nearest rivals, Manchester City, clinch the Division Two crown and secure promotion to the top flight of English football. A home match programme cost one penny and beneath the listings for the two teams the following notice appeared: *NOTE – In case of any alteration in the teams a notice will be sent round the ground giving the name of the substituted player and the number of the position in which he will play.* It is worth noting at this point that substitutes were not officially sanctioned by the Football League until the 1965-66 season.

On 7 February 1903, Harry Stafford became the first Manchester United player ever to be sent off when he was dismissed during a 2-1 FA Cup First Round win against Liverpool at Bank Street (Jack Peddie scored both goals). The match referee sent Stafford off in the second-half after the United defender had been warned about his conduct for persistent fouling and failed to heed the referee's warning.

During the 1902-03 season an unusual incident happened involving the Manchester United team when they travelled to Goodison Park on 21 February 1903 to face Everton in Round 2 of the FA Cup. The game was played in appalling weather conditions with a non-stop barrage of rain almost making the pitch unplayable as it cut up and began to resemble a quagmire. In the first-half United wore their red jerseys but when they took to the pitch for the second-half they wore blue and white striped shirts. The change of kit at the interval wasn't enough to prevent them from losing the tie 3-1, and it wasn't the only time they would do a shirt swap at half-time in a game. The team wore this blue and white striped jersey in those away games where their red home jersey clashed with the opposition's home jersey until the 1920s with a couple of exceptions. During the 1907-08 season, United wore a white home jersey and in the 1909 FA Cup final they swapped their red jersey for an all-white kit with a red 'V' and the rose of Lancashire whilst their opponents, Bristol City, were also forced to change their red jerseys and instead wore blue. Just a few weeks before the FA Cup final, United visited Bristol City for a Division One game and wore a white jersey but this time minus the red rose.

Ironically, a similar incident occurred 93 years later when United visited The Dell to face Southampton in the Premier League on 13 April 1996. United, the soon to be crowned Premiership champions for a third time, wore their second choice away kit, an all-grey number, and after trailing 3-0 at half-time they reappeared for the second-half wearing their second choice away kit of blue and white stripes. According to the players, their dismal first-half performance was because they were finding it difficult to pick one another out against the backdrop of the crowd. However, as with the 1903 occasion, the switch did them no good whatsoever, losing the game by the very same score, 3-1.

In August 1903 Dr Bishop was replaced as club Chairman by J. J. Bentley, President of the Football League and a vice-President of the Football Association and who, at the time, was the most powerful man in the English game. The following month, 20 September 1903, James West resigned from his role as club Secretary and was replaced by former Burnley boss, Ernest Mangnall, an old friend of J. J. Bentley.

Then on 12 December 1904, the Football Association suspended James West and Harry Stafford for two and a half years each for making 'illegal payments' to players, a regular practice among clubs in England at the time. When he was asked to give his side of the story at an FA inquiry, the ever-loyal Stafford, said, 'Everything I have done has been in the interests of the club', However, this is not entirely an accurate record of events. It has been claimed that Stafford and West took the rap for Davies and Bentley and were rewarded accordingly. West became the landlord of the Union Inn on Princess Street, Manchester and Stafford was given the stewardship of The Imperial Hotel on Manchester's Piccadilly.

Stafford hung-up his boots and resigned his place on the Board of Directors. He was the first of only four Manchester United players who went on to be appointed a director of the club (the other three were Harold Hardman, Bobby Charlton and Les Olive).

Despite his 5 feet, 9 inches height, Stafford weighed almost 13 stones (12 stones, 9 lbs) and was as solid as a rock in his position at full-back. Not too many opposing players fancied taking on Stafford who in boxing terms for his size was a welterweight (10 stones, 7 lbs) but was more like a light heavyweight (12 stones, 7 lbs) and when he tackled a player it felt like a freight train hitting him. Such was Stafford's reputation, many left sided outside-halves switched wings to avoid the thunder which came with a Stafford crunch tackle.

Stafford played 200 games for the club (Newton Heath Football Club/Manchester United Football Club) from season 1895-96 to 1902-03, and scored one goal. Stafford's only strike for the club came on 5 January 1901, in a 3-0 home win over Portsmouth in the FA Cup.

Did You Know That?

ACCORDING TO MANCHESTER United folklore, Harry Stafford left Manchester in the summer of 1909, just two months after the club won the FA Cup for the first time in their history, and in 1911, he emigrated to Australia due to an unnamed illness. Stafford even tapped Davies for £50 to flee the country.

In reality, Stafford was actually bound for another railway company in the United States of America, taking up employment in Schenectady, New York State as a boilermaker for the American Locomotive Company. In 1917 Stafford moved to Quebec, Canada after obtaining the position of boiler inspector at the Montreal Locomotive Works but during the Great Depression of the 1930s he lost his job and struggled financially throughout the decade. Despite claims that Harry had made a vast fortune as a hotelier, he passed away penniless on 24 October 1940, aged 70, at his home on Erie Street, Montreal, Canada. His remains are interred in an unmarked grave in Mount Royal Cemetery, Plot No.G733-L. There is no statue of Stafford at Old Trafford, but on the same equilibrium as Sir Christopher Wren and his architectural masterpiece, St. Paul's Cathedral in London, Manchester United fans searching for a monument to celebrate Stafford's contribution to the very fabric of the club, just need to look around Old Trafford today. Had it not been for Harry Stafford and his dog Major in 1902, and their chance meeting with John Henry Davies after Major got lost and turned up at the door of the wealthy Manchester brewer, Manchester United would quite simply not exist today.

THE UNITED REVIEW

Manchester United's official matchday programme, *United Review*, was first published in season 1946-47. The first edition was snapped up by the 41,025 fans who attended United's opening First Division game of the season on 31 August 1946, a home game played at Maine Road. Old Trafford was still under reconstruction. The programme cover depicted a fan wearing a suit and a trilby hat shaking hands with a United player (not an actual player from the club) and cost 3d (pre-decimalisation, 35 pence today). United won the game 2-0 with goals from Charlie Mitten and Jack Rowley. The cover remained unchanged for 13 seasons. On 24 August 1949, United were once again playing home games at Old Trafford and the first *United Review* purchased by fans at their spiritual home was for the visit of Bolton Wanderers, a 3-0 victory with Mitten and Rowley again on the scoresheet along with an own goal from the visitors.

Chelsea were United's first opponents in a home league game in season 1959-60. The publishers of the programme decided to remove the trilby hat of the fan and replaced it with a peaked flat cap to reflect the changing dress fashions towards the end of the decade. The price of it was 4d and the London club won the game 1-0. The next change to the *United Review* came in season 1966-67, a change to the font, although the trademark symbol of a unity between fan and player remained in the form of the famous handshake. The fans who bought it for the Red's opening game of the new league campaign paid 6d for it but it was a souvenir worth having as United beat West Bromwich Albion 5-3 on 20 August 1966 (scorers: Denis Law two, George Best,

David Herd and Nobby Stiles). However, in season 1966-67, the handshake was removed and did not appear again until United drew 0-0 with Nottingham Forest on 11 August 1981, it cost 35p. The old leather brown football was replaced with a white football behind the handshake.

Another change occurred for season 1986-87, the season Alex Ferguson arrived at Old Trafford. The player, as always, was depicted wearing the home shirt at the time but on this occasion the clothes of the fan were changed. Yet another fashion change. The programme cost 40p and West Ham United lost their opening First Division home game 3-2 to West Ham United (scorers: Frank Stapleton and Peter Davenport).

At the start of the 1993-94 season, perhaps as a thank you for his 13 loyal years of service, 'Captain Marvel' himself, Bryan Robson, replaced the computer image of a Manchester United player shaking hands with a United fan who was wearing a grey SHARP UMBRO hoodie. Another fashion change in an era when football club shirts were becoming fashion items in their own right. Robbo left United at the end of the season. Manchester United were the reigning Premier League champions, having won the inaugural Premier League title the previous season, when Sheffield United were beaten 3-0 on 18 August 1994. Robbo played in the game which United won 3-0, thanks to two goals from Roy Keane (his first for the club since joining them from Nottingham Forest on 19 July 1993, a £3.75 million transfer) and Mark Hughes. Bryan Robson remains the only ever player to appear on the front cover of the *United Review*, a testimony to his esteem at the club.

Two actors appeared on the front cover for the 1996-97 season handshake, which lasted until the end of the Treble winning season in 1998-99. The white match ball had the name of the shirt sponsor, UMBRO, at the top of it. The new millennium brought about a new design of the programme's masthead, with the curved writing replaced by a bolder font and the handshake placed in the centre of it. This new era design lasted two seasons. It cost £1.50.

In season 2002-03, the traditional, indeed historic front cover handshake, was removed from the front cover and moved to the inside pages, and over the course of the following seasons it appeared as a header to a miscellany of articles inside the match programme.

But, much to the delight of all Manchester United fans, the handshake reappeared in season 2010-11. It proved to be a lucky change of design. On 16 August 2010, United defeated Newcastle United 3-0 in the opening Premier League game of the 2010-11 season with goals from Dimitar Berbatov, Ryan Giggs and Darren Fletcher. United went on to win their 12th Premier League title in season 2010-11 as well as finishing runners-up to FC Barcelona in the 2011 UEFA Champions League final.

The fashion world took charge again in season 2012-13 with the fan wearing a pair of jeans and a United scarf whilst the player wore his AON sponsored shirt and the latest football boots. The style, including the front cover of the *United Review*, was altered the following season. The black background was replaced with a red background and the curved heading was reintroduced.

A retro style cover was introduced in season 2013-14, with a red background replacing the traditional black background. It paid homage to the original 1946 design. It cost £3. Three seasons later, 2016-17, *United Review's* emblem was switched to the back cover and this stayed in place for a few seasons. Season 2019-20 saw the handshake feature a real fan in a wheelchair whose image was drawn along with a fictitious player who was also drawn.

Did You Know That?

THE PUBLISHERS OF the *United Review* changed the entire front cover for the first time in its 32-year history on 7 August 1978. It was a very special occasion, the club was celebrating its centenary. Manchester United played Real Madrid at Old Trafford to celebrate the formation of the club as Newton Heath Lancashire and Yorkshire Railway Cricket and Football Club in 1878. The cover represented a football pennant and cost 50p. United beat the Spanish side, six-times champions of Europe, 4-0 thanks to two goals each from Joe Jordan and Sammy McIlroy in front of 49,937 fans. Alex Stepney, the only player in the United side who won a European Cup winners' medal in 1968, saved a penalty during the game.

A CLUB ON THE BRINK OF EXTINCTION

In season 1899-1900, Newton Heath Football Club finished in fourth place in the Second Division. It was the club's eighth season in the Football League and their sixth season in English football's lower tier. The Wednesday (they became Sheffield Wednesday in 1929) were crowned champions, Bolton Wanderers were runners-up and Small Heath (they became Birmingham City in 1943) took third place. In the 1899-1900 FA Cup, The Heathens were beaten 3-1 away to South Shore on 28 October 1899, in the First Qualifying Round (scorer: William Jackson). The club's home kit was a white shirt with navy blue shorts and navy blue socks. Their away kit was a green & yellow striped shirt, navy blue shorts and socks, whilst a third alternate kit comprised a red and navy blue striped shirt, navy blue shorts and socks.

Going into the new football millennium, season 1900-01, Newton Heath's finances were in the red, blood red, at the bank. They were in financial terms, bankrupt. Their home kit remained the same whilst the previous season's third kit became the club's away colours, there wasn't a third option because they couldn't afford one. Indeed, so financially destitute were Newton Heath Football Club at the start of season 1900-01, the club had to call upon the generosity of fans and ask them to help contribute financially to the cost of the railway fares to away games. A Victorian era 'Whip-Round' was conducted every other week during the season. At the time there was no such a thing as an overnight stay at a hotel for the players with a team meal followed-up by a team de-briefing of the opposition. Players left Manchester for the game on the morning and ate their lunch on the way to their opponent's ground, which comprised a bottle of beer and a block of cheese. Bread was a luxury.

These were days of great strife at the club and if a new player was signed, it would cause a great deal of excitement which resulted in hundreds of fans congregating at the railway station, to welcome the club's new star arrival. But, the club's performances on the pitch were not good enough to attract big audiences at home games which was so needed to keep the club afloat, or in legal terms, solvent.

In season 1900-01, the highest home attendance was 10,000 (a 4-0 win over Blackpool on 26 December 1900), but their lowest home gate receipts was for the game versus Chesterfield on 27 April 1901 when only 1,000 fans watched the game. The average home attendance for the 1900-01 season was 5,658. The fans were not happy and the players were very unhappy as their wages were paid according to gate receipts.

Newton Heath finished in tenth place in the 1900-01 Second Division and were beaten 7-1 by Burnley at Turf Moor in an FA Cup First Round replay after a 0-0 draw at Bank Street, Clayton in the first game. Alf Schofield scored for Newton Heath.

Despite their financial problems, the club managed to play another season, 1901-02, but not many fans believed that Newton Heath Football Club would exist at the end of this league campaign.

Did You Know That?

DURING THE 1900-01 season, one player is reported to have excused himself from playing after he had seen the meagre attendance in the stands at Bank Street prior to kick-off. Apparently, he informed James West, the Secretary/Manager of the club, that ,'I don't think I can play today, my foot isn't right'. He then put his clothes back on and watched the game as a fan.

ROY KEANE – UNITED's MIDFIELD GENERAL

Sir Alex Ferguson described Roy Keane as the best he's ever worked with, and aspiring footballers and Reds everywhere worshipped the ground he walked on but, above all else, Keano epitomised the unwavering spirit and desire to succeed which Manchester United stands for. The Cork-born midfielder began his career with Cobh Ramblers after failing to gain an apprenticeship in English football. However, the legendary Brian Clough took him to Nottingham Forest for a bargain £47,000 in 1990 before he completed a then-record £3.75 million switch to Old Trafford in the summer of 1993, spurning advances from Arsenal and Blackburn Rovers to join the inaugural Premier League Champions of 1992-93. Two goals on his home debut, a 3-0 win over Sheffield United, served notice of what would follow and the gladiatorial Keane won the first of seven Premier League winners' medals, the first of four FA Cup winners' medals and the first of four FA Community Shield winners' medals in his debut season, helping United win the Double for the first time with a 4-0 thumping of Chelsea on a rain-soaked pitch at the old Wembley Stadium in the 1994 FA Cup final. Along the way he added a UEFA Champions League and Intercontinental Cup winners' medals.

Following the retirement of the enigmatic French genius, Eric Cantona, in May 1997, Fergie handed Keano the captain's armband and the Irishman repaid the Boss's faith in him as he rallied United's troops in the heat of some fierce battles at home and abroad, and commandeered the midfield. However, his first season as skipper was cut short by a cruciate knee ligament injury sustained in a tackle with Leeds United's Alf-Inge Haaland at Elland Road, Leeds in September 1997.

The 1998-99 season more than any other saw Keano rise to legend status among the United faithful but it was a season of mixed fortunes for the fiery Irishman. On his way to leading United to their historic Treble, a sending-off in the FA Cup semi-final replay victory over Arsenal was followed by a yellow card during arguably his greatest display in a United shirt, the UEFA Champions League semi-final second-leg tie away to Juventus, forcing him to miss that unforgettable night in Barcelona when United were crowned Champions of Europe after defeating FC Bayern Munich 2-1 at Camp Nou.

In addition to his fifth Premier League winners' medal Keano scooped the prestigious Professional Footballers' Association Players' Player of the Year Award and the Football Writers' Association Footballer of the Year Award in 1999-2000. Prior to the start of the 2002 FIFA World Cup finals in South Korea and Japan, Keano was involved in a huge bust-up with his Republic of Ireland manager Mick McCarthy, which led to Keane's premature departure from the finals and what looked to be the end of his international career. Irish sport had never witnessed a bigger controversy than the Roy Keane-Mick McCarthy explosive disagreement in Saipan which became known as 'The Saipan Affair'. However, he made a shock return to international action under Brian Kerr in May 2004, a year which also saw him inducted into the English Football Hall of Fame, but retired from the international scene in the autumn of 2005 following Ireland's failure to qualify for the 2006 FIFA World Cup finals. Prior to his decision to quit international football he broke a metatarsal bone in his foot in United's Premiership match against Liverpool at Anfield on Sunday 18 September 2005 which proved to be his last ever game for United. On 19 November 2005, United fans all over the world were in shock when their Caesar announced that after conquering the south he was moving north across the border to join Glasgow Celtic, a team he had supported ever since he was a young boy. 'Whilst it is a sad day for me to leave such a great club and manager, I believe the time has now come for me to move on,' said Roy on the day of his departure. Paying tribute to his out-going general on the pitch Fergie said, 'Roy is the best midfield player in the world of his generation and one of the great figures in our club's illustrious history'. Six months after joining Celtic and helping them secure the Scottish Premier League title and Scottish League Cup, Keano announced his retirement from professional football on 12 June 2006 following medical advice.

His contribution to the history of Manchester United is indelibly recorded in the club's history books and along with Eric Cantona, who like Keano was not afraid to speak his mind in front of the media, particularly if he felt his colleagues were not reaching the high standards he expected, define the 1990s for Manchester United.

Roy Keane pulled on a Manchester United shirt 480 times from 1993-2005 and scored 51 goals for the club. He made 67 international appearances for the Republic of Ireland and scored nine goals (1991-2005).

Did You Know That?

BEFORE EMBARKING ON a career in football, Keano took-up boxing when he was just nine years old and trained for a number of years, winning all four of his bouts in the novice league. His favourite footballers when he was growing up were fellow Irishman, Liam Brady, Glenn Hoddle of Tottenham Hotspur (another team he supported as a boy) and United legend Bryan Robson.

A SEASON OF HIGHS AND LOWS

The 1892-93 season was Newton Heath Football Club's first in the English Football League, they were in the First Division. It was an eventful season on and off the pitch. They drew two and lost four of their opening six league games and in Game No.7, they not only recorded their first ever league victory but they also set a club record score when they beat Wolverhampton Wanderers 10-1 at North Road, Newton Heath. The 1892-93 campaign was only the club's 14th year in existence, founded in 1878 as Newton Heath Lancashire and Yorkshire Railway Cricket and Football Club, and it proved to be a hugely unsuccessful season as they finished rock bottom of the League.

At the time, the Football League had a Test Match game in place, a modern-day play-off game. Newton Heath faced a Victorian two-legged tie which would decide their Football League status for season 1893-94, and their opponents were Small Heath.

Small Heath (later became Birmingham City) won the Second

Division Championship in season 1892-93 and thereby secured the right to play the team which finished bottom of the First Division Championship table in a two-legged encounter. That team was Newton Heath Football Club.

The winner would be playing their football in the First Division the following season. The Heathens escaped relegation by the skin of their teeth, winning the two legged tie 7-3.

The highest home attendance of the season (15,000) was a 5-0 loss to Sunderland on 4 March 1893. However, Sunderland went on to clinch their second First Division Championship at the end of the season. The lowest home attendance of the season was 3,000 fans and was set twice: a 7-1 mailing of Derby County on 31 December 1892 and a 3-3 draw versus Accrington Stanley in the final game of the campaign, which was the club's last ever game at their North Road, Newton Heath home on 8 April 1893. Accrington Stanley ended the season one place above Newton Heath in 15th place in the table (16 teams made up the division) whilst Derby County finished in 13th position. Just as The Heathens had to do, Accrington Stanley played in a Test Match at the end of the season to determine their status for 1893-94. They lost 1-0 to Notts County at The Castle Ground, Nottingham in a one-off game and rather than play a season in the lower tier of English football, Accrington Stanley tendered their resignation from the league, thereby becoming the first of the 12 founding Football League clubs in season 1888-89 to leave the League permanently (Stoke City failed to achieve re-election for season 1890-91 after finishing the previous season in last place, but re-joined the Football League a year later).

Bob Donaldson was the club's leading goalscorer in all

competitions with 16 goals, all in the league. The club lost 4-0 away to Blackburn Rovers in Round 3 of the FA Cup and 4-0 away to Bury in the First Round of the Lancashire Cup. On the bright side, Newton Heath beat Bolton Wanderers 3-1 in the final of the Manchester Senior Cup.

Did You Know That?

DURING THEIR INAUGURAL season in the English First Division Championship, Newton Heath had to play a league game with only 10 men. On 7 January 1893, the team played Stoke City away but they were without their goalkeeper, James Warner, who failed to meet-up with the team for the train journey to Stoke. Warner joined the club from Aston Villa in July 1892, and played in all 20 of their league matches prior to the encounter with Stoke City. In his absence, half-back William Stewart went into nets and conceded seven times in a 7-1 defeat (scorer: James Coupar in the opening minute of the game). Warner only played twice more for the club following his no-show and in September 1893, he moved to Walsall Town Swifts.

AN AUDIENCE WITH THE POPE

Towards the end of the 1972-73 season, a season which saw Manchester United finish 18th in the First Division Championship, they were invited to participate in the Anglo-Italian Cup. Manchester United were placed in Group One along with fellow English clubs Crystal Palace, Hull City and Luton Town. Bari, Fiorentina, Lazio and Verona made up the Italian contingent in the group. Each team played against the four teams in their group from the opposing nation. In each group, the best team from each nation progressed to the semi-finals. The semi-finals were two-leg matches played between each nation's highest placed team. The winner of each nation's semi-final then met in a final.

The tournament was established in 1970 by Luigi 'Gigi' Peronace, a Calabrian football agent who specialised in organising transfers between English and Italian clubs. Many football historians consider Peronace the first ever football agent in England.

The 1970 tournament comprised six English clubs and six Italian clubs, split into three groups with two teams from each country in each group playing games home and away. The final was contested between the best team from each country, and Swindon Town played S.S.C. Napoli at the Stadio San Paolo on 28 May 1970. The game was abandoned after 79 minutes with Swindon leading 3-0 much to the anger of the home crowd who caused trouble in the stands. Swindon Town were declared the inaugural winners of the trophy. The following year Blackpool defeated Bologna FC in the final and were runners-up in 1972, losing out to AS Roma.

On 21 February 1973, Manchester United drew 1-1 at Old Trafford with Fiorentina (scorer: Jim Holton) in Group One. A month later, United travelled to the Italian capital and drew 0-0 with AS Roma at Stadio Olimpico, Rome, Italy on 21 March 1973. The day before the game United's travelling party of officials and players were given a very special audience. They were invited to the Vatican City to meet Pope Paul VI. Sir Matt Busby had the Order of Saint Gregory the Great bestowed upon him by Pope Paul VI in 1972. This very prestigious honour is bestowed upon Roman Catholic men and women (and sometimes in rare cases to non-Catholics) in recognition of their personal service to the Holy See and to the Roman Catholic Church, through their employment, their support of the Holy See, and the examples they set in their communities and in their countries. The Holy See is also known as the 'See of Rome', which is the jurisdiction of the Bishop of Rome, known as the Pope.

Next up for United was a home tie versus S.S.C. Bari who they beat 3-1 on 4 April 1973, with goals from Denis Law, Ian Storey-Moore and Mick Martin. United's last game in their Group was a 4-1 victory over Hellas Verona FC, with two goals from Bobby Charlton and one each from Patrick Olney and Peter Fletcher.

Manchester United finished second best between the English clubs in Group One with Crystal Palace gaining seven points from their four matches and United accumulating six points. Fiorentina topped the Italian side of Group One with only four points. Newcastle United and Bologna FC won their respective tables in Group Two. Newcastle United beat their London rivals 5-1 over two legs in the English semi-final, whilst Fiorentina defeated Bologna 3-2 in the Italian semi-final. The 1973 Anglo-Italian Cup final was played at Stadio Artemio Franchi, Florence, Italy, the home of ACF Fiorentina, with Newcastle United winning 2-1.

Did You Know That?

THE GAME VERSUS Hellas Verona FC was Bobby Charlton's last ever game in a Manchester United jersey, and the last time he scored for the club he so loyally served as man and boy for 20 years, having signed as an apprentice for the club in January 1953 when he was just 15 years old.

POSING WITH A HOLLYWOOD ICON AND HIS HORSE

On 13 October 1962, Manchester United played Blackburn Rovers in the First Division Championship at Old Trafford. A crowd of 42,252 attended the game which United lost 3-0. The fans who bought a *United Review* for 6d going into the game must have taken a double glance at the front cover of the matchday programme which featured the legendary American actor, Charlton Heston, and his horse.

Manchester United beat Real Madrid 2-0 (scorers: David Herd and Mark Pearson) in a friendly match at Estadio Santiago Bernabeu, Madrid on 19 September 1962, and during their visit to the Spanish capital they visited a film studio where the movie *55 Days at Peking*, starring Heston, David Niven and Ava Gardner was being filmed. The team posed for a photograph with the Hollywood star outside the studios which were located on the outskirts of the city.

Did You Know That?

BOBBY CHARLTON PLAYED his first game of the 1962-63 season in the 3-0 defeat to Blackburn Rovers having injured himself at the end of season 1961-62.

UNITED'S UEFA CHAMPIONS LEAGUE PIONEERS

In season 1992-93, the European Cup, which was first competed for in season 1955-56, and won by Real Madrid, was rebranded as the UEFA Champions League. Manchester United were not one of the participants in the inaugural new version of European football's most prestigious competition, having finished runners-up to Leeds United in the last-ever First Division Championship season in 1991-92. An ex-Red, Gordon Strachan, and a future Manchester United player, Eric Cantona, played for Leeds United in the competition and were beaten 4-2 on aggregate over two legs in the Second Round by the Scottish Champions, Glasgow Rangers.

Cantona scored in Leeds' 2-1 loss at home, in the second leg. The 1993 final was contested by AC Milan, the favourites to win the inaugural UEFA Champions League title, having previously won the European Cup on four occasions (1963, 1969, 1989 and 1990), and the French Champions, Olympique de Marseille, runners-up to Red Star Belgrade in the 1991 European Cup final. Against all odds, the French Ligue 1 reigning champions defeated the reigning Serie A holders, AC Milan, 1-0 at the Olympiastadion, Munich, Germany. Future Manchester United goalkeeper, Fabien Barthez (2000-04), played in goal for the French side in the 1993 UEFA Champions League final.

Did You Know That?

BARTHEZ IS FRANCE'S joint-fifth most capped player in the FIFA World Cup with 17 games for his country, and he shares the highest number of clean sheets in the competition, 10, with England's Peter Shilton. Following his retirement from the game in 2007, Barthez began a new sporting career, taking up Motorsport in 2008.

KIDD IS THE KID

When Manchester United, managed by Ole Gunnar Solskjaer, played Villarreal CF in the 2021 Europa League final, United's Mason Greenwood, aged 19 years and 237 days on the day of the final, was dreaming of becoming only the second English teenager to score in a major European club football competition final after Brian Kidd. Brian scored on his 19th birthday for United in the 1968 European Cup final, when they beat SL Benfica 4-1 after extra-time at Wembley Stadium on 29 May 1968. Alas, Solskjaer's kid never matched Matt Busby's Kidd, as United lost the 2021 Europa League final in a penalty shootout after the game ended 1-1 following extra-time.

Did You Know That?

BRIAN KIDD PLAYED in the Manchester Derby for United and City (he played for City from 1976-79), played in the North London Derby for Arsenal (1974-76) versus Tottenham Hotspur, and in the Merseyside Derby for Everton against Liverpool. Kidd has also been a coach at both United and City.

PART 11
A VERY SPECIAL RELATIONSHIP
MATT BUSBY RETURNS HOME

GIGGS KNOWS GREATNESS

BUSBY TAKES UP THE PEN

THE BIG FREEZE

BEST OF THEM ALL

A VERY SPECIAL RELATIONSHIP

The Munich Air Disaster on 6 February 1958, ripped the life and soul out of Manchester United Football Club and broke the hearts of all United fans with the claiming the lives of 23 passengers, eight of whom were part of Matt Busby's first team squad.

When Jimmy Murphy went to visit Busby in his hospital bed at the Rechts der Isar Hospital in Munich the United manager was only able to whisper a few words to his trusted number two, 'Keep the flag flying Jimmy'. Murphy almost broke down in tears as he was still grieving the loss of the players who lost their lives. And, when he went to see how Duncan Edwards was doing, he could not hold back the tears. When Duncan saw Jimmy approach his hospital bed he was upbeat and asked Murphy what time the game was at on Saturday. In his autobiography entitled *Matt .... United and me*, Murphy wrote, 'As my mind dwelt on the full appalling horror of it all I thought I would go mad, although I was doing my best to think about the future'.

The previous season, 1956-57, United became the first English club to play in the European Cup, a competition which began in season 1955-56, and reached the semi-finals where they lost

5-3 on aggregate to Real Madrid following a 3-1 loss in Madrid in the first leg and a 2-2 draw at Old Trafford. These two games were the beginning of a very special relationship between the two sides. The Anglo-Spanish War from 1585-1604 played no part in the rivalry of the English and Spanish football giants. When Real Madrid visited Manchester on 25 April 1957, this particular Spanish Armada were made most welcome.

Real Madrid's legendary Argentinian striker, Alfredo Di Stefano, one of the greatest footballers of all-time, later spoke quite movingly about the moment when he first learned of the Munich Air Disaster. Di Stefano was in his garden when his telephone rang. 'My heart was filled with sadness. I felt I had lost many, many friends. But I was more sorry for the game of football… for this Manchester United team was magnificence itself. It contained some of the world's greatest players, said the Real Madrid legend. Those who survived the crash were offered free holidays in Spain by Santiago Bernabeu, the President of Real Madrid, which some gratefully accepted. But, Bernabeu and Real Madrid went the extra mile and helped Manchester United out financially to help them build a new team.

Murphy was in charge of Manchester United's two ties versus AC Milan in the semi-finals of the 1957-58 European Cup. The first leg was played at Old Trafford on 8 May 1958, United winning the game 2-1 with goals from Ernie Taylor (penalty) and Dennis Viollet. But a 4-0 defeat in Milan, Italy six days later ended Busby's and Murphy's hopes and dreams of winning the trophy which they would undoubtedly have dedicated to the memory of the eight Busby Babes who died from their injuries in Munich. Real Madrid beat the reigning Hungarian League

Champions, Vasas SC, 4-0 in Madrid in the first leg of their semi-final tie but lost 2-0 in Budapest. However, they progressed to their third consecutive final with a 4-2 aggregate victory over the two legs. The Spanish giants then beat AC Milan 3-2 after extra-time in the 1958 European Cup final which was played in the Heysel Stadium, Brussels, Belgium on 28 May 1958.

Santiago Bernabéu, was a huge admirer of the Babes' style of play and he dedicated his club's 1958 European Cup victory to Manchester United. He also offered the trophy to the club, who politely refused the kind gesture. Prior to the start of the 1958-59 season, Bernabéu offered his club's most prized asset, Alfredo Di Stefano, the most coveted player in the world on a short-term loan deal. Both parties agreed to Di Stefano's temporary move to England, but incredibly the Football Association blocked the move in the belief that it would halt the progress of a British player.

Another legendary striker was linked with a move to Manchester United around the same time. In season 1956-57, Budapest Honvéd represented Hungary in the European Cup. The Hungarian National League champions were handed a bye in the Preliminary Round of the competition, a round in which Manchester United, English First Division champions the previous season, defeated RSC Anderlecht 12-0 over two legs. The draw for Round 1 saw United matched with the German National Champions, Borussia Dortmund, whilst Budapest Honvéd were drawn against the Spanish La Liga Champions, Athletic Bilbao. The winners of the United versus Borussia Dortmund tie would play the winners of the Athletic Bilbao versus Budapest Honvéd tie in the quarter-finals of the competition. United won their two-legged tie 3-2 on aggregate whilst Budapest Honvéd lost 6-5 on aggregate.

The Hungarian Revolution began on 23 October 1956, and although it only lasted until 10 November 1956, the Budapest Honvéd players refused to return to their country after they lost the first leg 3-2 in Bilbao on 23 November 1956. The Hungarian club arranged for the second leg to be played in Belgium at the Heysel Stadium, Brussels on 20 December 1956, with the game ending 3-3. The players, including Ferenc Puskas who scored in the 3-3 draw, brought their families out of Hungary to join them on a World Tour of Brazil, Italy, Spain and Portugal. The tour was vehemently opposed by the Hungarian Football Association and European football's controlling organisation, FIFA.

During his self-imposed exile Puskas played a few unofficial matches for RCD Espanyol in Spain and attracted the attention of two Italian giants, AC Milan and Juventus. But, any attempt by a club to sign him was effectively scuppered when he was given a two-year ban from the game by UEFA for refusing to return to Hungary and his club. He then moved to Austria and then to Italy and when his ban was lifted in the summer of 1958 he was not able to find a top-flight club in Italy who were willing to sign him, as Italian managers were concerned about his age, 31, and his weight. It was at this time that Murphy and Busby took an interest in signing Puskas for Manchester United but as a direct result of the Football Association Rules in place at the time on signing foreign players, coupled with the fact that Puskas could not speak English, he joined Real Madrid.

In the summer of 1959, Busby travelled to Madrid along with his club Chairman, Harold Hardman, in the hope that Real Madrid would help Manchester United build from within. There was a great deal of respect between Busby and the Spanish side which was based on their respective ideology to building attacking teams who played with a certain kind of flair which pleased the fans.

Busby asked Bernabeu if he would agree to his reigning European Cup winners playing Manchester United in a series of friendlies in Madrid and in Manchester. Real Madrid were the best team in the world at the time and were a box office attraction wherever they played. Their team was a 'Who's Who?' of the world's best players, including Di Stefano, Puskas, Didi a Brazilian midfield maestro and Francisco 'Paco' Gento, a very tricky and stylish Spanish winger. Bernabeu informed Busby and Hardman that the usual price for such a friendly was £12,000, a massive sum of money at the time. Matt, ever the diplomat but also a shrewd negotiator, explained that the Munich Air Disaster had ruined Manchester United not only physically with the loss of eight of the club's most talented players but also financially and asked Bernabeu for special consideration. Bernabeu looked at his Board of Directors and declared, 'We must treat Matt and Manchester United generously'.

Real Madrid said that they would come to Manchester to play United in a friendly at Old Trafford for half of their normal fee with an agreement to play four more matches. Busby had no hesitation in accepting the generous offer as he wanted to test his latest crop of young players against the best team in Europe. Busby and Murphy knew only too well that if their new batch of young players post-Munich could perform well against Real Madrid in these friendly fundraising games, then perhaps a new exciting Manchester United team would evolve. And, just as importantly, the series of friendly games would provide

Manchester United with a much needed cash injection to buy new players.

The first friendly game was played at Old Trafford on 1 October 1959, and it was shown live on television which added to the gate receipts United were struggling in the league and had lost their three previous games before the Kings of European Football arrived in Manchester. The Spanish giants had only played three La Liga games before the friendly with United and had beaten Real Betis 7-1 at home, lost 2-1 away to Valencia CF and defeated Espanol 4-0 at Estadio Santiago Bernabeu. When Real Madrid walked out of the tunnel at Old Trafford the floodlights made their all white kit look almost angelic. The Manchester United players formed a guard of honour for their famous visitors while the 63,000 United fans in attendance gave them a thunderous ovation. However, there was nothing angelic about the Spanish side's performance, they were ruthless and put United to the sword winning 6-1 in what was billed as a 'Grand Challenge Match'. The United players were simply no match for the artistry and guile of the visitors who were clinical in front of goal and miserly at the back.

Manuel Fleitas Solich, the coach of Real Madrid, praised Bobby Charlton after the game saying that the United forward was, 'World class in any country, anywhere'. The following month it was United's turn to do the travelling and flew to Spain for Round 2 of their five-game exhibition matches. The Madrilenos expected a similar result in the return game but the United players were not in the mood to allow their opponents to just walk over them without putting up a much better fight than they gave in Manchester. Outside the stadium Real Madrid were selling a specially commissioned football pennant with the names of those who lost their lives in the Munich Air Disaster printed on it. The pennant carried the title 'Champions of Honour', with the sale proceeds being donated to Manchester United.

The 80,000 fans who turned up were treated to a feast of entertaining, all-out attacking football, an 11-goal thriller in which the home side triumphed 6-5 after going 2-0 down and trailing after an hour of play. *The Daily Sketch* praised the performance of United: *United supermen nearly beat Real!* When Di Stefano was interviewed sometime later by *The People* he was asked about United's improvement from the first game and said, 'In many, many ways they were the better team. Certainly they gave us the biggest fright we've had for many, many home matches. The inside forwards, Quixall, Viollet, Charlton attacked our defence that day like men with sabres. They cut us to pieces. The young left-half Wilf McGuinness is a wonderful prospect too… with players like these and with Matt Busby to inspire them all, Manchester United must be strong again before long'.

Matt Busby had nothing but the utmost respect for Di Stefano and openly said that the Argentinian was the greatest centre-forward he had ever seen. After watching Real Madrid beat FC Barcelona 3-1 at Estadio Bernabeu in the first leg of their European Cup semi-final on 15 April 1960, Busby was asked by *The News Chronicle* what he thought of Di Stefano's performance in the game as he had scored twice (Puskas also scored), 'Di Stefano marshalled his men like the genius he is. I wish my youngsters could have been here to see these soccer aristocrats play in such an electric atmosphere'. Two days later FC Barcelona were crowned the 1959-60 La Liga champions on goal average, after finishing level with Real Madrid on 46 points from 30 games played. On 6 May 1960, Real Madrid won the second leg of the semi-final, defeating FC Barcelona 3-1 at Camp Nou, Barcelona (Puskas two and Gento).

On 18 May 1960, an 18-year-old Alex Ferguson was a spectator among the 127,621 crowd which poured into Hampden Park, Glasgow for the 1960 European Cup final. Ferguson was still a player with Queen's Park at the time (he moved to St Johnstone a short time later) whilst Hampden Park was the home ground of Queen's Park. Real Madrid were playing in their fifth consecutive European Cup final whilst their West German opponents, Eintracht Frankfurt, were playing in their first. The fans witnessed one of the greatest ever displays of football by a team when Real Madrid, with Di Stefano, Gento and Puskas all at their peak, destroying their opponents. The Kings of European football for the previous four years exuded exquisite majesty as they tore their opponents apart, winning a sensational game 7-3. The King and Crown Prince of Real Madrid, Di Stefano and Puskas, scored all seven goals with Puskas netting four times including a penalty. Without question, as his later career in management showed, Ferguson took a lifelong inspiration from the game.

When United and Real Madrid met a third time on 13 October 1960, the match at Old Trafford was once again televised. Again, United's league form was dismal, as they languished near the bottom of the First Division with just two wins in their 10 outings. However, only the second-half was shown on TV with the visitors winning 3-2 but Busby remained true to his football values. He always said that he wanted to see how his young players could handle themselves against the best club side in Europe and for this game he played a very young side which included: 17-year-old Nobby Stiles, who was making only his second first-team appearance; 17-year-old Belfast born James Nicholson (the youngest player on the pitch); 18-year-old Tony Dunne who was making his first team debut (he made his league debut two days later) and 19-year-old Mark Pearson. *The Daily Mail's* reporter was impressed with the United kids writing, *United are beaten by Real, but share the glory.*

The press were in love with Manchester United again with The *Daily Express* stating, *Teenage trio shock Real.* Despite having lost all three friendlies Busby and Murphy knew they were on the right track as they gradually built a third great Manchester United side. The youngsters while being fearless, occasionally heroic, were still merely pupils in football parlance but more importantly, they were learning quickly from their Spanish masters. The defeats meant nothing to Busby who was more concerned about how his young charges handled themselves against more experienced, and in the case of Di Stefano and Puskas, vastly superior opponents. Indeed, in an interview with the *Daily Herald*, Puskas praised the 'Proud men of United'. Puskas went on to say that he thought Albert Quixall and Charlton had a tendency to run with the ball too often rather than passing. An observation the 23-year-old Charlton paid attention to as his career blossomed for both club and country.

When Round 4 of their head-to-head took place, Manchester United were sitting precariously second from bottom of the league. The game was played at Old Trafford on 13 December

1961 and going into it United had only won once in 11 games. A dark cloud of possible relegation to Division Two was hanging over Old Trafford that winter night whilst it was reported that Busby had received abusive letters from some fans who were not happy with the club's latest domestic slump. But the United manager had the full support of his Board of Directors which was still led by Harold Hardman. Perhaps Busby shared the letters with his players or just told them that it was time to start turning things around on the pitch, but whatever he did it worked as United beat Real Madrid 3-1 to send 43,000 fans home very happy with the team's performance. Phil Chisnall, aged 19, opened the scoring in the game, only his third appearance for the club, whilst new signing David Herd, who joined from Arsenal in July 1961 in a £35,000 transfer, scored twice. After the game, the captain of Real Madrid, José María Zárraga Martín (winner of five European Cups with the club), generously presented the victors with some silverware.

The Spanish side may not have been the force they once were with SL Benfica replacing them as European Cup winners in 1961 but they still went on to win La Liga in season 1961-62 and were beaten 5-3 by SL Benfica in the 1962 European Cup final.

The fifth and final instalment of the Anglo-Spanish entente took place at Estadio Santiago Bernabeu on 19 September 1962. By this time the second member of the legendary Manchester United triumvirate was at the club, Denis Law who joined from AS Torino on 12 July 1962 in a £110,000 move, a British record transfer fee at the time. José María Zárraga Martín chose the game for his testimonial match (he joined the club in 1951) and 80,000 fans turned out to pay homage to one of the club's greatest ever players. However, the home fans turned on their heroes when United led 2-0 thanks to goals from Herd and Mark Pearson and many headed for the exits before the referee blew his final whistle. Those who were still inside the magnificent stadium rose to their feet and saluted the Manchester United players after their 2-0 victory, Law in particular who tortured the home defence with his aggressive play and darting runs into the penalty area, the first time Real Madrid had lost at home to an English club.

It was a fitting end to the five-game series of friendlies between the two famous football clubs with Real Madrid deserving Busby's and Manchester United's most grateful appreciation for their part in helping Manchester United rebuild a team and rise again once more to prominence after the most traumatic period in the club's history.

The two clubs enjoyed a very special relationship from 1959-62.

Did You Know That?

THE WEEKEND BEFORE Real Madrid were due to face Manchester United at Old Trafford in the first-leg of their European Cup semi-final on 24 April 1968, the Spanish club's 72-year-old President, Santiago Bernabeu, spoke with remarkable warmth about his old rivals at a dinner held to celebrate Real Madrid winning the 1967-68 La Liga title. 'I want Manchester United greeted and treated and respected as the greatest club in the world. As our friends for many years, nothing must go wrong. If we are beaten in the European Cup by Manchester United on Wednesday then we shall have lost to a great team. We have met them on many occasions and it's about time their luck changed.'

Manchester United defeated Real Madrid 1-0 at Old Trafford and drew 3-3 in Madrid to make it to their first European Cup final where they defeated SL Benfica 4-1 after extra-time at Wembley Stadium on 29 May 1968. Real Madrid had most certainly played their part in helping Matt Busby wipe away the sorrowful tears he shed in Munich on the day his second great team died, to helping the United boss celebrate the lives of his eight lost Busby Babes when his third great side were crowned Champions of Europe.

Speaking after Busby's and Manchester United's triumph, a most gracious Santiago Bernabeu quite simply said, 'If it had to be anyone, then I am glad it was them'. Very touching words spoken straight from the heart by a man who had more than played his own part in their resurrection.

GIGGS ON GREATNESS

In February 2011, *Inside United* magazine asked Ryan Giggs for his thoughts on the other nine players, apart from him, who made up Manchester United's Top 10 Greatest Ever Players according to the latest poll as voted for by readers of *Inside United* and *ManUtd.com*, but first asked for his opinion on who he would have voted for, which he gave in descending order.

He said, 'Peter Schmeichel, Roy Keane and Paul Scholes. Obviously there have been some unbelievable players here down the years – Best, Law, Charlton; Duncan Edwards… so many. But I've gone for the ones I've played with, purely because I've seen what they did first hand and what they bring to the team.'

And his thoughts on the Top 10?

No.2 Eric Cantona – 'Eric was a match winner. With him in the team, you always felt he was going to create a chance or score a goal, and he scored so many important ones for us. He was a great guy off the pitch too, and really was just one of the lads.'

No.3 George Best – 'Obviously I only saw videos of him playing, but some of the things he did on the pitch and the goals he scored were incredible. His movement was unbelievable, and he could tear defences apart both here and in Europe. He played during a time when there were some pretty tasty tackles flying in which you wouldn't get away with these days, but he had such great balance and seemed to skip past anyone in his path.'

No.4 Sir Bobby Charlton – 'A legend at this club and someone who has had a massive influence on me. He was a hugely talented footballer who could score goals with either foot. He used to train with us before Champions League away games a few years back, and you could see he still had it even then, that dip of the shoulder and the ability to shoot with either foot.'

No.5 Cristiano Ronaldo – 'Like Best, Cristiano was a very brave player. He went from being a fantastic winger and dribbler to being an unbelievable goalscorer as well. Right foot, left foot, free-kicks, penalties, headers… he can score all types of goals. He really is the all-round package.'

No.6 Paul Scholes – 'I'd go for Scholesy as the club's greatest ever player. I've seen him do things that no other player can do. The way he can control the tempo of games, and his range of passing, are both incredible. We've seen over the years that players just haven't been able to get near him. And you can't forget his goals either.'

No.7 David Beckham – 'The best crosser and passer of a

ball over long distances I've ever seen. Becks not only had great technique, his work-rate was first class: he never stopped. He wasn't the quickest, but he had great movement and always popped up in those little pockets where he was hard for defenders to pick up.'

No.8 Roy Keane – 'Keaney was the driving influence in the squad – he was someone you'd always want in your team. You always felt that when he was on the pitch you had a chance. A great captain.'

No.9 Peter Schmeichel – 'Like Eric, Peter was simply a match winner. He was such an imposing figure in goal – he saved us so many times in games and won us a lot of points.'

No.10 Wayne Rooney – 'A technically brilliant footballer and someone who gives everything to the cause. Wayne is physically and mentally strong, can score goals and is capable of producing the moments of magic which win you games.'

Giggs was typically magnanimous when he found out he had topped the poll. 'When I got told I was really chuffed. I couldn't believe it to be honest, especially when you look at the list of other players who are up there.'

Did You Know That?

IN APRIL 2020, Manchester United supporters voted Sir Bobby Charlton as the club's greatest-ever English player. The 1966 FIFA World Cup winner amassed an impressive 35% of the vote to beat Wayne Rooney into second place, with Paul Scholes third. David Beckham, Duncan Edwards, Bryan Robson, Rio Ferdinand and Gary Neville also featured in the club's shortlist to mark St George's Day.

POLL RESULT

Sir Bobby Charlton – 35%

Wayne Rooney – 26%

Paul Scholes – 14%

David Beckham – 12%

Duncan Edwards – 6%

Bryan Robson – 5%

Rio Ferdinand – 1%

Gary Neville – 1%

MATT BUSBY's FIRST PROGRAMME ARTICLE

On 31 August 1946, Manchester United kicked off the 1946-47 First Division Championship season with a home game versus Grimsby Town. However, the match was played at Manchester City's Maine Road ground which United were renting after Old Trafford had been badly damaged during a bombing raid on Manchester during the Second World War.

Matt Busby, who had been appointed the manager of Manchester United in February 1945, had steered the club to fourth place in the Wartime Football League North in season 1945-46, his first season in charge of the club. In season 1946-47, League football returned and United were in Division One.

In the *United Review* for the Grimsby Town game, Busby

addressed the fans for the first time.

To all United Fans I say 'How do you do?' This is my first opportunity of having a word with you since my arrival here last year, and what better means than by the Club programme? This represents the written words and thoughts of the Manchester United F.C., and I am certain you and I have an equal interest in it. As it is intended that I have a regular article to discuss football from many view-points, I hope it will bring us even closer together. You and I look forward to the opening of the 1946-47 season and what it has in store for us. How often have I felt that tingle run through me, known to all players on the first match of a new season, wondering in what form it would find me and how kindly the ball would run. I am finding all the same reactions as a manager.

A great number of people have asked me about our prospects for the coming season. To this I have replied that our boys are in good heart and excellent physical condition, and will hold their own. Others have remarked that the team should do very well if they start off as they finished last season. Yes, I would be a very happy man if they start off as they finished, but I realise from experience the number of things that can crop up to influence this. After all, each player is human and not a mechanical engine which, when you press a button, goes through its work every minute of the day. I do wish all followers of football would remember this very important point when a player has an 'off day'.

However, we must get on to the battle which starts this afternoon. We will all find the pace of the game stepping up, the tackling keener and the teamwork improved with a view to getting back to 1939 standards – which is all to the good of the game. Whether we start off on the right foot this afternoon or not, I do feel our boys will provide many happy afternoons for us all.

When I came here, I set out to have a team play methodical and progressive football. Without making progress after creating an opening or a position, the opportunity is lost and the team is back where it started. This will always be my policy, so I leave it to the players to supply the answer, and I hope you will have something good to shout about!

M. Busby
Manager

United beat Grimsby Town 2-1 with goals from Charlie Mitten and Jack Rowley.

Busby's impact was immediate with United ending the 1946-47 season in runners-up position in the league to champions Liverpool. A single point separated the Lancashire rivals, 57 to 56, whilst United enjoyed a far superior goal average, 1.759 to 1.625 over the course of 42 games. A case of 'Only If', as United beat Liverpool 5-0 at Maine Road on 11 September 1946 (scorers: Stan Pearson three, Mitten and Rowley). If United had drawn or beaten Liverpool at Anfield, Liverpool on 3 May 1947, their fourth last game of their league campaign, they would have been crowned champions of England for the first time in 36 years, season 1910-11. But they lost 1-0 to the champions-elect.

Did You Know That?

IN THE SAME edition of the *United Review* (Volume 1, Number 1) of 31 August 1946, an article entitled *Walter Crickmer Still Smiling* read, *It is indeed like old times to see Walter Crickmer, our general secretary, in his usual office. The war years have not left the marks upon him which we might have expected. He was on police duty during the blitz and the station received a direct hit by a high explosive bomb. Walter was a lucky one who escaped alive. Also he has been doing tremendously strenuous and important work during the war – of which storage of Government supplies was not the least. In spite of these troubles and trials he is bubbling over with enthusiasm for the old team. His great grudge against the universe is that it has proved impossible to rebuild the stands – thus the games at Maine Road.*

THE BIG FREEZE 1962-63

Between Boxing Day 1962 (United beat Fulham 1-0 away in the First Division) and 23 February 1963 (United drew 1-1 at home in the League to Blackpool), Manchester United never played a competitive game of football because of what became known as 'The Big Freeze of 1963'. Fifty-nine days without a single ball kicked in anger and not even the FA Cup avoided the snow and blizzards that ravaged England in the winter of 1962-63. Round 3 of the FA Cup is traditionally played on the first or second weekend of January but United were unable to play their FA Cup tie versus Huddersfield Town until 4 March 1963 (United won 5-0 at Old Trafford). Indeed, it took 66 days just to complete Round 3 games up and down the country which encompassed 261 postponed matches. The 1963 FA Cup Final, won by United, was not played until 25 May 1963 whilst the two-legged final of the Football League Cup was played two days either side of the main Wembley attraction in which United beat Leicester City 3-1 (scorers David Herd two and Denis Law). It is the only time in the history of the League Cup (1961-present) that a player lifted the League Cup aloft after the FA Cup had already been handed out.

Birmingham City, captained by Trevor Smith, beat local rivals, Aston Villa 3-1 at their home St. Andrew's ground on 23 May 1963 and drew 0-0 at Villa Park, Birmingham on 27 May 1963. Aston Villa were managed by Joe Mercer, who went on to guide Manchester City to the Second Division Championship in season 1965-66; the First Division Championship title in season 1967-68 when City prevented United from winning the league and European Cup Double as United finished runners-up to their Derby rivals by two points; the FA Charity Shield in 1968; the FA Cup in 1969; the League Cup in 1970 and the European Cup Winners' Cup in 1970 making him legendary status as a Manchester City manager.

The country was battered by a tsunami of blizzards, freezing fog and icy temperatures which plunged as low as -22°C. All across England, towns and cities were covered in a thick blanket of snow, many lakes and rivers froze over, children found it difficult to make their way to school and many factories resembled a ghost town as workers were unable to get to work. In the 'Central England Temperature' (CET) records which dated back as far as 1659, only the winter of 1683-84 had been colder. It was also the coldest winter on record since 1740. The cold snap began on 22 December 1962 with the snow arriving via a 36-hour blizzard on Boxing Day resulting in places experiencing snow drifts in excess of 20 feet. Power lines buckled under the freak weather conditions, brought down in high winds which reached Gale Force 8, roads and railway lines were closed and many villagers in remote areas of the country were stranded for weeks at a time. Freezing fog made it almost impossible to make any type of long journey. At times it was if the Ice Age had returned to Britain. For the Manchester United players training at The Cliff was impossible as the pitch was covered in six inches of snow and was rock hard, although the first team players and apprentices enjoyed several snowball fights to keep themselves occupied. In January 1963, the country started to freeze solid with temperatures dropping as low as -16°C in many places. On the Isle of Man, wind speeds were recorded at 119mph, which was faster than most cars could do at the time.

In January 1963, temperatures dropped so sharply that a one-mile stretch of sea out from the shore at Herne Bay, Kent froze over and parts of the River Thames in London were used as an ice rink by winter revellers in the capital. The Big Freeze effectively wiped out the UK sporting calendar for over two months; football games in the English and Scottish Leagues were called off, both rugby codes (League and Union) suffered as did National Hunt horse racing with 94 race meetings cancelled during the period of the freeze. There was no horse racing in England between 23 December 1962 and 7 March 1963 although amazingly one meeting did manage to take place for the equestrian starved punters on 5 January 1963, in Ayr, Scotland. Only a handful of the top clubs had under-soil heating at the time. Everton was the first club to install under-soil heating in 1958, but even warm pipes under the soil at their Liverpool home, Goodison Park, were no match for the extreme coldness of the pitch.

Football clubs were faced with the dilemma of how to keep their players fit so as they would be ready to play when the weather finally abated. A small number of clubs, thanks to the ground staff and dedicated fans, managed to defrost their pitches only for them to freeze over again almost immediately. Second Division outfit, Norwich City, used flame throwers borrowed from the British Army to defrost the pitch at Carrow Road and ended up flooding it! Blackpool, from the First Division, managed to defrost the pitch at Bloomfield Road only for it to freeze over again leaving their players, including England internationals Jimmy Armfield and Tony Waiters, free to skate on it. A number of clubs opted to train indoors but this was not the ideal preparation for a game whilst a few clubs, notably Manchester United, decided to travel to Ireland which had inexplicably escaped the worst of the Big Freeze. Meanwhile, Halifax Town took full advantage of their frozen pitch at The Shay and kept the club's Treasurer happy by turning their pitch into a public ice rink and charged an entrance fee for the locals to skate on its surface.

The Pools companies were getting anxious at the amount of games called off and what that was doing to business so on 26 January 1963, they set up the Pools Panel which comprised a group of men who predicted what would have happened had the games been played. The first sitting panel consisted of Conservative MP Gerald Nabarro, former players Ted Drake, Tommy Lawton and George Young, and former referee Arthur Ellis.

On 2 February 1963, Matt Busby's Manchester United met Jimmy Hill's Third Division Coventry City in Dublin. The game took place thanks to the ingenuity and creative marketing thinking of the Coventry City manager, Jimmy Hill. It was Hill who played a pivotal role in the abolition of the maximum wage in England, his advocacy of the three-points-for-a-win system and the introduction of football punditry on TV (Match of the Day) which is legend, who persuaded seven other English clubs (Birmingham City, Bolton Wanderers, Burnley, Liverpool, Manchester City, Stoke City and Swindon Town) to take part in 10 matches in Dublin, Cork and Limerick in just 17 days. They were fitted in with scant consideration given to the League of Ireland fixture list which had already racked up 12 back matches. Between them, the friendlies attracted 100,000 paying spectators, proving to be a far bigger draw than League of Ireland matches at the time.

More than 20,000 Southern Irish Reds from all parts of Dublin including Ballsbridge, Coolock, Crumlin, Donnybrook, Drumcondra, Finglas, Glasnevin, Merrion, Ringsend and Sandymount poured into Milltown on the southside of the city to watch the game played on Shamrock Rovers' rock hard pitch at Glenmalure Park. Coach loads of Northern Irish Reds left Belfast in the early hours of the morning for the 100 miles trip across the border, which separated Northern Ireland from the Republic of Ireland, into the Irish Free State, many of whom had never even ventured out of Ulster before such was the appeal a visiting Manchester United attracted. The match ended 2-2 (scorers: Albert Quixall and Bobby Charlton). The fans were so excited to see their Manchester United heroes, including their septuplet of Irishmen, Shay Brennan, Tony Dunne, Johnny Giles, Jimmy Nicholson, Samuel McMillan, Noel Cantwell, captain of the club, and the Hero of Munich, Harry Gregg, that they invaded the pitch at half-time clamouring for autographs.

After expenses, the £600 gate receipts was split between United, Coventry and hosts Shamrock Rovers. To put that in context, the Irish club's gate receipts for a Football Association of Ireland cup tie against Bohemians that season brought in £30.00.

United would go on to beat Coventry City 3-1 at Highfield Road in the quarter-finals of the FA Cup on 30 March 1963. With the weather not getting any better in Manchester, Busby took the players back to Ireland 11 days later where they played fellow First Division and Lancashire rivals Bolton Wanderers in Cork at Flower Lodge, home to Cork City FC. The game had been proposed by the Cork Schoolboys League and, after expenses, it shared whatever was left over with the two English clubs. However, when they arrived in Cork the heavens opened and rain fell incessantly making the pitch a quagmire.

The two teams trudged through the mud onto the pitch much to the delight of the 6,000 plus crowd who had braved the weather conditions to see two giants of the English game go head-to-head in this friendly. In the United team was Pat Crerand – his parents came from Gweedore, County Donegal – who was playing his first ever game for Manchester United having just been purchased from Glasgow Celtic a few days earlier, costing the club £55,000. Crerand had a debut to remember scoring in United's 4-2 victory (other scorers: Albert Quixall penalty, Johnny Giles and Denis Law) although given the atrocious conditions the players, and the fans standing on the terraces had to endure, had the game been a First Division game it would probably have been abandoned after the first half hour. At times the game looked more like a mud wrestle than a game of football.

Before the game, Busby said, 'We are looking forward to Flower Lodge. Jimmy Hill recommended the pitch to us. He told us the pitch was a very good one'. After the game Crerand said, 'I've never seen as much mud in my life'. Manchester United's first visit to the Republic of Ireland's second city created a huge sensation for the locals. The two teams were met at Cork's Glanmire Road Station Railway Station (renamed 'Cork Kent Railway Station' in 1966 on the 50th anniversary of the Easter Rising) by the Lord Mayor of the city and factory workers started their shifts earlier in order to get out in time to see local hero Cantwell who would go on to captain United to FA Cup glory a few months later.

Then on 19 February 1963, Manchester United faced a Combination Irish XI side (made up from players of Bohemians and Shamrock Rovers) in Dublin, and ran out comfortable 4-0 winners with David Herd scoring twice along with goals from Bobby Charlton and Denis Law. The team returned home to Manchester having won all three games on their mini-Irish tour designed to beat the Big Freeze and drew 1-1 with Blackpool four days later, a game which saw Crerand make his senior debut having already played in two friendlies.

Finally, on the morning of 6 March 1963, Britain woke up to a frost-free morning and fans all around the country could once again don their hats and scarves and attend football matches. Gloves were an option.

Did You Know That?

WHEN NOEL CANTWELL, who was born in Cork, Republic of Ireland on 28 February 1932, captained Manchester United to FA Cup final glory in 1963, he became the second Irishman to hold aloft the most prestigious domestic cup in world football as the captain of the club, following Dublin-born Johnny Carey in 1948 (born 23 February 1919). The only other player at the time to captain a Manchester United FA Cup wining side was England's Charlie Roberts in 1909.

THE BEST YEARS OF OUR LIVES

On 14 September 1963, a 17-year-old very shy teenager from East Belfast made his debut for Manchester United and went on to become the Greatest Player in the World.

His name is George Best.

> *'To me, a genius is someone with a brilliant mind who has had great accomplishments in a challenging field, and changed the world in some meaningful way. As vague as this definition may seem, the essence of genius is limitless. There appear to be no bounds to what geniuses can accomplish. To define it much further, is to limit something that is supposed to be limitless.'*
>
> (I. C. Robledo)

George Best was a Genius.

On a bright sunny day on Wednesday May 22, 1946 a baby boy was born in Belfast who would literally change the face of football forever. In June 1945, Dickie Best married his sweetheart Anne Withers and 11 months later the couple witnessed the birth of their first child and named him George after Anne's father. Has any footballer ever been born with a more suitable name and into such a humble background?

Dickie was a modest working-class man and a hugely respected figure in the local community of Castlereagh in East Belfast where the Best family lived at Burren Way. Dickie worked at an iron turner's lathe at the world-famous Harland & Wolff shipyard at Queen's Island, where the Titanic was built. Anne worked on the production line at Gallaher's tobacco factory, the largest tobacco factory in the world, located in North Belfast. Dickie was 26 years old when Geordie, as the family called him, was born and played amateur football until he was 36, whilst George's mum was an outstanding hockey player.

From the moment he could walk, all George ever did was play football and it was his Granda George who would kick a ball about all day with his grandson. On the other side of the family, it was his Granda James 'Scottie' Best, who took him to his first football match to see Glentoran play at The Oval in East Belfast, close to James' house. Well, there wasn't much else for the kids growing up on the streets of post-war Belfast to do except play football as very few families had a television set at the time and the only 'net' young boys were concerned about in the early 1950s was a make-shift goal net made from placing jumpers on the ground.

> *'In school, children learn that there is only one answer for each question and are requested to conform to conventional social wisdoms. The difference between geniuses and most of us is that they managed to not lose their childhood creativity.'*
> (Andrii Sedniev)

The young George attended Nettlefield Primary School in Radnor Street, and on his way to and home from school he took a tennis ball out of his coat-pocket and dribbled it along the pavement, throwing his hips from side to side as he weaved in and out of men and women on their way to work. These unsuspecting early morning workers were, in George's mind, defenders he had to snake past en route to the goal. When the bell rang to announce the mid-morning break no one at the school had to go looking for George as he was the first out on the school playground waiting for one of the older boys to produce a football for a kick-about. Lunchtime was the same at school, a game of football with jumpers for goalposts, and after school George played football on a strip of grass near his home.

It was no wonder George was a skinny kid with all that running about he did, and food was the last thing on his mind when his mum had to go looking for him at tea time. It was usually quite dark by the time George got home, perhaps having played football for four hours or more at the end of the school day. When all the other kids had been dragged home by their parents, George improvised and kicked his tennis ball against the kerb so as it would bounce back to him, with George controlling it and passing it against the kerb again. Shooting practice for George was placing the tennis ball on the ground and aiming for the handle of a garage door.

George loved Christmas time because that was when he would either receive a brand-new football from his parents or a pair of football boots, depending on whether his current ball had seen its best days or if his feet had grown too big for the football boots he was wearing at the time.

However, despite football taking up all of his spare time George was an excellent pupil and a very quick learner. He passed the 11-plus and went to Grosvenor Grammar School on the Grosvenor Road. He hated the school but not for academic reasons; none of his mates were at the school and worst of all, Grammar Schools in Belfast played rugby, not football. In his first year at Grosvenor George found himself running with an oddly shaped ball in his hands rather than having a football at his feet doing whatever he wanted it to do. But George gave rugby a go and was a half decent fly-half although for George no sport could replace his love for football. George hated going to the school and used to trick his teachers into sending him home thinking he was ill as the shrewd young Best used to suck on a certain brand of 'hot' sweet which made his throat turn red.

When George started to 'go on the beak' (Belfast slang for playing truant) at Grosvenor, his parents, sensing he was unhappy there, managed to get him into Lisnasharragh High School. And whereas other young boys at the time, including Alex 'Hurricane' Higgins, who were similarly avoiding a school day, would make their way to a nearby snooker hall, the young Best made his way to a patch of grass to kick his ball about. George's new school was in Stirling Avenue and much closer to his home than Grosvenor but, more importantly to George, all of his mates attended the school and they played football there, not rugby. Despite rugby being the number one sport at Grosvenor High School their rugby team only ever won the top prize in Northern Ireland schoolboy rugby on one occasion, lifting the Ulster Schools Challenge Cup in 1983, long after the best days of George's playing career were well and truly a distant memory. Goodness only knows how many times Grosvenor Grammar School would have won the Ulster Schools Challenge Cup had George chosen rugby ahead of football. And so, when George walked out of the gates at Grosvenor for the last time, little did the school know it at the time but they were effectively giving a free transfer to a teenager who would go on to become the greatest ever footballer in the world; a player who in today's crazy football transfer market would cost well in excess of the world record fee of £198m paid to FC Barcelona by Paris Saint-Germain for Neymar da Silva Santos Júnior in August 2017.

Apart from his local team, Glentoran, when George was a young boy, he also supported an English League side but it wasn't Manchester United. He supported Wolverhampton Wanderers who were as successful in the 1950s as Manchester United was in the 1990s. Managed by the legendary Stan Cullis, and captained by the England international team captain Billy Wright, Wolves won the First Division Championship in 1953-54, 1957-58 and 1958-59 (runners-up in 1954-55 and 1959-60). Cullis invented the famous 'kick and rush' style of football.

In the summer of 1953, Wolves became one of the first clubs to install floodlights at their Molineux ground which enabled them to play some very high-profile friendly games against some of the world's best teams. Clubs such as Real Madrid (Spain), Racing Club of Argentina (Argentina), First Vienna (Austria), Spartak Moscow (USSR) and Honved (Hungary) all visited the Black Country to take on Cullis' all-conquering side. The Wolves v Honvéd FC game was televised by the BBC on Monday 13 December 1954 and an eight-year-old George Best sat in front of the black and white television set at home cheering his heroes in gold and black on. At the time, the national game had taken a bit of a battering after England has been knocked out of the 1954 FIFA World Cup finals after a 4-2 defeat to Uruguay in the quarter-finals and, earlier in the year, Hungary embarrassed England in Budapest (May 23, 1954) putting on a master class of football winning 7-1 (scorers: Lantos, Puskás two, Kocsis two, Hidegkuti and Toth). Hungary's international side at the time were known as the 'Mighty Magyars' and had finished as runners-up to West Germany in the 1954 Fifa World Cup Final. Seven months before the hammering they gave England in Budapest they beat England 6-3 at Wembley Stadium (scorers: Hidegkuti three, Puskás two and Bozsik). Honvéd's team which ran out at Molineux to face Wolves before a crowd of 55,000 included five of the 'Mighty Magyars' who had humbled the English on both occasions; József Bozsik, Gyula Lóránt, Sándor Kocsis, Ferenc Puskas & Zoltán Czibor.

The nation watching on TV, including the young Best, held their breaths in anticipation wondering how the pride of England, Wolves, the reigning English First Division champions, would fare against the winners of the Double in Hungary in 1953-54. From the outset, George was completely captivated by the Hungarian's style of play which was centred around their two magnificent strikers, Puskas and Kocsis, and driven on from midfield by the majestic Bozsik. The Hungarians just seemed to be moving that much quicker than their hosts and led 2-0 at half-time with goals from Kocsis and Machos inside the first 15 minutes of play. Would this be another dent in the already frail football suit of English body armour or could Wolves rise to the occasion, led by Wright, who had tasted defeat captaining England in both losses to the Hungarians?

Incredibly, whatever Cullis said to his players at half-time, or whatever pick-me-up he put in their cup of tea, worked wonders and Wolves scored three times (Roy Swinbourne two and a penalty from Johnny Hancocks) to win the match 3-2 before a delirious partisan Molineux crowd. George danced around the living room with delight whilst Cullis hailed his team as the 'Champions of the World'.

When he was 13 years old, George played for his local youth club, Cregagh Boys. The team was run by Bud McFarlane, a close friend of Dickie Best, and he was also coach of the Reserve team at Glentoran. McFarlane knew from day one that this young skinny boy from Burren Way had what it took to become a footballer and mentored the young Best. Bud would constantly offer George advice on all aspects of his game and, on one occasion, he told George that he felt he was concentrating too much on playing with his right foot and suggested that he practice playing with his left foot. George took Bud's advice on board and over the following week he never touched the ball with his right foot; he was still practising with a tennis ball at the time.

When he turned up for Cregagh Boys' next match he only brought one football boot with him, his left one. George put the boot on and wore a *guddy* (Belfast slang for a plimsole) on his stronger right foot. Best scored 12 goals in the game and never once used his right foot to kick the ball. Quite amazingly, someone, somewhere, decided that George was not good enough to represent Northern Ireland at Schoolboy level! And this unbelievable decision was actually taken after George played for his youth club against a Possibles Northern Ireland Schoolboys XI which the kids from the Cregagh won 2-1, and George was the best player on the pitch by a country mile.

Bob Bishop was Manchester United's Chief Scout in Northern Ireland from 1950 to 1987 and in his early years Bishop helped coach the famous Boyland Youth Club football team which earned a reputation as nursery club for many teams in the English First Division. Bud McFarlane was a close friend of Bob and he persuaded him to take George away for the weekend to one of the many training camps Bishop held at Helen's Bay, County Down. Bishop agreed and so George set off from his home making the short journey to the camp which was located just outside Belfast. George was an extremely shy lad, not at all extrovert, but Bishop liked what he had seen and decided to keep a close watchful eye on him.

Leeds United had a useful scouting system in Northern Ireland at the time but according to their scout George was far too skinny to cope with the demands of life in the English Leagues. But McFarlane believed in George and refused to give up on securing his young star-in-the-making a trial with a major English club. Bud asked Bishop to organise a friendly match between Boyland FC and McFarlane's Cregagh Boys under-16 team. At McFarlane's request, the Boyland team was made up of their best 17-18 year-olds. Bishop stood on the sidelines watching the 15-year-old Best weave his magic on the pitch scoring twice in a 4-2 win against his much bigger and stronger boys. It was at that moment that Bishop realised that McFarlane had been right all the long, the young dark haired skinny kid had what it took to become a professional footballer and he sent his now infamous telegram to the Manchester United manager, Matt Busby, with the message reading: 'I think I've found you a Genius'.

Matt Busby invited George over to Old Trafford for a trial in the summer of 1961 during the school holidays. Best, and another young player who Bishop thought could make the grade at United, Eric McMordie, boarded the Belfast to Liverpool ferry in June 1961. George wore his best clothes for the journey, his school uniform! Speaking shortly after George died in 2005, Eric fondly recalled that journey to Manchester: 'I'd played for a club in East Belfast called Boyland since I was 11. There was a man called Bob Bishop who spent his days watching Boyland and sent kids from there to the big clubs. It was like a nursery for Manchester United. George became one of the first to go to United who didn't play for Boyland. Bob's eye for talent was equal to none – he was a very special man. But a match between us and Cregagh Boys, who George played for, was set up. I've never seen a player with so many bruises on his body as George. He was picked on not just because he was wee but because he was so talented. But he fought back and that's what made George the great player he was.'

None of the boys were accompanied by any of their parents or a guardian for the trip and were simply told to make their way to Lime Street Train Station in Liverpool and take the train to Manchester, where a taxi would be sent to meet them and take them to Old Trafford. The entire journey was a terrifying ordeal for two kids from the streets of Belfast who had never been out of Northern Ireland before. When the boys arrived in Manchester there was nobody holding a sign with either of their names on it and so they jumped in a taxi and asked the driver to take them to Old Trafford. Unknown to George and Eric, there were two Old Traffords and the driver took them to Lancashire County Cricket Club as the football season had ended and the cricket season had just begun.

The taxi driver thought the two boys were just young cricketers hoping to join Lancashire County Cricket Club. When the pair finally made it to United's home ground they were met by the club's Chief Scout, Joe Armstrong, who took them to the Cliff training ground. At the Cliff they met a number of the first team players including Northern Ireland's Harry Gregg and Jimmy Nicholson, before being taken on to their digs. Armstrong drove the two bewildered young boys to a terraced house in Chorlton-cum-Hardy, a suburb of Manchester, and introduced them to Mrs Fullaway. Little did George know it at the time, but Mrs Fullaway's house would be his home on and off for the next 10 years.

The Belfast boys were homesick on their first night away from their families and when Armstrong called at Mrs Fullaway's house early the next morning to pick them up, George told him that both he and Eric wanted to go home. So, the boys made their way back across the Irish Sea to their Belfast homes. Sometime later in life, McMordie, who went on to play for Middlesbrough (1964-75) winning 21 caps for his country, recalled the journey: 'It was an incredible time. There was George in his Lisnasharragh school uniform with his prefect's badge and me. We were just a pair of kids who had never been out of Belfast. It was like another world. But it all became too much and we ended up back home in less than a couple of days. We were both overawed. A short while later George went back and the rest is history.'

Dickie telephoned Busby to find out what had happened and Busby persuaded George's dad to send his boy back over again to see if he possessed the necessary talent and ability to become a professional footballer. George had planned to take-up an apprenticeship as a printer in Belfast when he left school but, thankfully, Busby persuaded him to sign amateur forms at United in August 1961 and George ended up keeping printers all over the country busy over the following 12 years and more. It took the young Best a while to get over the homesickness and to keep him occupied after training, United got him a job as a clerk at the Manchester Ship Canal. George hated the job, having to make countless cups of tea all day long. On May 22, 1963, the day of his 17th birthday, George signed professional forms with Manchester United. Three days after celebrating his birthday and becoming a professional footballer, George was sitting in the stands at Wembley Stadium, a member of United's travelling non-playing party at the 1963 FA Cup final versus Leicester City, a game United won 3-1 (scorers: David Herd two, Denis Law). Goodness knows how many United fans brushed past George that day without even knowing who the skinny dark-haired kid was. However, exactly five years and six days later, George would be back at Wembley and this time he'd be out on the pitch playing in Europe's premier club competition, the European Cup final. And everyone who followed football knew exactly who he was that night in 1968.

Speed, athleticism, bravery, cunning, dare, agility, timing, skill… all words to sum up what the perfect athlete would require to be the best in the world at their sport. And yet all of these attributes were mere strands in the DNA of George Best. Paddy Crerand, a teammate of Best, once said that 'George was a God'. Paddy wasn't far off the mark in his high praise of the Belfast Boy but George was much more than a God in the Roman mythology meaning of a God. George's teammates who made up the United Trinity, Bobby Charlton and Denis Law, may well have been Gods to all United fans. George made his debut for Manchester United aged just 17 on September 14, 1963, a 1-0 First Division victory over West Bromwich Albion (scorer: David Sadler) at Old Trafford. Best and Sadler, who was three months older than George, were part of Manchester United's 1964 FA Youth Cup winning side. Best scored in the 1-1 draw away to Swindon Town and Sadler grabbed a hat-trick in United's 4-1 victory at Old Trafford (John Aston Jr. also scored). Manchester United: Harry Gregg, Tony Dunne, Noel Cantwell (capt), Bill Foulkes, Maurice Setters, Paddy Crerand, Nobby Stiles, Philip Chisnall, David Sadler, Bobby Charlton, George Best.

The young shy Belfast teenager took the place of the fans' cult hero in the side, Denis Law, who was ruled out of action with an injury. Bobby Charlton played in the game and not before long the names of Law, Best and Charlton would not only sound shivers down the spines of the players of English clubs when the opposing players glanced at the Manchester United team sheet, but this famous trio was feared throughout Europe. They were liquid, crushing, potent, forceful, lethal, devastating and merciless in front of goal. The world's most famous front trio scored a staggering 665 goals for Manchester United: Charlton 249, Law 237 and Best 179.

However, whereas many of the game's true greats began to mature and reach their peak as professional footballers in their mid-20s, George packed the game in aged just 27. George once famously said: 'I spent a lot of money on booze, birds and fast cars. The rest I just squandered'. Two First Division League Championships medals with United in 1965 and 1967, a European Cup winner's medal in 1968 and Manchester United's top goalscorer on four occasions, George had the world at his feet. After playing his last game for United on New Year's Day

1974, a 3-0 First Division loss away to Queens Park Rangers, George turned his back on football.

And as for fortune, and as for fame, George never invited them in, though it seemed to the world they were all that he desired. His ability with a football was what opened that particular door to the sponsors and reporters who clamoured for his attention. Apart from an odd deal or two with a chewing gum company or a hair cream manufacturer, footballers were not targeted by companies to help promote their products before George Best burst on to the scene. The world of personal sponsorship deals was the domain of movie stars and pop artists. But Best changed all that at a time when English football did not have any sponsored competition or a club had a sponsor other than sponsoring the match ball.

Indeed, the first English Football League tournament whereby clubs could sell their naming rights was the Watney Cup, sponsored by a brewery company, Watney Mann, which was played from 1970-73. Best played in United's first ever Watney Cup game, a 3-1 away win over Reading on August 1, 1970 (scorers: Charlton two, Paul Edwards).

But by his time, the face of George Best had already adorned millions of fashion and glamour magazines around the world, his signature appeared on Fore aftershave boxes and Stylo football boots. In his native Northern Ireland, he appeared in a television advertisement sitting down for a meal with his mum, dad and siblings, when the family were eating Cookstown Family Sausages. Best's strapline was: Cookstown are the Best family sausages. George was football's first Superstar.

The press hounded his every move. They devoured his every

action. True creative geniuses are those who understand that a stage or a paintbrush is not required for making the highest art of all. George Best expressed his art on a football pitch where he painted many masterpieces. But for Best the fame and fortune he had achieved playing football were merely illusions, not the solutions they promised to be. And so, the most gifted player ever to play the beautiful game, decided to bring the curtain down on his glittering - yet so unfulfilled to its full promise - career in 1974 aged just 27.

He had entertained United fans in 470 appearances for the club scoring 179 goals: English First Division 361 games/137 goals, FA Cup 46 games/21 goals, League Cup 25 games/nine goals, Charity Shield two games/one goal, European Cup 21 games/nine goals, European Cup Winners' Cup two games/0 goals, Inter-Cities Fairs Cup 11 games/two goals, Inter-Continental Cup two games/0 goals.

Over the following eight years George flirted with comebacks including a season, 1976-77, in the Second Division when he and another football maverick, Rodney Marsh, along with England's 1966 World Cup winning captain, Bobby Moore, packed Craven Cottage with their entertaining football. Best scored for The Cottagers on his debut after only 71 seconds to give them a 1-0 win over Bristol Rovers. Best also played in the North American Soccer League (NASL) for the Fort Lauderdale Strikers, Los Angeles Aztecs and San Jose Earthquakes. But his football away from Manchester United never quite touched the same highs.

And of course, George reached some lows: constant battles with alcoholism, marriage splits, a liver transplant and a 12-week jail sentence in 1984 for drink-driving, assaulting a police officer and failing to answer bail. But it is the good times that fans will forever remember George for, which was what George himself wanted to be remembered for. His magical performance in 1966 against SL Benfica in their own backyard when he scored twice in United's 5–1 win, a performance that earned him the nickname 'El Beatle'. Or his six goals for United in the FA Cup against Northampton Town; and who will ever forget that night at Wembley on May 29, 1968, when George scored in the European Cup final in their 4–1 win over SL Benfica of Portugal.

In season 1967-68, George scored 28 times in the League, one goal in the FA Cup and three times in United's successful European Cup campaign. United's Holy Trinity of Law, Charlton and Best had delivered the Holy Grail, the European Cup, for their manager, Matt Busby to help United erase the memory of the Munich Air Disaster some 10 years earlier. George was voted European Player of the Year in 1968.

On 20 November 2005, the *News of the World* newspaper published a photograph of a very seriously ill George Best lying in his hospital bed at the request of the Manchester United legend. The caption with the photograph read: 'Don't die like me'. Sadly, George died in Cromwell Hospital, London five days after the photograph was published.

> *'One of the strongest characteristics of genius is the power of lighting its own fire.'*
> (John W. Foster)

When George Best had a football at his feet, he could make the poppies dance and set fire to the rain. The Belfast Boy could thread a needle with his toes. Grand Masters painted their masterpieces on canvas.

George Best painted his on football pitches all over the world.

Did You Know That?

A 17-YEAR-OLD George Best made his debut for Northern Ireland in the British Home International Championships on April 15, 1964. The Irish travelled to Swansea to play Wales at The Vetch Field, home to Swansea City. Pat Jennings, the legendary Arsenal, Tottenham Hotspur and Northern Ireland goalkeeper, also made his international debut in the game aged 18, which the Irish won 3-2. Pat paid a beautiful tribute to George after his death: 'He was the finest player I ever played with or against. I treasure my memories with him even though on occasions he made me look rather foolish.' However, whereas Jennings went on to win a record 119 caps for his country and play at two World Cup final tournaments (1982 and 1986), George only managed 37 caps, scoring nine times, and football fans around the world never saw him display his skills on the international world stage at any major finals.

EPILOGUE

I have been a Manchester United fan all of my life and I am very privileged to have followed the Greatest Football Club in the world and seen them play home and abroad. For me personally, away games are tremendous experiences because Manchester United's travelling Red Army make it a hostile atmosphere for the home fans. And, we sing our hearts out to them: 'You only came to see United, now F**k Off Home'.

I have seen United play in many away games in England and across Europe, not forgetting the odd cup final played at the Millennium Stadium, Cardiff. Our sea of Reds that follow United on their journeys in pursuit of the Premier League title, FA Cup, Caraboa Cup, UEFA Europa League or UEFA Champions League are in my opinion die hard Reds like my good mate, and lifelong Red, Addy Dearnaley from the Stalybridge Manchester United Supporters' Club. Addy, and I will refrain from giving away his age, has seen Manchester United play in every country the famous Red Devils have visited whether for a friendly or a competitive fixture.

For some young Reds reading this book you may not have heard of other European competitions Manchester United played in which include the UEFA Cup and the European Cup Winners' Cup. Well, the UEFA Cup is now the Europa League and the European Cup Winners' Cup was contested by the winners of each one of UEFA's domestic Cup winners on an annual basis from 1960-99. In England, the FA Cup winners qualified for the European Cup Winners' Cup. Alex Ferguson guided Manchester United to FA Cup glory in 1990, his first trophy success as the Boss of Manchester United. In season 1990-91, Manchester United beat FC Barcelona 2-1 in the 1991 European Cup Winners' Cup final at Feyenoord Stadium, Netherlands. Mark Hughes scored both of our goals that glorious evening. I adored Sparky and when my first son was born on May 21, 1990, I named him Marc, after our striker, and a Pop Star I loved as a child, Marc Bolan. My second son, Paul, was born on June 4, 1993, not long after we won the inaugural Premier League title.

Addy does not chart his Manchester United odyssey in books, like I do. His Manchester United passport is his own personal testimony, just as it is to so many tens of thousands of my fellow Reds across the globe - the various border stamps proof of his support and undying love for Manchester United.

For Manchester United fans visiting Old Trafford to see United play, we come in expectation. Full of hopes and dreams. We come for the promise of greatness. To be seduced by genius. We come to Old Trafford for more than just a game. We come to see United, the greatest football club in the world.

In my life as a Red there have been sacrifices and discouragements, triumphs and set-backs, trials and tribulations, some lows and so many wonderful highs. The path upon which we United fans have set our course following our beloved club is not an easy one. The trail is often difficult to find and sometimes throws up an obstacle in our path. However, we must make our map as we go along, and step by step continue on our path to greatness. But I know I travel in good company with my fellow Reds around the globe. Men, women and children all expressing their unified love for United as one.

Success on the field of play is like freedom to an oppressed nation. It is elusive, hard to come by and much harder to maintain. It cannot be put into a pocket or a wallet and zipped there to stay. It is the constant pursuit of success from our team, on behalf of us their army of loyal followers, that drives the men in red forward to glory. Long gone are the halcyon days of our most famous, unrivalled, triumvirate of Best, Charlton and Law, but that notwithstanding, our current team march on without jealousy or fear to maintain our status as the most feared, most hated, most famous and most successful club in the history of English football.

Without United we would walk alone, living a mundane life without fear or expectation. A life hamstrung by the absence of celebrating a moment of pure ecstasy or enjoying a sweet tasting victory with a fellow Red. A boring existence condemned to an endless struggle to survive in a world void of a sense of belonging, a world ruled by uncertainty instead of confidence and hope. We United fans have endured seasons of great expectations that ended with shrinking horizons. But with every low there is a high and United have lifted our hearts and voices time and time again. Let me assure you that my voice is the steadier for support of United for seasons yet to come, that I move more firmly into the task ahead, knowing that millions of my fellow Reds are joined with me in the resolve to make this support of our team endure. We will forever keep the red flag flying high.

A treasured few were born to play for United, players we still hold in high esteem long after they walked out of the exit door at Old Trafford. Great moments are born from great opportunity and I can't help recalling Al Pacino's famous 'Inch by Inch' speech from *Any Given Sunday* and somehow imagining Sir Alex giving a similar speech to his team, our team, at half-time in the 1999 UEFA Champions League final:

> *I don't know what to say really.*
> *Three minutes to the biggest battle of our professional lives all comes down to today.*
> *Either we heal as a team or we are going to crumble.*
> *Inch by inch*
> *play by play*
> *till we're finished.*
> *We are in hell right now, gentlemen*
> *believe me and we can stay here and get the shit kicked out of us or we can fight our way back into the light.*
> *We can climb out of hell.*
> *One inch, at a time.*
>
> *Now I can't do it for you.*
> *I'm too old.*
> *I look around and I see these young faces and I think… I mean I made every wrong choice a middle age man could make.*
> *I uh… I pissed away all my money believe it or not.*

I chased off anyone who has ever loved me.
And lately, I can't even stand the face I see in the mirror.

You know when you get old in life things get taken from you.
That's, that's part of life.
But,
you only learn that when you start losing stuff.
You find out that life is just a game of inches.
So is football.
Because in either game life or football the margin for error is so small.
I mean one half step too late or too early you don't quite make it.
One half second too slow or too fast and you don't quite catch it.
The inches we need are everywhere around us.
They are in every break of the game every minute, every second.

On this team, we fight for that inch
On this team, we tear ourselves, and everyone around us to pieces for that inch.
We CLAW with our finger nails for that inch.
Cause we know when we add up all those inches that's going to make the fucking difference
between WINNING and LOSING
between LIVING and DYING.

I'll tell you this
in any fight it is the guy who is willing to die who is going to win that inch.

*And I know if I am going to have any life anymore
it is because, I am still willing to fight, and die for that inch
because that is what LIVING is.
The six inches in front of your face.*

*Now I can't make you do it.
You gotta look at the guy next to you.
Look into his eyes.
Now I think you are going to see a guy who will go that inch with you.
You are going to see a guy who will sacrifice himself for this team
because he knows when it comes down to it, you are gonna do the
same thing for him.*

*That's a team, gentlemen and either we heal now, as a team,
or we will die as individuals.
That's football guys.
That's all it is.
Now, whattaya gonna do?*

History has shown that in Manchester United we have a team that never gives up, a team that fights for every ball for every minute of every game. We want a team which possesses an insatiable thirst for success. We expect the Manchester United players to tear themselves and everyone around them to pieces in the pursuit of glory for us the fans. They have to fight with everything they have because they know that we the fans expect nothing less from them, nothing else will do for us in the team's constant pursuit of success to be celebrated on the pitch by the players and on the terraces by us the fans. And make no mistake about it, have no doubt whatsoever in your mind, that every United player is fully aware of what we expect from him every time he crosses that white line. The players more than any of us know fully that what they do in a game wearing the famous shirt of Manchester United will ultimately make the difference between them WINNING and LOSING and for us the fans, the difference between LIVING and DYING.

Our deepest fear as Reds is not that we are inadequate. Our deepest fear is that we are powerful beyond measure. It is our strengths, not our weaknesses, that most frightens us. All Reds are meant to shine as children do. It's not just in some of us; it is in all of us.

And as we let our own lights shine, we unconsciously give other people permission to do the same. But we are far greater than our foes and our light shines like a beacon amid rocks surrounded by a crashing sea.

I want to march shoulder to shoulder and stand in solidarity with my fellow Reds. The time to stand up and be counted, to make a difference and to support United is now.

Your Fellow Red,
John

BIBLIOGRAPHY

WEBSITES

http://www.mufcinfo.com/

http://englandfootballonline.com/

https://talksport.com/football

http://www.historicalkits.co.uk/Manchester_United/Manchester_United.htm

https://www.englishfootballleaguetables.co.uk/season/S1974-75/1975-04-19.html#d2

https://www.bbc.co.uk/sport/football/15776021

https://www.theguardian.com/football/2020/oct/30/dennis-walker-manchester-united-first-and-only-black-busby-babe

https://www.unitedkits.com/kits/seasons/1884.php

http://barryhugmansfootballers.com/

https://www.footballsite.co.uk

https://distromanchasterutd.blogspot.com/2013/07/the-theatre-of-dreams-old-trafford.html

https://everythingorient.wixsite.com/everythingorient/post/blast-from-the-past-mike-pinner

https://www.mirror.co.uk/sport/football/news/incredible-letter-emerges-manchester-united-12555474

https://duncan-edwards.co.uk/

https://thesefootballtimes.co/2015/08/13/duncan-edwards-boy-wonder/ – Andrew Flint

https://beyondthelastman.com/2020/12/15/duncan-edwards-there-is-a-light-that-never-goes-out/

https://www.espn.co.uk/football/club/manchester-united/360/blog/post/3224618/duncan-edwards-manchester-united-legend-lives-on

https://www.mirror.co.uk/sport/football/news/come-on-mum-home-cant-11976919

https://www.nmrs.org.uk/mines-map/accidents-disasters/cheshire/hyde-colliery-explosion-hyde-1889/

https://footballpink.net/2019-2-2-eddie-colman-the-spirit-of-salford-and-heartbeat-of-the-busby-babes/

https://www.skysports.com/football/news/11096/11610094/denis-law-huddersfield-manchester-city-and-bill-shankly

https://www.examinerlive.co.uk/sport/football/news/bill-shankly-case-what-might-12134125

https://readtheleague.com/the-big-feature/the-british-transfer-record-breakers-denis-law

https://www.manchestereveningnews.co.uk/sport/football/football-news/matt-busby-bill-shankly-tribute-915254

https://www.theguardian.com/football/2018/jan/08/hibernian-british-team-european-cup-hibs

https://manchesterunitedmemories.wordpress.com/2018/04/01/martin-buchan-a-very-classy-manchester-united-defender-of-the-1970s/

https://www.scotsman.com/sport/football/interview-martin-buchan-scotland-and-day-largs-1453271

https://www.totalfootballmag.com/features/columnists/the-gordon-hill-column-a-birds-eye-view-of-becoming-a-top-player/

https://the-football-archive.com/2020/06/27/manchester-united-and-the-f-a-youth-cup/

https://www.theguardian.com/football/2009/dec/23/albert-scanlon-obituary

https://www.independent.co.uk/news/obituaries/albert-scanlon-busby-babe-who-survived-the-munich-disaster-but-never-fulfilled-his-potential-as-a-footballer-1849125.html

https://www.manchestereveningnews.co.uk/news/greater-manchester-news/busby-babe-albert-scanlon-left-899129

https://api.parliament.uk/historic-hansard/commons/1958/feb/07/bea-aircraft-accident-munich

https://www.nationalarchives.gov.uk/wp-content/uploads/2014/03/fo1042-391.jpg

https://thebusbybabe.sbnation.com/2014/2/28/5456162/manchester-united-jack-rowley-forgotten-goalscorer

http://www.englandfootballonline.com/TeamPlyrsBios/PlayersR/BioRowleyJF.html

https://www.greensonscreen.co.uk/gosdb-players2.asp?pid=724&scp=1,2,3,4,5,6,7

https://www.lcfc.com/news/2160781/former-manager-remembers-frank-ofarrell/featured

https://www.whufc.com/news/articles/2021/october/09-october/happy-birthday-frank-ofarrell-oldest-living-west-ham-united

BOOKS

Keane The Autobiography - Roy Keane with Eamon Dunphy - Published by Michael Joseph, August 2002

Sir Bobby Charlton - My Manchester United Years - The Autobiography; Bobby Charlton with James Lawton (2007); Headline Publishing Group

Ian Morrison & Alan Shury – *Manchester United: A Complete Record 1878-1992* – The Breedon Books Publishing Company 1992

Irish Reds – Iain McCartney – Britespot Publishing Solutions Limited – 2002

Manchester United Pictorial History & Club Record - Charles Zahra, Joseph Muscat, Iain McCartney and Keith Mellor – Temple Nostalgia 1986

The United Alphabet – A Complete Who's Who of Manchester United – Garth Dykes – ACL & Polar Publishing (UK) Limited 1994

The Official Manchester United Miscellany – John D T White (2005); Carlton Publishing Limited

The Official Manchester United Almanac – John D T White (2008); Orion Publishing Limited

Kicking Through The Troubles – How Manchester United Helped To Heal A Divided Community - John D T White (2017) - Empire Publications, Manchester

Manchester United – The Making of a Football Dynasty – John D T White (2021) - Empire Publications, Manchester

Printed in Great Britain
by Amazon